RAMPIN

'A fascinating and rigorous journey through a century of disability activism, and a powerful, urgent call for societal and cultural change centring the lives and voices of disabled people.'

Elinor Cleghorn, author of *Unwell Women*

'Young people should be taught this book in schools. A much needed take on disability history and our power in protest.'

Frances Ryan, *Guardian* columnist and author of *Crippled*

'A book of rage, power and hope. This is a testament to collective power, a resounding rejection of the silencing of disability history, and a story of the community's fight for survival in a dehumanising system. I wish I could go back and gift newly disabled me this book. She would have felt less alone.'

Bethany Handley, Shaw Trust Disability Power 100 finalist and author of *Cling Film*

'A vital, overlooked history, reminding us we can make a better world for disabled people.'

Lucy Webster, journalist, campaigner and author of *he View from Down Here: Life As a Young Disabled Woman*

'More than a history lesson, this is a call to arms. Igniting a fire for today's battles, and unflinchingly chronicling past struggles, this book is a must-read for anyone who cares about equality, justice and fairness.'

Kamran Mallick, Chief Executive of Disability Rights UK

'This book traces disability justice across generations, yet feels so current and pressing. A damning indictment of the state's treatment of disabled people, it's also an ode to our creativity, perseverance and resilience. Charlton-Dailey gives voice to the voiceless, and tells these stories with grace and elegance.'

Grace Spence Green, doctor and author of *To Exist As I Am*

'This is an incredibly important book, tracing the much-overlooked history of how disability rights have been fought for, won, and lost in the UK over the last century, and how the fight is continuing. Filled with passion, rage, and hope, this should be required reading in schools across the country.'

Laura Elliott, disability journalist and author of *Awakened*

RACHEL CHARLTON-DAILEY

Ramping Up Rights

*An Unfinished History
of British Disability Activism*

HURST & COMPANY, LONDON

First published in the United Kingdom in 2025 by
C. Hurst & Co. (Publishers) Ltd.,
New Wing, Somerset House, Strand, London, WC2R 1LA
© Rachel Charlton-Dailey, 2025
All rights reserved.

Distributed in the United States, Canada and Latin America by
Oxford University Press, 198 Madison Avenue, New York, NY 10016,
United States of America.

The right of Rachel Charlton-Dailey to be identified as the author
of this publication is asserted by them in accordance with the
Copyright, Designs and Patents Act, 1988.

A Cataloguing-in-Publication data record for this book
is available from the British Library.

ISBN: 9781911723950

This book is printed using paper from registered sustainable
and managed sources.

www.hurstpublishers.com

Printed and bound in Great Britain by Bell & Bain Ltd, Glasgow

*For Nana and Granda, for always believing in me.
I'll keep you with me forever.*

CONTENTS

Trigger Warnings and Language Notes   xiii
Foreword by Ellen Clifford   xv

Introduction   1

PART ONE
ROOTS AND RECKONINGS

1. My Freedom of Spirit: Early 1900s   17

2. Does He Take Sugar?: The Pan-Disabled Movement, 1950s–70s   31

3. Let Us Live: The Social Model, 1970s   43

4. Coalition: The Decade of Disabled Persons, 1980s   53

5. Piss On Pity: Direct Action, 1980s–90s   61

6. Disabled Anarchist Blues: The Arts Movement, 1980s–2000s   75

7. Cuts Kill: 1990s–2010s   87

8. We Shall Not Be Removed: Covid, 2020–2   115

9. Heating or Eating: 2022–4   141

PART TWO
TODAY AND TOMORROW

10. Don't Make Me the Problem: Ableist Media Narratives   155

11. A Decent Life: Independent Living and Equal Access   183

12. Does the Minister Really Think This Is Supporting People?: Work and Education   205

13. Assist Us To Live: Birth, Death, Genetics and Assisted Dying   225

| Conclusion: Just Ask | 247 |

Afterword: The Community Speaks	263
Acknowledgements	273
Bibliography	277
Index	311

TRIGGER WARNINGS AND LANGUAGE NOTES

This book, whilst meant to inform and educate, also includes subjects and words which could be triggering or upsetting to many, especially disabled people. Please take care and prioritise your own mental health and wellbeing.

This book includes mentions of:

- Systemic abuse of disabled people
- Deaths of disabled people by government
- Suicide
- Covid
- Euthanasia
- Eugenics
- Assault, abuse and neglect of disabled people

Some parts of the book also include language about disabled people that would be considered outdated or offensive nowadays. This includes past names of associations and charities which were considered acceptable by the disabled community at the time.

TRIGGER WARNINGS AND LANGUAGE NOTES

This book uses both the terms 'ableism' and 'disablism'. When I talk about 'ableism', I mean an attitude or policy that centres non-disabled people as the norm. When I say 'disablism', I mean an attitude or policy that amounts to discrimination against, or oppression of, disabled people.

FOREWORD

Ellen Clifford

"One of us" is the phrase that went through my head during my first interaction with Rachel Charlton-Dailey. Taken from the 1932 film *Freaks*, the phrase has been adopted by disabled activists as well as other fringe communities to signify a person who shares our politics and culture, someone we feel comfortable with and safe around, someone who fits.

Although our paths had not previously crossed, I was aware of Rachel's work as a disabled journalist writing in a mainstream newspaper. Not only was she writing about the issues that matter most to disabled people, but doing so from a position informed by both lived experience and good disability politics.

Despite being a not insignificant minority (according to the latest figures there are 16.1 million disabled people across the UK although this is likely to be an under-estimate), media coverage is overwhelmingly unfavourable

FOREWORD

to us. Mainstream media either repeats government rhetoric demonising us as benefit cheats, presents us as passive victims deserving of pity and charity or ignores us.

A major bone of contention to disabled activists has been the lack of media attention given to what the Chair of the United Nations Committee on the Rights of Disabled People, Theresia Degener described in 2017 as a "human catastrophe".

She was referring to cuts introduced by the UK government adversely impacting disabled people on such a scale and depth as to meet the threshold for grave and systematic violations of our rights. This was the finding, published a year earlier, of an unprecedented investigation by the UN Committee.

Rachel's work on the Mirror's *Disabled Britain* column and subsequently for The Canary stood her apart as one of only a handful of disabled and ally journalists, including John Pring, Frances Ryan, Steve Topple and Chaminda Jayanetti, committed to exposing mass harm consciously inflicted on disabled people.

That was why I was so happy to be contacted by her in August 2023.

I was mid-preparation for a trip to Geneva where a delegation of Deaf and Disabled people from across the UK would be giving evidence to the UN disability committee as part of their follow up to the 2016 special investigation.

The government would not be joining us. They said they were too busy and would go in March 2024 instead.

FOREWORD

The evidence we were due to present covered benefit deaths, denial of disabled people's basic human rights through social care support cuts and a recent ramping up of hostile rhetoric from government ministers targeting disability benefit claimants.

These are issues that matter immensely to disabled people and the general level of press interest was underwhelming to say the least.

This made Rachel's interest in covering the proceedings even more valuable.

I felt an instant connection with her.

Despite her profile and reach, she was warm and friendly, non-judgemental, didn't hold back on talking about her own life and the barriers she faces, and she worked at odd hours like me.

Those first impressions were confirmed at our first in person meeting on a cold Lake Geneva beach in March 2024.

I was late as usual but it didn't matter: the gaggle of activists from various Deaf and Disabled People's Organisations, trade unions and families of benefit death victims were already ensconced in creating social media content to tell the story of how we were back at the United Nations. This time the government was due to show and our delegation was even bigger and more united.

One of my biggest aims in co-ordinating that delegation, besides exposing further serious regressions in disabled people's rights, was to involve new and younger disabled campaigners.

FOREWORD

So long as we live under a socio-economic system that puts profit before people, disabled people will be forced to struggle for the resources we need to survive. In times of prosperity, we will be granted concessions, but in times of recession we will always be the first to face cuts.

This means that disabled activists must always be mindful of the need to bring in new blood and bring on the next generation.

Our movement, in particular, is beset with burn outs and early deaths. This is a consequence of the toll it takes on us to actively campaign on top of living with our impairments and conditions, on top of the need to constantly fight to justify and access the support we need to survive and on top of coming up against barriers and discrimination on a daily basis.

Disabled people have no more of an automatic understanding of disability politics than non-disabled people. Similar to members of the LGBTQ+ community, we may well be born into families whose ideas of disability are dominated by disempowering mainstream notions.

Opportunities to educate and mentor new and younger Deaf and disabled campaigners need to be actively created.

Presenting role models and sharing learning that evidences the power of our own agency is an essential part of this.

I am therefore delighted that Rachel has devoted an entire book to doing just that.

But this isn't just a book for disabled people.

It records a world that the majority of people in society don't even know exists.

Time and again, exhibitions and books dedicated to civil rights movements and the history of protest omit disabled people's struggle.

It's not intentional. Rather, society sees us as individuals—whether a superhero who has overcome personal challenges or a tragic victim of personal circumstances—and misses the truth of the matter which is the deeply political and collective nature of disability.

As this book evidences, disabled people in Britain have been actively involved in resistance for as long as a disabled identity has existed. And more than that, we have been at the forefront of wider political struggles such as the Chartist and suffragette movements.

International history confirms this picture: disabled Black social activist Harriet Tubman made some thirteen missions to rescue approximately seventy enslaved people; disabled revolutionaries were involved in events in Russia in 1917 as the "crippled warriors" mentioned by Trotsky and as patients liberating their asylums in partnership with Marxist psychiatrists; returning German soldiers disabled on the frontline played a key role in ending the First World War; US campaigners who were born disabled used radical tactics to fight for rights to jobs during the Great Depression of the 1930s.

Disabled people occupy a unique position on the margins of society that allows us to fundamentally question society and the supposedly common-sense ideas which underpin it. Our inclusion comes with a cost that is rarely considered worth it. This makes us a minority that remains largely un-co-opted by the establishment.

Increasingly though, the main aim of government is not to co-opt us but to push us even further into the margins with no concern for if we live or die.

Without a solution to low productivity growth, the Labour government elected in 2024 has taken up the playbook used by the Tories before them to scapegoat disability benefit claimants. In the high court, they ferociously defended a legal challenge against a consultation undertaken by the previous government with proposals to change eligibility for out of work disability benefits.

Under these proposals, another 100,000 disabled people would be pushed into absolute poverty, from a total of 450,000+ who would be adversely impacted by 2028/9. They would increase mental distress among disabled people at risk of self-harm and suicidal ideation and undoubtedly lead to more benefit deaths. The plan to get away with this deliberate causation of mass harm involved withholding key information from the public and spin.

In the White House meanwhile, is a president who is openly eugenicist and believes that people with learning difficulties should be left to die.

The odds are stacked against disabled people like never before in the history of modern social policy. In late-stage

Capitalism, however, it is not only disabled people who are facing existential threat but all of humanity.

In a situation this extreme, it's the outliers who are most likely to come up with the answers. More than ever, society needs disabled people with our ability to think outside the box, our creativity and resourcefulness, born of the need to find ways to survive.

Disability history is a history full of courage, determination and fortitude. In a world where many would rather be dead than disabled, where we are denied equal life chances while being blamed for not raising ourselves up, what we know best is struggle.

This book is testimony to the lives lived well of disabled activists in Britain.

It's a book society needs and also one to enjoy.

Thank you, Rachel. ♥

Ellen Clifford
February 2025

INTRODUCTION

I've had some pretty amazing opportunities in my working life over the last few years, but the most incredible and life-changing one was sharing a stage with disability rights legend Barbara Lisicki.

If you don't know me, I'm a freelance journalist, writer, editor and author. In my career I've written about disability for some of the biggest publications in the UK and the US. I've challenged the way disabled people are portrayed in the media, interviewed some of the biggest disabled stars, and worked to hold the government to account and inform the public about disabled life.

I've spoken at the Labour Party annual conference, and I regularly crop up on TV and radio to speak up for disabled people and our rights. I was one of the few disabled journalists covering Covid from the very beginning in March 2020. I was also one of the few British journalists invited to the United Nations in Geneva in April 2024 to attend the Committee on the Rights of Disabled People at which the UK government was asked to respond to its "grave violations" of the Convention on the Rights of Disabled People.

But getting this kind of platform for disability has been a long, hard, lonely road. After I witnessed how tough it was for disabled stories to get into newspapers, I decided we had to create our own online publication, and I founded *The Unwritten*, where disabled people can tell their stories without the media turning them into tales of trauma or inspiration.

I even won a British Journalism Award for my work on *The Unwritten*. This led to me editing *Disabled Britain: Doing it for Ourselves* with *The Daily Mirror*, the first series in a national newspaper focusing on the realities of disabled life written by disabled people, as opposed to about us. I became one of the handful of disabled columnists in the country.

But without a doubt, the best experience of my career was when I got to chair an event with Barbara Lisicki at the National Education Union's Disabled Members annual conference. When the NEU came to me asking if I'd host this conversation with Barbara in 2023, I was absolutely taken aback—surely not me and her on the same stage?

Barbara's work has changed countless lives, and yet most people don't even know who she is. This is why I wanted to write this book. We'll go into much deeper detail about Barbara in Chapter 5, but let me give you a quick rundown now of why someone like Barbara should be a household name.

Barbara Lisicki is one of the founders of the Disabled People's Direct Action Network (DAN) which fought in

INTRODUCTION

the 1980s and 1990s for accessible transport, other disability rights, and respect for disabled people as members of our society. DAN were the ones chaining themselves to buses, picketing charity telethons and shouting the now iconic slogan 'Piss On Pity' at the likes of Chris Tarrant. This became the battle cry against media portrayals of disabled people, demanding equality instead of condescension. The work of Barbara and her peers led to the creation of the Disability Discrimination Act of 1995.

While I was onstage with Barbara, I realised two things. The first was just how important disability journalism was to disabled people. Whilst so many of the questions from the audience were directed at Barbara, her incredible work and her views on the situation for disabled people in the UK today, a good chunk were aimed at me and the awful state of media ableism.

The second realisation didn't make me feel anywhere near as helpful to the community. A teacher in the audience spoke about the importance of teaching their students about recent disability history, and how difficult it was. Suddenly this really resonated with me.

Despite being a prominent disability rights journalist, whose job it was to fight for change for disabled people by exposing the injustices we face, I felt ashamed at the lack of knowledge I had about those from past generations who had fought for the rights I now have.

I knew so little about our history, and about those still fighting to maintain and improve our rights and freedom. It was there and then that I vowed to change this.

* * *

Though many argue it wasn't enough, and was full of loopholes that left it easy to discriminate against disabled people, the Disability Discrimination Act was a landmark law. It enshrined for the first time the right of British disabled people to live free from discrimination—twenty years after women had won the same protections in the Sex Discrimination Act, and thirty years after the Race Relations Act had outlawed racial discrimination.

I was six when it came into effect in 1995, but I don't remember once hearing about it growing up. It was only after I interviewed the writer and presenter Cerrie Burnell about her documentary *Silenced: The Hidden Story of Disabled Britain*, which hit our screens as late as 2021, that I fully grasped how little I knew about the treatment of the UK's disabled people right up until the late twentieth century. Or how the social values and assumptions behind that treatment are connected to the struggles our community still faces today.

To give just one example: of course I knew that disabled people had been shut up in asylums a very long time ago, but it was a lot to take in when watching Cerrie's documentary that this still happened routinely far into the 1900s—and that thanks to neurodivergent kids

INTRODUCTION

being misdiagnosed or inappropriately farmed out to the wrong services, it essentially still happens now (see Chapter 12).

At first I blamed myself for this lack of knowledge. The impostor syndrome kicked in and I thought I must not have researched or studied hard enough to be able to do my job. Could I be the wrong person to report on disabled people? But then I thought about the way disability had always been portrayed to me as a child and young adult.

I grew up in the 1990s and 2000s when you would regularly see non-disabled parents crying on TV about the fate of their disabled kids. My twenties were spent in the dark times of the 2010s, when 'documentaries' like *Benefits Street* and endless tabloid news stories painted anyone who claimed unemployment disability benefits as a scrounger or defrauding the system.

On top of the damage done by media representations of present-day disability, I realised I'd grown up in a society where the disabled past wasn't represented at all. Despite being interested in history for as long as I can remember, I can't recall ever learning anything about the disabled people who were an integral part of Britain's story and an integral part of the history of civil rights in the UK—not just disability rights.

British schoolchildren learn more about the civil rights movement across the ocean in the US than they do about disabled people's fight for civil rights in their own country. This shows just how much the history of disability rights has been erased.

And when the history of British activism does get taught, disabled campaigners are almost always missing from the story. When I was nine, I was obsessed with everything about the suffragette movement and of course the Pankhursts, but I was never taught anything about Rosa May Billinghurst. Known as "the Cripple Suffragette", Billinghurst used to hide rocks in the blankets on her wheelchair to throw at police and would use crutches on either side of her chair to propel herself towards police trying to block the protesters. How had I never heard of such a badass?

The erasure of both disabled people and their champions throughout history has been so pervasive that entire generations of young people have no idea who came before them, or that the rights disabled people have today weren't generously 'bestowed' on us by non-disabled society or the British state—we claimed the rights that were ours, and we fought for them, tooth and nail. The fact that people, disabled and non-disabled, don't know about this is unacceptable, especially now, when our rights are more at risk than ever.

* * *

The world is a mess right now, there's no denying that. Years into both a global pandemic and the biggest cost of living crisis in many people's lifetimes, people in the

INTRODUCTION

UK are struggling to survive. This is an even harder task for disabled people.

The charity Scope estimates that 23% of working-class adults are disabled, yet disabled people are almost twice as likely to be unemployed than non-disabled people. Scope also estimates that it still costs disabled people on average £1,067 more a month to live compared with non-disabled people, yet disability benefits are woefully low.

Disabled people are also more likely to live in poverty, at 27% compared to non-disabled people at 19%. Between July and October 2023, 5% of adults told the Office for National Statistics they had run out of food in the past two weeks and were unable to afford more. The proportion was 8% among disabled adults.

Even before the crisis of the 2020s, disabled people in the UK were already struggling. After fourteen years of the Conservative party in power, disability rights have taken a tumble. Back in 2016 the United Nations Committee on the Rights of Persons with Disabilities had found that the UK had committed "grave and systemic" violations of disabled people's rights. It finally felt like things were going to change.

But, on 18 March 2024, there I was, standing outside the United Nations, hearing again about how the UK government had shirked their responsibility to disabled people from that same UN Committee on the Rights of Persons with Disabilities. It reported there'd been no progress since the original 2016 investigation, stating that "the State party has failed to take all appropriate measures to address grave and systematic violations of the human rights of persons with disabilities and has failed to eliminate the root causes of inequality and discrimination."

The UN even went as far as saying there was evidence of regression. I do want to stress how important this is—from a position of grave violations, the situation has grown worse. And we'll see in the parts of this book about 2000–2020s policy (Chapters 9–12) that there's not much reason to hope the Labour party in power since July 2024 will take a totally different approach. I was one of the handful of journalists there at the UN in 2024, and no one seemed to want to commission me to write about it.

According to the 2021 census, there are 16 million disabled people in the UK, in a total population that's around 68 million—but it's believed this figure could already be out of date and much higher as among other things many are now identifying as disabled after Covid lockdowns. Disability also intersects with other minority groups, compounding the disadvantage in today's society: the census showed that disabled people were more than twice as likely to be lesbian, gay, bisexual, or another minority sexuality than non-disabled people.

A survey of trans people that same year found that just under half of respondents were disabled, and more

INTRODUCTION

than half were neurodivergent; a 2019 government report found that 30% of trans women, 40% of trans men and 37% of non-binary people had accessed mental health services, compared with 24% of cis people—yet LGBTQ rights are being pitted against disabled people's rights in an ever ridiculous culture war about toilets and rows about same sex care.

According to the 2021 census, the second largest ethnic group among disabled people is 'mixed White and Black Caribbean' (22.4% of this group are disabled in England, and 26.7% in Wales), followed in England by Bangladeshis (20.7%). For over-65s, Muslims are the biggest religious group identifying as 'disabled and limited a lot'—one in three Muslim women and one in five Muslim men within that age bracket.

There are 16 million disabled people in the UK, roughly double the entire population of London—but we are still underrepresented. There are, as of the July 2024 election, just nine Members of Parliament who openly identify as disabled—though this is an improvement on the previous five. There could also be more than nine—this is based on MPs self-reporting as disabled, and nobody should be forced to reveal their private medical information. But the figure can only be so off, and if Parliament were truly representative of society, there would be 136 disabled MPs.

Disabled people also make up just 8.7% of TV representation. This might explain why the on-screen narrative around disability is still often limited to scrounger villains demonised for their needs versus inspirational heroes praised for 'overcoming' their bodies. But disabled people wouldn't have to be inspiring if we didn't live in such an ableist society. And we have so many more stories to tell, if we can only win the space. As Ruth Madeley who played Barbara Lisicki in the BBC dramatisation *Then Barbara Met Alan* said when asked about another of her roles, "Her disability is the least interesting thing about her."

For now, we mostly seem stuck with narratives that alienate, other and isolate disabled people—and in turn this allows the state to continue to chip away at our rights. You might think that the poisonous prejudice of something like *Benefits Street* is behind us, a kind of cultural relic from the years of austerity rhetoric after 2010, but sadly this isn't the case. The coalition government that fanned those flames to justify its cuts might be gone, but public understanding hasn't changed as much as we'd like to think.

The Leonard Cheshire charity, which supports disabled people around the country, estimates that there were 10,740 disability hate crimes between 2022 and 2023, and 11,157 in 2021/22. After the pandemic fuelled new levels of anti-disability rhetoric, that 2021/22 figure represented a 25% increase in a single year for all hate crimes, and a 27% rise in violent hate crimes. That's why it's important for us to harness the unfinished history of the

INTRODUCTION

disability rights movement and use this knowledge to help us move forward. We will not allow our rights to regress when they're so paltry to start with.

* * *

This book isn't meant to be an encyclopaedia. I've actually been struggling with the idea of writing it because I feel so humbled by all the people who came before me, and by all the stories I've still not dug up. In some ways, I don't feel like I'm the right author for this book, because I know so little, but maybe that makes me the right person in other ways.

While I haven't been there for all of the fight, I'm determined to preserve the memory of the people who were, so that others can find their stories more easily than I did. I will not let the work of all who came before me go to waste. Instead, I'm seeing this book as a starting point for anyone who wants to know more about where disability activists have been and where we're headed. I will also highlight many of the difficulties disabled people encounter when trying to get their voices heard.

There will no doubt be things I missed so in addition to this book, I will create an online resource to keep adding to our shared knowledge bank. I'm still learning our history, and bringing you along for the ride in the hope that you can learn more too.

As well as looking at where we came from, I will also be looking at where we are now, which is definitely more my area of expertise. The questions of visibility and exclusion in our recent history are more important to discuss than ever, because the situation today is about more than just ideas or attitudes. It's not only cultural representation that's outdated beyond belief in the twenty-first century: the government has been stripping away rights from disabled people before our very eyes—from benefits reforms and making travel inaccessible to their woeful policy during Covid and the crisis in care, to name just a few. I will lead you through to where the fight is going.

This book is for the whole disabled community and I wanted to include the voices of as many others who belong to it as I could. The British establishment is at great pains to make all of us, both disabled and non-disabled, believe that disabled people are a minority too small to accommodate, that we're too different from each other for all of our needs to be met, that we're not organised and, most importantly, that we have no power.

They also rely on our disability being a hindrance to the more usual forms of protests—many of us can't stand up or march for our rights, we can't shout into microphones, but it doesn't mean we aren't fighting for our right to be heard. The campaigners who came before us used incredibly inventive tactics to protest and we have so much to learn from them. We also now have something they didn't—a strong online community that enables us to regroup, spread awareness and raise issues.

INTRODUCTION

I'm by no means an expert in British disability rights history, and I don't claim to be. But I'm lucky to know many people who are, and I am deeply passionate about the work of these incredible, fierce, ferocious campaigners who were there, in the thick of making change happen, fellow disabled people in the media and politics who are fighting for change, and campaigners out there on the ground still working against the constant barrage of hatred. In these pages their work will finally come centre stage.

The year 2025 marks the thirty-year anniversary of the Disability Discrimination Act. This should be a cause for celebration, and a time of looking back to what was achieved so that we can look forward to building on it until we get justice. My hope for this book is that by discovering where our movement came from, and why it's still needed in the 2020s, everyone who cares about the rights of disabled people, even those who are unsure how to get involved, can learn how we can best come together and ensure the world is better for the next generation.

PART ONE

ROOTS AND RECKONINGS

1

MY FREEDOM OF SPIRIT

EARLY 1900s

Disabled people have always existed, but before the late nineteenth century, records of disability activism are patchy. The twentieth century is where we start to start to find reliable sources showing disabled people working together to enact change for themselves, from political revolts and protests to social movements for women's rights, from civil rights to labour rights.

Collective and social actions to improve the lives of large sections of the British population have always included disabled people but their role has often been overlooked by history, and so it's only at the turn of the twentieth century that disabled activists come into focus—once the UK starts seeing collective action specifically focusing on disability issues.

Public consciousness of the mistreatment of disabled people rose in the nineteenth century with the criticism of conditions in asylums and workhouses. Bethlem

Asylum (commonly known as Bedlam) had been founded all the way back in 1247, and for a long period of its history inmates were exposed to the general public as if they were animals in a zoo, with people even poking and hurting them. When public access ended in 1707, this should've meant an end to patient abuse, but it only meant that the staff could do what they wanted without public scrutiny.

Before the modern era, there was no professional, state-controlled system: anyone could open an asylum, and anyone could work in one. The 'patients' weren't only mentally ill people, but often those with other disabilities, or people who were considered troublesome to society and its values—the poor, the homeless, single mothers, women who'd suffered abuse.

It's not that the staff all just happened to be individually cruel and evil people who liked torturing their fellow man—it was an entire cultural problem that didn't see patients as fully human. It was generally believed that all these groups suffered from a kind of moral weakness, or sickness: if they were often treated as less than fully human by their 'keepers', it's because that's how they were understood by society.

In the early nineteenth century, a change in attitude emerged in the treatment of mentally ill people. External control and punishment became the norm rather than physical isolation in institutions. But still nothing was done to help patients overcome their conditions. If your 'illness' was down to your moral character, then it was an essential part of you—could you even *be* helped? But, gradually, other changes took place in Victorian Britain: with the Industrial Revolution, more and more people were becoming wealthy enough to take up charitable causes, and philanthropy was in fashion; and more and more people came to know about the living standards of the 'lower classes'.

The press was booming, with new technologies of mass production and rising literacy rates, especially after primary education became compulsory in 1880: 'true crime' reporting was taking journalists into poor communities, and novels, usually first published as a 'serial' in the press, were enjoying a golden age, often including social issues as themes.

There was a growing sense among politicians that the government should have a bigger role in taking care of vulnerable people, and a new awareness of the importance of hygiene for the safety of all. Modern medicine was emerging and professionalising, including the body known today as the Royal College of Psychiatrists. The scandals of forced incarceration and the appalling conditions of asylums began to be scrutinised.

Workhouses had also existed for a couple of centuries, but it was the Victorian author Charles Dickens who made them (in)famous. Over time, they had evolved into refuges for elderly and disabled people who were having difficulties living and working, in the days before the safety net of a welfare state.

But even if they were originally intended to provide work and shelter for the poorest in society, by the time Dickens was writing workhouses were known for their terrible conditions, forced child labour, long hours, malnutrition, beatings and neglect. In 1834, the Poor Law Amendment Act (otherwise known as the New Poor Law) centralised all welfare (or 'poor relief') to be distributed through the workhouses, rather than through local parishes, which had been the system supporting British society's poorest for centuries—which meant people who needed extra support had nowhere else to turn.

But in the age of industrialisation, most owners of workhouses were seeking profits and saw people as commodities. Dr Colin Barnes, Emeritus Professor of Sociology at the University of Leeds, notes in his foreword to *Disability Politics* that the nineteenth century saw the birth of a multi-billion-pound 'disability industry' in Britain and most other Western societies. Businesses still seek to profit from disability today (see Chapter 11), but especially in the Victorian age, the 'industry' relied very much on disabled people remaining dependent, and the workhouse was a huge part of this. The conditions were so harsh that they often created disabled people, and both poor people and disabled people could spend a lifetime moving between the workhouse and the asylum.

Towards the end of the nineteenth century, the general public's attitude shifted against the cruelty displayed. By 1929, new legislation would be introduced so that local authorities could take over workhouses as hospitals—further showing the blurred lines in UK history between 'healthcare' for disabled people and the policing and segregation of all of society's vulnerable members. Workhouses would be formally abolished in 1930, though many continued in their new incarnation as Public Assistance Institutions under the control of local authorities.

* * *

As the public's attitude to the plight of the less privileged shifted, a growing movement of collective action began fighting for the rights of working class people, people of colour, women and many others. Disabled people were at the forefront of each of these fights.

The Chartist movement was the first mass political movement of the British working class. At its peak in the 1840s, millions of workers nationwide would sign parliamentary petitions demanding major reforms to democratise elections and protesting economic hardship. William Cuffay, a mixed race man born in 1788, became one of its leading figures. Cuffay would have been considered disabled today due to limb differences. He helped form the Metropolitan Tailors' Charter Association in 1839 and in 1842 went on to be elected to the national executive of the National Charter Association.

He was also voted president of the London Chartists, campaigning for the right to vote. But it would be decades before more men were enfranchised, and many of the Chartist leaders were arrested and convicted of various crimes in the crackdown: Cuffay was sentenced to transportation in Australia. While there, he played a crucial role in campaigning against the Master and Servant Acts which allowed employers to prosecute servants if they sought higher paying work. In 1864 alone over 10,000 working men were imprisoned because of their masters.

The Chartists themselves might not have been victorious, but the electoral reforms they'd demanded would be met, one by one, over the decades that followed. Chartism was also an important inspiration for the political campaigns that started later in the century, like the women's rights movement—which also featured many disabled women in its ranks.

Born in 1875 in Lewisham, Rosa May Billinghurst, who went by her middle name May, was a social campaigner widely known as the "Cripple Suffragette" as she used a tricycle wheelchair for most of her life. She joined the Women's Social and Political Union (WSPU) in 1907. The group had been founded by the Pankhursts in 1903 and was known for asking its members to deliberately avoid peaceful protests and embrace civil disobedience and direct action. May started the Greenwich chapter of the WSPU.

May was arrested multiple times, which would have had a negative impact on her health, but persisted in her activism, which ultimately helped women secure the right to vote in the UK, partially in 1918 and universally in 1928. She quite literally clashed with the police at numerous protests by ramming into officers with her tricycle and smashing windows with hammers and stones. On 18 November 1910, known as 'Black Friday', 300 suffragettes gathered outside Parliament demanding to talk to Prime Minister Asquith. When he refused they tried to storm the building and were violently manhandled by the police: May was forcibly removed from her tricycle and injured.

In March 1912, she was sentenced to a month's imprisonment after being part of a window smashing campaign during which she reportedly hid rocks under the rug she used to keep herself warm in her chair. On seeing that May was disabled, her prison guards were confused as to why she, a seemingly weak and feeble woman, had been sentenced to forced labour. They gave her no extra work, which she used to her advantage, continuing to campaign from inside the prison.

In 1913, she was sentenced to eight further months in prison, on the ridiculous charge of damaging a postbox—but then property has always been protected more than people. May represented herself in court and her defence speech, "The Guilt Lies on the Shoulders of the Government", was published in *The Suffragette*. During this prison stint, she was force-fed after going on hunger strike and injured again. She became so ill that she was released after two weeks and the WSPU awarded her the hunger strike medal of valour, given to suffragettes who had experienced the harsh torture of force feeding.

None of the indignities she endured from the police stopped her. In May 1914, she chained herself and her tricycle to the gates of Buckingham Palace where the police attacked her once again. In her trial statement, she said,

> The government may further maim my crippled body by the torture of forcible feeding, as they are torturing weak women in prison today. They may even kill me in the process, for I am not strong, but they cannot take away my freedom of spirit or my determination to fight this good fight to the end.

May died in 1953, leaving her body to medical science.

May wasn't the only disabled suffragette; there were others such as Eliza Adelaide "Addy" Knight who came from a tough working class background. She was born with a limb difference and following accidents in childhood suffered from poor health and used a walking stick or crutches. She married a Black sailor called Donald Adolphus Brown, at a time when mixed race couples were very uncommon. In 1906, Adelaide joined the WSPU and was quickly arrested for her role in protest actions. She was offered the chance to be spared jail if she agreed to give up protesting for one year. Despite knowing jail would make her health worse, she chose the six weeks in prison.

When Addy grew unhappy with the lack of democracy within the WSPU (and with Christabel Pankhurst seeming increasingly hellbent on only giving women who owned property the right to vote), she resigned to be able to campaign for the rights of working class women. She joined the Adult Suffrage Society, and later, with Donald, both the Social Democratic Federation (a socialist group) and the Labour Party. In 1920, she became a founding member of the Communist Party of Great Britain.

* * *

Inspired by the various successes of the labour and women's rights movements, by the late nineteenth century, many disabled people who had experienced hardship decided to make a change, and to organise. We can go all the way back to the early Industrial Revolution to see how some disabled people started to raise awareness of their living and working conditions locally: in 1791, for example, the Liverpool School for the Indigent Blind was created by Edward Rushton. It was the first school of its kind in the UK specifically for blind children. Rushton had lost his sight and continually sought to raise awareness of the difficulties blind people experienced living and working.

Right at the tail end of the nineteenth century, we can see the first larger movements organised by disabled people for disabled people starting to appear. The first two were the British Deaf Association founded in 1890 (originally as The British Deaf and Dumb Association) and the National League of the Blind, which was registered as a trade union in 1899. The Deaf Association came about because of a situation which still feels very familiar to us now: a designated group of non-disabled people making decisions about disabled people's lives without inclusion of the people affected. The 1889 Royal Commission on the education of deaf children completely failed to consult any deaf people, and a controversial movement was campaigning to ban sign language teachers in classrooms and cut down class sizes by getting rid of deaf students. The community were pushed to unite for their own interests.

It's important to understand that the disability rights movements didn't just follow on or take inspiration from other groups and campaigns—disabled activists were also some of the trailblazers setting the blueprint for UK protests. The National League of the Blind rose to national prominence in April 1920 with the Blind March, which kickstarted other protest movements between the world wars, like the Jarrow March of 1936 against unemployment and poverty from my own North East of England.

It was organised to protest blind people's poor education and work opportunities and the poverty they experienced as a result, and to demand a financial grant for blind people. Its leading slogan was 'Social Justice Not Charity' and it involved 250 blind men (they only permitted men to march as the conditions were expected to be tough—a little sexist, but okay) marching on London from across the UK over twenty days (with 171 marching from the beginning). The march ended in a demonstration at Trafalgar Square with over 10,000 people attending.

The marchers were initially refused an audience with Prime Minister David Lloyd George so instead they had tea with Lady Astor, the UK's first woman MP, in the House of Commons while they waited, and refused to leave London. Five days later, he gave in and met four of the organisers but said budget issues meant he could not give them what they wanted. Despite this, the march was still seen as a success due to the awareness of the cause it had raised. That and subsequent political action led to the Blind Persons Act of 1920, which was the first disability-specific legislation to be passed in the UK and worldwide. The league gave their affiliation to the Trade Union Congress (TUC) in 1902, and to the Labour Party in 1909.

Because the national blind rights movement had coalesced around issues of economic hardship and working conditions, there was a strong link between this side of disability activism and the labour movement. Ben Purse, one of the founding members of the National League of the Blind, was a living example of this.

Born in 1874, Purse lost his sight at thirteen years old, and became the League's first secretary general in 1897, then its president between 1905 and 1916. In 1914, he successfully campaigned for neonatal conjunctivitis (which could lead to blindness in newborns) to be registered as a notifiable disease, which requires any cases to be reported to government authorities so that they can be monitored.

Purse was an advocate of self-representation and was keen to use parliamentary as well as direct action: he became a founding member of the government's Advisory Committee for the Welfare of the Blind in 1917 and held this role for twenty-five years. But after the Blind Persons Act of 1920, Purse moved on from the League to work with charities to improve the lives of blind people. He set up a breakaway union, the National Union of Industrial and Professional Blind.

It's probably not a coincidence that the Blind Persons Act was passed not long after the First World War ended. In the short term, the conflict got in the way of disability activism: it put a brief end to some of the social and collective work of direct action groups, including disabled rights campaigners, with organisers realising the need to get behind the war effort; and, although a big section of the National League of the Blind were veterans, they were not allowed to join the 1920 Blind March, as organisers did not want its success to be unduly credited to patriotism. But once the war was over, the need for disabled rights was even greater, and could no longer be ignored.

By the end of the First World War, two million soldiers had returned home with some level of permanent disability. Over 40,000 lived with limb difference due to amputations or injury and many others dealt with blindness or physical injury from head wounds. Shell shock (now known as post-traumatic stress disorder) was a very common issue.

Help to support disabled veterans came in the form of government support and charities like St Dunstan's (now Blind Veterans UK) and the Douglas Haig Memorial Homes Trust (now Haig Housing Trust). It was noted that a clean, peaceful and rural setting brought the best health benefits and the Scottish Veterans Garden City Association created in 1915 pioneered this form of treatment. But charities weren't enough (and arguably shouldn't be the only support) and soon ex-soldiers organised into a number of campaigning groups—many of these came together in what is now the Royal British Legion.

The British Legion is a charity providing financial, social and emotional support to members and veterans of the British Armed Forces, their families and dependants. One of the active veteran campaigners involved in its founding at the start of the 1920s was Major Sir Benn Jack Brunel Cohen KBE. After being wounded at the Third Battle of Ypres in 1917, the major had both of his legs amputated above the knee and he would use a wheelchair for most of his life. In 1918, he'd been elected as the MP for Liverpool Fairfield and his maiden speech a year later was on the needs of disabled veterans. He dedicated his time to raising awareness about the people wounded in war and the issues of their employment and training, as well as campaigning for war pensions.

Cohen also chaired the Ministry of Labour's national advisory council on employment for disabled people. His work contributed to the passing of the Disabled Persons (Employment) Act in 1944 which meant employers had to meet a certain quota of jobs for disabled people. The organisation Remploy was created as part of the law to directly employ disabled persons in specialised factories. Cohen would become its vice-chairman in 1946 and its chairman in 1955.

The earliest recorded beginnings of the British disability rights movement are especially remarkable, because rights were virtually non-existent at the time. Every fight was hard won, and as we shall see, the work of these activists and organisers in the late 1800s and the first half of the twentieth century paved the way for much of what was to come in the second half.

2

DOES HE TAKE SUGAR?
THE PAN-DISABLED MOVEMENT, 1950s–70s

For a good few years in the mid-twentieth century, disabled rights protests took a back seat while the world focused on the Second World War and its aftermath, with disability causes promoted through the kind of single-issue organisations that we saw in Chapter 1, including new ones founded in the postwar years.

In 1952, for example, three parents and a social worker met to create Scope (under its original name, which is now considered to be a slur, so I won't be using it). Today one of the UK's leading charities advocating against ableism and disablism and for disabled children in general, the charity was originally established to campaign for children with cerebral palsy to have an equal right to an education.

It was only in the 1960s that disabled people took to the streets and fought for their rights in the public eye again—and it was in the postwar decades that people with different kinds of disabilities first came together to form a united, 'pan-impairment' movement. The protests and gains in the early part of the century had focused on workers' rights, including the rehabilitation of soldiers, but the end of the world war era, the establishment of the National Health Service and the economic bump in the 1960s meant that some disabled people felt that this wasn't targeting the real issues and their voices weren't being heard—people who had become disabled during the war or in the workplace were entitled to significantly more help than the rest.

You could argue that this was the start of the welfare culture we still see today, deeming people in need to be worthy or unworthy of support based on whether they had "contributed" to their country either by inflating the economy or serving as cannon fodder. In 1965, the Disablement Income Group started to campaign for a full income for all disabled people through the social security system—whether they could work or not. It was one of the first pan-impairment pressure groups in Britain, which would lead "disabled people" to become a recognised minority in its own right.

The Disablement Income Group was founded by two Surrey "housewives" as they were described at the time: the British-born Megan du Boisson and the Norwegian-born Berit Moore (also known by her maiden name Berit Stueland), who were both disabled themselves, living with multiple sclerosis. (In 1966, Margaret Blackwood followed suit and created the Disablement Income Group Scotland; we'll hear more about her in Chapter 3.)

On 22 March 1965, du Boisson and Moore wrote a letter to the *Guardian* highlighting the deep inequalities of welfare provision for disabled people. At the time, not only did the level of disability payments depend on how the recipient had become disabled, but married disabled women were entitled to no financial support at all, as they were expected to be "kept" by their husbands. This meant many lifelong disabled people were still effectively imprisoned by the state as they were trapped in marriages with no financial support to leave bad situations; if they were abandoned by their husbands or did manage to leave, they had no option but to enter institutions.

Du Boisson and Moore argued that paying disabled people a state pension was more economical and morally justified than condemning people to institutions, and suggested the formation of a group "called the Disablement Income Group—or DIG. It would exist only to correlate the work of the other groups in regard solely to getting recognition for the *right* of disabled persons, irrespective of the reason for that disablement, to pensions from the State to enable them to live in a reasonable degree of independence and dignity *in their own homes*."

The Group changed British understanding of those with chronic conditions and all disabilities. As Charles Robinson wrote in *The Times* in 1967, its "sole reason for existence is to help disabled people live as human beings in a very unhelpful and uninterested society. It began because it was needed, and has flourished because the need for it is desperate."

At the time of Megan du Boisson's death in 1969, just four years after co-founding the DIG, *The Times* would write that "it was her doing, more than that of any other single individual, that public opinion is now so much more alive to the needs of the disabled."

Megan combined her personal experience and love of facts with passion in her advocacy. She contacted a number of MPs and peers from across the three main political parties who were sympathetic to the cause and supported them to table questions about welfare provision for disabled people in both the House of Commons and Lords. She worked not only to lobby for benefits for all disabled people, but also to bring mainstream attention to the struggles disabled people faced in everyday life: she was a vital part of the organising team for successful protest rallies in Trafalgar Square in 1967 and 1968—the 1968 one coincided with the United Nations Year of Human Rights.

Megan was killed in a car crash aged just forty-four, on her way to the fourth annual meeting of the DIG. While she didn't live to see the results of her activism, she definitely woke up the public to our fight. We still feel the importance of her arguments today in the modern debates not only about benefits, but about a whole range of issues we'll explore in later chapters, such as euthanasia.

Berit Moore lived all the way up until 2012 and as well as being an instrumental part of the DIG, she got herself into trouble by translating the controversial *Little Red Schoolbook* into English which instructed children and young people on how to reject societal norms. In the late 1960s, she assisted in the smuggling of a resistance fighter out of Greece, which was then a military dictatorship. She also worked with the Children Poverty Action Group from the 1970s. In her obituary in the *Guardian*, her daughter Ingrid wrote, "My mother was well respected in disability reform circles and is credited with providing the phrase that became the title to the BBC radio programme *Does He Take Sugar?*, while reflecting to a BBC producer on attitudes to disabled people."

The tendency of non-disabled people to address all their questions or instructions to a carer, even in the presence of the visibly disabled person themselves, was something experienced by people with all kinds of impairments—it resonated across the burgeoning rights movement. Berit, her daughter wrote, never allowed her disability to stop her fighting for what she believed in. Berit, Megan and others who fought under the Disablement Income Group are commemorated with a bench in Godalming, Surrey where the group was founded.

* * *

The 1960s also saw another scandal which would lead to legal change. From the 1950s, many pregnant women were prescribed the new drug thalidomide to treat morning sickness. Originally released as a non-addictive, nonbarbiturate sedative by the German pharmaceutical company Chemie–Grünenthal, it was seen as effective when used as an anti-sickness medication. It went on to be heavily promoted and prescribed as a safe drug for women experiencing morning sickness—it was even dubbed a "wonder drug" and its adverts emphasised it was "non-toxic" and had "no known toxicity".

Thalidomide was so widespread and heavily pushed that the manufacturer even gave out free samples to doctors to distribute to their patients before prescribing. It isn't known how many women took the drug around the world, but we know it must have been a huge number as it was prescribed in forty-six countries.

When word started to arise that some patients developed nerve damage and that children were being born with limb differences, it took a while before the dots were connected. It wasn't until 1961 that thalidomide was officially confirmed as the cause. The prescribing of thalidomide resulted in the biggest man-made medical disaster ever with thousands of miscarriages and over 10,000 babies born with limb differences, at a time when this sort of disability completely changed a British person's access to education and work, their social status, and potentially their ability to live independently.

The scandal completely changed the way drugs were tested and led to the creation of the Medicines Act in the

UK in 1968. Despite wrecking so many lives, no individual or company was prosecuted over the disaster.

In 1962, the Thalidomide Society was established in the UK by parents of babies affected by the drug seeking compensation to help meet medical and other associated costs. Unfortunately, despite the public support raised for disabled people in general in the 1960s, their legal battle had very little public or media support. Eventually, a settlement from Distillers, the UK distributor of the drug, was awarded to sixty-two of the affected children and their parents—but they only received the equivalent of 40% of the assessed damage.

It was only in 1972, when the *Sunday Times* launched a campaign on behalf of the thalidomide children that the needle started moving. This campaign was helped by a pivotal Commons motion sponsored by Jack Ashley, a disability campaigner and the first completely deaf MP in the history of the UK (maybe the world). It introduced a distinction between legal and moral obligation, meaning even if something was legal, the Commons recognised that didn't always make it right (something I think Parliament needs to remember today when it comes to many things!). A year later, a final settlement by Distillers was agreed and the Thalidomide Trust was founded to help support affected children and their families.

It was also Jack Ashley who inspired the development of live captioning on television for the benefit of deaf and hard of hearing people. He could follow the proceedings in the House of Commons through the help of the stenograph machines which he'd learned to read, but he knew many others didn't have such means at their disposal. In 1975, while he was visiting a BBC studio, an engineer commissioned a student to develop a computer programme that would translate stenograph output into text as subtitles.

* * *

The thalidomide scandal was an obvious injustice, with so many parents misinformed about the effects of the drug; but the outcome wouldn't have been such a catastrophe if it hadn't forced so many children out of mainstream society. This became an increasing focus of disability activism in the postwar decades, as groups formed to ensure that disabled people were able to participate equally in public life.

One important milestone tackled the Victorian legacy of the 'asylum': in 1959, the Mental Health Act abolished the distinction between psychiatric and other hospitals, so that mental health patients could be deinstitutionalised and others who'd been shut in asylums as 'moral imbeciles' would no longer be identified that way. Defining 'mental disorder' for the first time, as a kind of illness that was medically treatable (and on a voluntary basis, not by locking people away and throwing away the key), encouraged the development of social and community care for people with mental health issues, and for all disabled people.

Another of the key postwar battles for access to civic life would be over transport. The Disabled Drivers' Motor Club (DDMC) had originally been formed (like a lot of early disability rights groups) by First World War veterans in 1922. It was open to all disabled drivers of cars and cyclecars (if you don't know what those were, please go and google them; I can guarantee you won't be disappointed). In the 1930s, the group had successfully lobbied for the right of disabled people to hold a driving licence, and one of its members was the first disabled person to pass the advanced driving test. They were then officially recognised by the Minister of Transport as the representative organisation for disabled drivers.

After the war, their work continued. Through the 1950s, the DDMC campaigned for on-street parking and income tax concessions. We also have the Club to thank for what is now known as the Blue Badge: in the 1960s, their campaign culminated in the first "Yellow Badges", which gave disabled people free parking, being authorised by local authorities. In the 1970s, the DDMC was a huge part of the campaign which saw both the introduction of mobility allowance (which later became the mobility component of Disability Living Allowance), and the establishment of Motability, the scheme allowing disabled people to rent motorised wheelchairs, cars or scooters using their allowance.

The fact that 'even' a group with a specific focus like the DDMC has never run out of access, inclusion and equality issues to tackle shows what a terrible base the postwar disability rights groups were starting from. In the 1980s, they campaigned for and won the rights for hand controls in cars (among other adjustments for disabled drivers and passengers), VAT exemption and for disabled sixteen-year-olds to be able to hold a provisional driving licence. They're still going in the twenty-first century, building on their success in London and campaigning for Blue Badge users to be exempt from congestion charge schemes nationwide.

Another organisation that saw its remit grow and grow in the postwar years was the Invalid Tricycle Association—originally formed in 1948 to promote excursions and travel, it soon focused on mutual help and support and in 1963, it became the Disabled Drivers' Association (DDA). Both the DDA and the DDMC worked in tandem to campaign for change for disabled people on the roads, before in 2005 they merged, becoming Mobilise (now Disabled Motoring UK).

It's easy to imagine these kinds of associations as doing "activism behind a desk": the long, hard slog of working through state bureaucracy in order to challenge it on behalf of disabled people. But leading that kind of campaign and taking action in the streets weren't mutually exclusive in the late twentieth century.

Take Joe Hennessy, who first joined the Invalid Tricycle Association in 1959, who would serve on its governing body continuously for a few decades, including as National Chairman, and who would be appointed Governor of Motability (1977) and a Trustee of the Independent Living Fund (1988–93). In 1971, Joe chaired a mass protest rally in Trafalgar Square to campaign for better mobility provisions and led a delegation to meet Prime Minister Ted Heath afterwards.

The work of pan-impairment organisations in the 1960s and '70s led to disabled people of all kinds working together to create change for decades to come, and often remaining invested in the cause throughout their careers, moving from organisation to organisation and forging closer bonds with other activists. You don't stop disability campaigning: these pioneering groups of the disability rights movement showed that activists would be there for as long as there were ableist structures left to fight. And there certainly would be more to fight.

3

LET US LIVE
THE SOCIAL MODEL, 1970s

While disability campaigners in the immediate postwar decades had achieved greater public empathy and understanding, and acceptance of the principle that all disabled people were entitled to financial support, one of the biggest issues outstanding was their literal living situation: residential arrangements still treated disabled people as "others" separate from society, and by the 1970s they were getting pretty sick of it.

Paul Hunt is often described as the founder of the UK's disabled people's movement. He started out campaigning with the Disablement Income Group in the 1960s, but he would soon move on to a bigger basis of disabled life—the issue that had plagued his own young adulthood. Throughout his teens he had been forced to live on what was known as a "chronic" ward in a hospital in London, surrounded by other disabled people who had been left to die, essentially. These places weren't like care homes today, where spaces and timetables are geared towards helping residents to stay active, whether mentally, physically or socially.

Young Paul, who was born with an impairment, was housed with terminally ill people and the elderly, anyone considered an "invalid"—and all of them were left to lie in their beds, regardless of whether or not they could move from that position without assistance. Even if they could, there was pretty much nothing for them to do and nowhere for them to go: they weren't expected to have interests or needs, beyond physical assistance.

Wards and homes like these weren't built to allow disabled people to move around independently, with features like stair lifts; and if an institution couldn't understand why you would want to get around your home without being carried, it definitely wasn't going to occur to that same culture that it might be important for you to have full access to things like entertainment, activities and company. All of this set-up was standard in the 1950s.

Paul then moved to a residential disabled people's home which, unbelievably, was described by the *Radio Times* in 1955 as a place where "discarded wrecks regained their self-respect". Paul started campaigning with others on the rights of disabled people to make decisions about their own lives, both within his home and beyond, and he left the home in 1970, aged thirty-three. Today, he is most famous for his letter to the

Guardian in September 1972 about the need for disabled people to unionise against segregated living:

> Perhaps we all secretly wish that the severely disabled would go away somewhere together and be happy, leaving us to get on with the important business of leading normal lives. Large ghettos such as Het Dorp [a residential "village" in the Netherlands that was one of the first in the world to be built specifically and solely for disabled people], however imaginatively designed and run, are surely more a result of this feeling than of the actual needs of the handicapped themselves.
>
> It is true that a number of heavily disabled people either cannot or do not wish to rely on relatives for constant help, yet they find that hospital is quite inappropriate as a permanent environment. In Britain at present the only alternative may be an equally unsuitable residential hostel or home, probably isolated in the country, and certainly beset by the intractable problems of institutional living.
>
> What is needed, I believe, is not a big final solution like Het Dorp, but small groups of flatlets incorporated in housing schemes throughout the country. Perhaps half a dozen severely disabled people could thus live out in the community, each as a private householder in his own home, but sharing some facilities and with daily care provided.
>
> Such a scheme would not in itself solve the difficulty of participation in society, but also make it a lot harder for society to ignore the awkward fact of disability.

As a result of his letter, Paul joined up with Vic Finkelstein to found The Union of the Physically Impaired Against Segregation (UPIAS) in 1973. Judy Hunt, Paul's wife, explained in her book *No Limits* that Paul had become very interested in the Civil Rights movement in the US in the 1960s. Finkelstein, a wheelchair user born in South Africa, had come to the UK seeking political asylum: he had been heavily involved in anti-Apartheid activism back home. When they met, they felt that some elements of both these fights could be used in the disability rights movement.

UPIAS developed what later became known as the social model of disability. This was a key shift from the medical model of disability which saw the disabled body as a kind of machine needing to be fixed to conform to the norm—or else be thrown on the proverbial scrap heap and left to rot. The social model of disability instead identifies that although our ill health impairs us, we're mostly disabled by systemic barriers, exclusion, othering and the negative attitudes which make it difficult or impossible for disabled people to live their lives to the full. As UPIAS put it,

> In our view, it is society which disables physically impaired people. Disability is something imposed on top of our impairments, by the way we are unnecessarily isolated and excluded from full participation in society. Disabled people are therefore an oppressed group in society. It follows from this analysis that having low

incomes, for example, is only one aspect of our oppression. It is a consequence of our isolation and segregation, in every area of life, such as education, work, mobility, housing, etc.

The performer and activist Liz Carr tells me that she credits the social model, and the other disabled people who told her about it, for getting her involved in protests towards the end of the century: "I was becoming politicised and disability rights was the answer I had been searching for. The social model of disability was my saviour—as were all the disabled mates who introduced me to the disability rights movement." Fired up by the social model's real hope for change, "I grabbed every opportunity—events, conferences, meetings, committees, newsletters, training and protests. Once I learned that we could work together to create social change, to break down the barriers, I became addicted and committed to activism. I think, hope, in many ways, I still am."

UPIAS was unlike the apolitical disabled-led organisations that came before it due to its political bent, paving the way for other late-twentieth-century entities to follow suit. Its founding statement announced,

> All registered charities receive valuable tax concessions, but they are not allowed to campaign directly for political change. We regard political involvement as essential if disabled people are ever to make real advances. So in order to protect our independence of action we are not registered with the Charity Commissioners.

UPIAS also rejected the claim that non-disabled experts could know better than disabled people themselves, a precursor to the disability rights slogan "Nothing About Us Without Us", which would be made famous in the 1990s by US activists who inherited it from Central European constitutional campaigners via South African disability activists (quite the trip). The founding statement read:

> We as a Union are not interested in descriptions of how awful it is to be disabled. What we are interested in, are ways of changing our conditions of life, and thus overcoming the disabilities which are imposed on top our physical impairments by the way this society is organised to exclude us. In our view, it is only the actual impairment which we must accept; the additional and totally unnecessary problems caused by the way we are treated are essentially to be overcome and not accepted.

This quote, though almost fifty years old, feels like it could've been written by many disabled people and disability activists today.

By the time UPIAS got going in the early 1970s, a cultural shift could already be seen in Parliament. In 1969, the backbench MP Alf Morris had introduced a bill that would become the Chronically Sick and Disabled Persons Act of 1970, the first legislation anywhere in the world that made provisions for chronically sick and disabled people. Morris, a British Labour

Co-operative politician and disability rights campaigner, shared Paul Hunt's vision. He said,

> When the title of my Bill was announced, I was frequently asked what kind of improvements for the chronically sick and disabled I had in mind. It always seemed best to begin with the problems of access. I explained that I wanted to remove the severe and gratuitous social handicaps inflicted on disabled people, and often on their families and friends, not just by their exclusion from town and county halls, art galleries, libraries and many of the universities, but even from pubs, restaurants, theatres, cinemas and other places of entertainment ... I explained that I and my friends were concerned to stop society from treating disabled people as if they were a separate species.

The Act put a broad legal obligation on councils to ensure that disabled people had access to public buildings, and also for the local authority to assist with provision and adaptation in a disabled person's private residence, from the right to a useable phone, radio and television, to the right to a means of transport to and from home.

In 1974, he became the UK's first Minister for the Disabled. While he was not disabled himself, he knew what disabled people and their families had to face thanks to his father who had been injured in the First World War. In his obituary in the *Guardian* in 2012, he was quoted as having said in 2007:

> All our current disability benefits are founded on legislation promoted in my years as minister for disabled people from 1974 to 1979: incapacity benefit, the non-contributory invalidity pension ... the mobility allowance, the disabled housewives' allowance and the carers' allowance—all of them were aimed at reducing the socially handicapping effects of disability.

The landmark legislation Morris had sponsored wasn't a pure product of Parliament: it came out of collaboration between politicians and activists. The committee that was consulted over the drafting of the bill and its provisions was chaired by Mary Greaves, du Boisson's successor at Disability Income Group after her death.

Margaret Blackwood, who you might remember set up Disability Income Group Scotland in the 1960s, also took up the cause of disabled people's right to live a full and self-reliant life. She was instrumental in the Chronically Sick and Disabled Persons Act due to her government lobbying and protests, which meant that disabled people got mobility and attendance benefits under the new law.

In 1972, Margaret went on to found the Margaret Blackwood Housing Association which offered independent living homes for disabled people. The Association is now one of Scotland's leading housing and care providers with high quality housing, care and support for disabled people of all ages, providing over 1,700 homes across all twenty-nine mainland local authorities in Scotland. She was a relentless campaigner in the 1970s in Parliament and her impassioned rallying cry of "You haven't mentioned the disabled! Are we a dirty word?" was often heard in meetings and echoing through the halls of power as she refused to be ignored.

Margaret Blackwood was only one person, though. She worried about the lack of visibility of disabled people. In 1974, she led the famous March on Wheels where over 1,000 people (many using wheelchairs) took over the heart of Edinburgh, down Princes Street. She was quoted in the *Aberdeen Press and Journal* as saying, "Many people occasionally see a disabled person and are able then to forget about it. What we want to do is let the public see a large number of disabled people together. We want disabled people to be fully accepted into society."

Margaret also addressed a rally in Trafalgar Square with the slogan "We Exist. Help Us Live" being shouted—this cry has echoed right up to the late 2024 campaign against the assisted dying bill, with protesters outside Parliament demanding, "Assist Us To Live".

In 1974, UPIAS and a group of other disability organisations set up the Disability Alliance with the aim of campaigning for disability rights. Two years later, UPIAS went further and published its manifesto addressing all disabled people, not just existing campaigners. 'Fundamental Principles of Disability' encouraged disabled people to stop seeing their impairment as the source of their problem, but rather focus on the society which discriminated against them, and rally against it. The "right to exist" attitude of the 1970s was making way for the punky '80s and a demand for change beyond the paltry minimum—a need to organise on a grand scale all over the UK and demand our rights.

4

COALITION

THE DECADE OF DISABLED PERSONS, 1980s

After years of crying out for recognition as equal citizens with the right to an inclusive society, in 1976, the General Assembly of the United Nations voted that 1981 should be the International Year of Disabled Persons, calling for a plan of action at national, regional and international levels, with an emphasis on equality of opportunities, rehabilitation and prevention of disabilities. The theme of the year wasn't just to call on charity but rather to embrace "full participation and equality" so that disabled people could participate fully in the life and development of their societies.

The main outcome, aside from raising awareness, was that the World Programme of Action Concerning Disabled People was adopted by the UN General Assembly. This was followed by the International Decade of Disabled Persons (1982–93). For the first time, disability was put on the world stage and officially linked with human rights in the outlook of UN bodies. In 1980, the World Health Organization produced the first classification of disability, designed for a universal application and encouraging member states to enact new laws in accordance.

There were debates however over how these new goals should be met internationally in a multicultural world. The concept proposed by the UN was based on the Western notion of individual independence, when many Global South countries had a community-based approach involving care-giving and kinship—what was the best way for the Decade of Disabled Persons to encompass both?

Another controversy about the best approach to the Year of Disabled Persons was the on-the-ground organisation. Many disabled activists felt that it mostly involved events and debates about disabled people, rather than featuring many disabled people, or even being aimed at or inclusive of a disabled audience.

The singer Ian Dury, who was disabled himself, wrote the song 'Sp*sticus Autisticus' in protest against the UN's year, which he found to be "patronising" and "crashingly insensitive". The song was banned from the BBC due to its title and offensive lyrics, but in his defence Dury argued that they were supposed to be provocative and that the title was a play on Spartacus the famed gladiator, as his friend Ed Speight had suggested: "it should be Sp*sticus Autisticus—he's the freed slave of the disabled."

Dury used the offensive term *because* it was becoming taboo, used more commonly as a slur to throw at disabled people from outside than to talk about them. At the 2012 London Paralympics opening ceremony, Orbital and the Graeae theatre company would perform the song live on stage.

* * *

Dury wasn't the only one tired of being excluded from major conferences that impacted them. Disabled people were inspired to start their own grassroots organisations—not just to petition governments for specific changes, keeping up the work of the postwar decades, but also to formally discuss the issues in their own forums, and to come up with campaigning strategies and policies of their own.

Disabled Peoples' International (DPI) was formed in the UN's Year of Disabled Persons, 1981, and many disabled people and organisations attended a conference run by Rehabilitation International. People from around the world shared their thoughts, experiences and ideas around disability and discrimination. In 1984, Disabled Peoples' International successfully lobbied the United Nations to include disabled people in the Declaration of Human Rights.

The new energy on the international stage was happening back in the UK too. In 1981, the British Council of Organisations of Disabled People was set up, largely thanks to Vic Finkelstein's work, and he became its first chair. In the same year, he represented Britain at the first world congress, established by Disabled Peoples' International. He created one of the first university courses we know now as disabilities studies.

The coalition of Council organisations continued the British tradition of intersectional disability activism: one of the founding member organisations was Gemma, the national friendship and support group of disabled lesbians and bisexual women, co-founded by Elsa Beckett.

The Council's longest serving member, who was there right from the start, was Stephen Bradshaw. He was first involved in disability activism via the Disablement Income Group in 1968, going on to become the first director of the Spinal Injuries Association (SIA), founded in 1974. He would also go on to chair Rights Now!, the coalition of user-led and non-user led organisations founded in the 1990s to fight for civil rights for disabled people. His obituary celebrates him as one of the great "visionary leaders" of the disability rights movement.

The scaled-up national and international movements for disability rights inspired more local groups in the UK to get together and work towards equality. One such organisation was the Greater Manchester Coalition of Disabled People, which was established in 1985 after many years of work from activists. Individuals travelled around the UK to talk to other organisations to see how they were set up, coming up with a constitution and working out what to do in Greater Manchester. They continued collaborating with other organisations in their campaigns, and organised conferences for political change on transport, housing and social care.

They were also passionate about raising awareness and spreading information to the disability community. The Greater Manchester Coalition decided to produce and distribute their own factsheets and information bulletins—a crucial contribution to the coalition-building of the 1980s, given that there was no internet back then and the mainstream media doesn't publish a huge amount of disability stories. Disabled people who weren't directly involved in campaigning themselves had practically no way of knowing what was happening around their rights and what organisations were doing to fight for them. But the answer was, more and more.

The Greater Manchester Coalition was typical of the radical disability activism that could be seen popping up around the country in that decade. They kept their local foothold but often tackled nationwide campaigns. Half of the members were also members of UPIAS, upholding the social model of disability, and members were also heavily involved in the creation of the British Council of Organisations of Disabled People. The Coalition also set up the Disabled People's Archive, an essential national resource that is still running today.

The momentum building in the 1980s wasn't just about meetings and publications: it was also still taking place on the streets. In London in 1983, disabled people blocked the entrance to the Members' car park at Parliament to support one of the earlier (though unsuccessful) Anti-Discrimination Bills.

In 1985, disabled people successfully picketed the Manchester Town Hall when they found that its Disabled People's Steering Group was, ironically, inaccessible to disabled people due to the venue. They also lobbied for the posts in the Greater Manchester Council's Equal Opportunity Unit to be reserved for disabled people. (This was before positive discrimination and other employment inclusion schemes so despite these roles being about disability they weren't required to be offered to them.)

There were also huge calls during the 1980s for anti-discrimination legislation and a form of Civil Rights law for disabled people that would make it illegal for them to be discriminated against in all areas concerning daily life including housing, transport, education and work. (As we know, disabled people would have to wait until 1995 for the Disability Discrimination Act to be passed.)

There were national policy changes in the 1980s—the Disabled Person's Act of 1986 went further than the Chronically Sick and Disabled Persons Act (1970), in that it required local authorities to actually meet the needs of disabled people; and in 1988, the Independent Living Fund was set up to enable disabled people to live in the community rather than in institutions. But without anti-discrimination legislation, these measures could only go so far, both in terms of disabled people's access to public life and in terms of their place in British culture.

In 1988, Ian Stanton of the Greater Manchester Coalition, alongside sixty other people, demonstrated outside Granada Studio to protest the decision by the makers of the *Erasmus Microman* children's TV series to deny disabled actor Nabil Shaban work because they were worried he would scare children. The lack of representation on screen became an ever more significant issue during this time and would continue to do so into the '90s. As we carry on through the book we will see more and more protests around the issue of discrimination, as MPs kept delaying or "talking out" any debate.

But the decade had seen groups become more organised and connected: change was becoming something disabled people were prepared to insist on instead of asking for. In the late 1980s, disabled campaigners were done with playing nice. Soon they'd start to resort to much more extreme means.

5

PISS ON PITY

DIRECT ACTION, 1980s–90s

In the late 1980s and early '90s, the disability rights movement was in full swing, and organising combined with fury and a refusal to stay quiet. On 28 July 1988, when cuts were proposed to social security, the newly formed British Council of Organisations of Disabled People held a day of action, marching from Kennington to the Department for Health and Social Security head office in Elephant and Castle. The march was attended by over 1,200 people and as described in the poem 'The Battle for Elephant and Castle' by Simon Brisenden, "we were disabled, united and completely incited by an anger we knew to be true".

When the marchers reached Elephant and Castle, instead of just shouting slogans, several hundred either sat down in the road or planted their wheelchairs in place and refused to move, blocking the roads. One person who was of course there was activist Barbara Lisicki.

"It was hilarious cos the great and the good of the movement were coming to me and trying to get me to tell them all to stop, and I said no! And I sat down in the road too." Barbara laughed while telling me about that day. "I think it was one of the first examples of direct action we'd done on a huge scale that really disrupted. And it was all spontaneous. It was beautiful."

In 1989, Chesterfield Council pedestrianised their town centre, ignoring four protests by disabled people and a petition with over a 1,000 signatures. Derbyshire Coalition of Disabled People (DCDP) members, backed by disabled people from other groups, ignored the new rules about where they could park and continued to drive their vehicles into the new pedestrianised zone. This resulted in arrests and court hearings. Once again the court hearings showed just how much disabled people were shut out of public life as two of the arrested, Ken Davis and Jack Fitton, had to be lifted up the steps of the court by officials.

In court, the disabled people arrested refused to plead guilty and all read out the same defence, an extract from which explained their actions:

> We explained that the Order would affect our ability to go about our business; to shop; to find work; in some cases even to get to our places of work; or just to have the pleasure of going into our own town centre. We explained that the alternative parking would be too far away for some disabled people; that we would lose our

independence; that it would add to the stress on those who help us.

The court finally cracked, the charges were withdrawn and no fines were issued. A team was commissioned from Leeds University to determine the best course of action. Disabled people were of course right and eventually the council relented and allowed disabled people to park in the market square.

After this, these Derbyshire Coalition members formed the *Derbyshire Direct Action Now Network* (DDANN). One of the network's key protesters was Alan Holdsworth, who acted as community link worker for the Coalition. Alan, who was an ambulatory wheelchair user, is most notorious for his multicoloured hat which always made him one of the first to be picked out for arrest at any action. Later, during his time with the national Direct Action Network, he would coordinate all of their actions taking place in his area.

* * *

Over the following years there were many more disability rights marches organised by disabled networks aiming to disrupt. A key slogan of the movement was "Rights Not Charity" so when activists saw and heard of the trauma inflicted on disabled people by the increasingly popular TV telethon fundraisers in the early 1990s, they knew they had to put a stop to them—by making some trouble.

ITV London at the time held a biannual 24-hour event called *Telethon*, which was all about raising money for "needy", i.e. disabled, people. Despite apparently being about helping disabled people, no disabled people were involved in the presenting or production of the show. It was presented by an entirely non-disabled set of presenters and viewed by the community as a way to boost careers rather than support disabled people. It was also made primarily for non-disabled people to make them feel sorry for disabled people, assuming disabled people wouldn't be watching an entertainment show.

To this end, disabled people were shown as being desperate and miserable and almost living half lives (when they were shown at all); the shows mainly spoke about disabled people, not to them. It would parade them as objects of pity for the entertainment of people watching at home—much like the BBC does with *Children in Need*—with all proceeds going to charities.

Of course, these charities helped disabled people, but when disabled people were being discriminated against in the job market and couldn't even get on public transport, they found the tone of these broadcasts patronising, and objected to the lazy approach of chucking money at disabled people in a feelgood act of charity without confronting how society disabled them. There was also much frustration from disabled people about the way they were used in charity advertising. The "Cap in Hand?" one-day conference in 1990 questioned this particularly.

The first telethon protest (now known as Block Telethon) was, by Barbara Lisicki's own admission, pulled together at quite short notice, that same year. Alan Holdsworth, Barbara's partner at the time, told the BBC it was "the easiest action ever to organise" due to how many people hated the fundraiser broadcasts and were willing to take part. The action featured a few hundred gathered on the South Bank outside the studios of ITV London. There was a heavy police presence but disabled people refused to be intimidated.

Placards featured slogans such as "Ask Us, Not Aspel", referencing the presenter Michael Aspel, but there was one slogan that definitely struck a chord, mainly because it angered police. "Piss On Pity" became a rallying cry for the Direct Action Network after police threatened to arrest Alan if he didn't take it down, despite it not being as offensive as other signs.

What made this action different was that the media were now behind the disability rights movement; the Network's protests were always covered and Barbara was even invited to debate the head of *Telethon* Joe Simpson. In Barbara's own words, "I wiped the floor with him", but she says this was mainly because ITV didn't have a robust argument against disabled people's clear message that this wasn't how they wanted to be portrayed to the nation: "they were trying to justify it but people could see that *Telethon* was so grotesque and it was just full of stars looking to promote themselves."

The growing media platform and the power of the early protests fed each other and piled pressure on those responsible for the telethons: "Once people saw us on the news, they'd turn up. And, there was the media support that there just isn't now."

On 8 September 1991, realising that direct action worked, the British Council of Organisations of Disabled People hosted a weekend workshop led by Mike Auberger and Babs Johnson from the American Disability Rights Group ADAPT. It was held during the Council's tenth annual meeting in South Manchester and built on the international network-building of the 1980s, focusing on how British activists could learn from similar street protests in the United States. The workshop finished with a nice practical exercise where they all went outside and blocked three buses on the main road, as you do.

Between ITV telethons, there was also *Children in Need*, the biannual BBC telethon raising money for "needy" children, the overwhelming majority at the time being disabled. "I think the thing about *Children in Need* is the name of it, people wanted to help kids and it wasn't just disabled ones, so they thought it was a good thing to have," Barbara says. Disabled journalist Melissa Parker described it in 2022 as "the BBC turning disabled kids into Tiny Tim", referring to the angelically suffering Charles Dickens character with an unknown deadly condition—as of course *Children in Need* is still happening today.

PISS ON PITY

In 1991, disabled people protested outside the BBC studios in Leeds where *Children in Need* was being filmed; after the first Block Telethon though, police were onto disabled people. Barbara explained to me that protesters were tracked so much by police that they had to sneak in and out of hotels in cities where actions were taking place so as to not be bothered.

After protestors blocked the doors of the BBC in Leeds, officers got involved. "The police were nasty, really nasty," Barbara tells me, and "that was the first time I ever got arrested." Barbara says she was put in a cell on her own as she was the only woman. "The cops were bastards in Leeds, they wouldn't even give us a drink of water, they broke all the rules." This treatment wouldn't stop the campaigners from their work, though. A partner of a protester who worked with social services got the police to release them, and disabled organisers soon set to work organising the second Block Telethon to be held when it next aired in 1992.

Unlike the first protest, Barbara says this one took months of planning. They held meetings in houses and communicated with all the other disability groups around the country through fax and over the phone. Barbara tells me that it was important to have organisers they could trust as this was such a precarious time for disabled people.

After Alan's banner had been confiscated at the 1990 protest, Piss on Pity became the war cry of Block

Telethon 1992 with a hundred t-shirts printed with the slogan. Barbara was asked to remove the "offensive article" of clothing by police whilst setting up and she told him, "Certainly, Officer. I'm not wearing anything underneath but, if that's what you want, I will comply with your request. By the way, there are another 99 of these, all being worn right here, today…" The t-shirts, unsurprisingly, were not removed.

Whilst the 1992 action was a demonstration, organisers also describe it as a party, a celebration of what truly makes disabled people great, as opposed to how *Telethon* was portraying them. There was music, poetry, dancing, comedy and of course storming of police barricades, along with "accidental" denting of cars belonging to rich celebrities who'd come along for the free publicity. Protestors shook police barricades until they toppled and chanted for hours, interrupting the broadcast.

One of the celebrities who came out to try and confront protestors was Frank Bruno (who now identifies as disabled), who asked "What's wrong with you people?" Celebrities were baffled as to why disabled people weren't grateful for the fundraising and the spotlight. Chris Tarrant, an ITV presenter staunchly opposed to Block Telethon, saw his feet run over by a wheelchair user.

As Elspeth Morrison recounted in a 2018 Medium article collated by Barbara, "What I remember most clearly are the faces of celeb types … arriving in their limos. Their faces beaming generously to the grateful masses, then, when realising we weren't the grateful masses, turning to bewilderment and possibly horror." Disability rights champion Sue Elsegood said in the same piece, "We were claiming back our identities as being in control, pissing on pity and challenging patronising charity portrayals of disabled people." Sue, it turns out, was the one who "accidentally" trampled Tarrant's foot.

The 1992 action resulted in that year being the last ever *Telethon*, but Block Telethon's organisers realised that after bringing together so many people they had to use it— "it would've been such a waste to have organised so many people and then not do anything with that momentum," Barbara says. "We just basically said, we know direct action works, and what we're going to do is set up a direct action group—and it was never an organisation. It was always just like a group of people. So we decided to set something up. And that thing was, DAN."

So in 1993, along with Alan Holdsworth and Sue Elsegood, Barbara founded the Disabled People's Direct Action Network (DAN), a national network of disabled people and allies that would come together across the UK to fight for disability rights. The organisation fed from a national committee of disabled people which many of DAN's organisers sat on. Disruptive protest and civil disobedience was moving well beyond Derbyshire.

* * *

Alongside DAN's efforts to destroy TV telethons and charity "displays" of disabled people as objects of pity, protests were mounting against exclusion from public transport. Wheelchair ramps and low floors for buses were nowhere to be seen in this period: if you couldn't climb on board, you couldn't board. Step-free stations were also a rarity: in London, only the recently opened Docklands Light Railway had been built with level access to the trains, and wheelchairs were actually banned on parts of the Tube.

Between 1990 and 1993, the Campaign for Accessible Transport fought for disabled people's right to travel. The organisers included Kate Brown, Tracey Proudlock, Victoria Waddington, Sue Elsegood, Ruth Bashall (who later founded Stay Safe East, an organisation that supports disabled abuse survivors) and Allan Sutherland, who was their press officer.

The Campaign held street demonstrations as they couldn't actually board buses to protest about them. In 1990, the group shut down Oxford Street, and Sue Elsegood said the protest made her realise that her impairment wasn't the problem, it was the ableist society she lived in. "I realised then that buses should be for everyone, including us. Up to that point, I just thought it was my fault I couldn't walk and couldn't get on."

Fifteen people were arrested that day, including Sue, but the charges were eventually dropped. Many people think this is because the courts themselves were inaccessible—attempting to prosecute disabled activists for action in the name of equal access often involved an embarrassing scene of officials having to carry the "defendants" into the courtroom.

In the spring of 1993, the Direct Action Network held their first weekend residential in Norwich to decide who they wanted to be and what they wanted to do. The group had to decide which battles to fight—for civil rights in general, or on specific issues. The vote eventually went in favour of specific targets and equal access to public transport was an obvious one for DAN's first campaign.

In 1995 the Network began targeting many train stations and buses around the country. As the Campaign for Accessible Transport had been finding, "It was something very visible that people could see and get behind," Barbara says. In February 1995, DAN caused pandemonium on Westminster Bridge by stopping traffic and handcuffing themselves to buses or pulling themselves under vehicles to stop them from moving. Barbara got into an argument with a furious bus driver whilst police attempted to carry Sue off in her very heavy electric wheelchair and Alan chained himself to another bus.

It became a routine. "We'd handcuff ourselves to each other. We'd hang ourselves up to the fronts of buses, the backs of buses, climb on top of buses if we could. And we just wouldn't stop even when we knew we'd be arrested," Barbara laughs.

In train stations up and down the country protestors chained themselves to trains to protest the fact that wheelchair users couldn't travel with the rest of the passengers. Alan was arrested in Cardiff at one of these actions. Sue was initially arrested but then let go. When the police told her off for stopping people from catching the train, she told them, "Well, I can't access platform three."

Police often intervened and carried activists away from the scene kicking and screaming, but they typically struggled to actually hold and charge them. Due to how inaccessible stations and police vans were, protesters would often walk away without going to jail and, as with the Oxford Street protest, magistrates' courts were also often too inaccessible for any charges to stick.

Whilst the actions of DAN seemed radical and unacceptably disruptive, that's only because the activist had done their research. "We went out and did our homework, we used the suffragettes for inspiration," Barbara said, and drew attention to how the climate protesters getting a lot of attention now are also drawing from past actions that have ultimately been recognised as just, and led to change—"but the press don't want to tell people that when they're getting outraged about soup being thrown on art."

The 1990s bus protesters were named the wheelchair warriors; one of their chants was "They call us wheelchair warriors, we're kicking up some fuss. And we will keep on marching 'til you let us on the bus."

During the most outrageous and public facing direct actions, DAN was heavily criticised, especially by other disabled organisers. Much like the split in the suffragettes, many thought protests should remain lawful and nonviolent so as to not ruin the image of disabled people and put non-disabled people off—but they weren't deterred. Barbara said, "We were really ripped into, even by disabled people saying 'you shouldn't be breaking the law.' And we said, 'Well, you tell us a better way. What's happened so far? If you think that you can be more effective, tell us how.'"

Between 1982 and the mid-nineties, there were fourteen attempts to get rights for disabled people put into laws and all failed when they reached the stage of Commons debate. One of the MPs who was a strong opponent to disability rights laws was Robert Hayward, a Conservative who'd deliberately wasted time in a filibuster during the January 1992 debate on a disability civil rights bill, blocking its passage, though he was not the only MP to resort to "talking out" tactics in this period.

Hayward would be forced to apologise the following month for misleading the House, and would go on to lose his seat in that year's general election. In the next year's election he attempted to win the safe conservative seat of Christchurch, but disabled people weren't prepared to let that happen. In DAN's first public action, disability activists spent the day chasing after him in their wheelchairs and informing his would-be constituents what he'd done. He eventually lost the election to the Liberal Democrats by over 35%.

This was an example of using the suffragettes for inspiration, as there had been many cases of their activist forebears following around politicians who were opponents of their cause, in particular the case of Mary Maloney who in 1908 followed Winston Churchill with a bell demanding he apologise for insulting women's suffrage every time he spoke.

Given the resistance they were up against in Parliament, it's obvious that the passing of the 1995 Disability Discrimination Act wouldn't have happened without both the direct action of DAN but also traditional campaigning from groups such as Rights Now. On 9 November 1995 the Act came into law, describing itself as finally making it "unlawful to discriminate against disabled persons" in the jobs market and in the availability of "goods, facilities and services or the disposal or management of premises"; the new law also made specific "provision about the employment of disabled persons; and to establish a National Disability Council."

6

DISABLED ANARCHIST BLUES
THE ARTS MOVEMENT, 1980s–2000s

While disabled people had hoped an anti-discrimination bill would give them the same sort of legal protections that were already available to other oppressed groups under the 1970s Sex Discrimination and Race Relations Acts, they were left bitterly disappointed by the law that was actually passed. While the Disability Discrimination Act of 1995 officially outlawed state or business discrimination against disabled people for the first time, activists said its definitions and provisions were flimsy and didn't offer enough protections to disabled people in practice.

"We were very critical of it as we all felt that this isn't what we'd campaigned for," Barbara Lisicki says. Unlike the others, there was no legal body set up to police the disability anti-discrimination law. The Disability Rights Commission wasn't even established until 1999, four years after the Act. The measures set out in the act, including a requirement of reasonable adjustments to make services and organisations accessible, also had implementation timelines of up to a decade; and key things DAN had fought for such as accessible transport would require further legislation (the Act wouldn't be strengthened until 2003).

At the time, Andy Gill of DAN said: "It is not addressing the real concerns of what disabled people need. We need legislation to ensure that all disabled people have the right to live as full participants in society."

So, the work of disabled campaigners was far from done after the Disability Discrimination Act was passed, and DAN kept up its activism for a few more years before its focus became more political, as you'll see in the next few chapters. The Network held more than 100 actions between 1993 and 1998 and sixteen national actions between 1993 and 2002.

Other groups and campaigns were also still pushing for change. In 1996, the British Council of Organisations of Disabled People and its chair Baroness Jane Campbell set up the National Centre for Independent Living. This completely changed both the services offered to disabled people and the way they could independently live their lives, the Centre being instrumental in lobbying the government to legalise direct payments for social care that year.

From 1997, disabled people relying on community care funded by their local authority could independently manage their finances, receiving council money to pay their assistant's salary. Before this, disabled people either had to employ their own carer privately without financial support, or they had to receive grants from the council indirectly through a non-profit (where the council had this sort of scheme in place—because direct payment was not allowed).

Campbell, who has specialised in disability rights and independent living for most of her life and co-wrote the academic book *Disability Politics*, has seen the Council through some of its most pioneering work in the field of independent living, civil rights, peer counselling and equal opportunities.

Campbell's *Disability Politics* co-author Mike Oliver was a founding Council member and a member of DAN. He was the first Professor of Disability Studies in the world and the one who coined and popularised the term "social model" to describe the distinction UPIAS had made in the 1970s between "impairment" and "disability".

Researchers and academics are important for disability rights not only so that we can support political fights with theory, but so that we are represented in academia and researched in a way that benefits and considers us. Mike Oliver, keen for academics to serve the interests of disabled people and not bother them as a means to an end in their research, was a key proponent of what he described as "emancipatory disability studies".

In fact, many leading figures in the disability rights movement of the late twentieth century weren't just energetic campaigners, but brilliant minds, including Liz Crow, and the DAN co-founders. Aside from their role in direct action, Barbara Lisicki and Alan Holdsworth performed as a comedy cabaret duo in the 1990s, touring the UK, Europe and US, including Glastonbury in 1993, to spread the word about disability rights and direct action.

This had started in 1988, when Barbara performed a stand-up routine at a London Disability Arts Forum Cabaret—that impromptu performance ended up kickstarting her career as the UK's first female disabled comedian. Their alter-egos, Barbara's sharp-witted Wanda Barbara and Alan's profanity-laden musical act Johnny Crescendo, drummed up support for the cause at their "Tragic but Brave" roadshows—an uncompromising double act that was seen as both irreverent and radical.

The show title was borrowed from one of the songs sung at Block Telethon 1992, by Ian Stanton, one of Britain's foremost disabled singer-songwriters. Stanton himself used humour to expose the prejudice disabled people faced and some of his most famous songs quickly became anthems of the movement with titles such as "Chip on Your Shoulder" and "Talkin' Disabled Anarchist Blues"; the trio made for a tough act to ignore. Alan told the BBC, "We went around disability organisations performing and telling jokes. We then talked to them in the bar afterwards to see what they wanted to do."

When a venue cut Barbara and Alan's microphones over "blasphemous language", Barbara and Alan penned a poem that I really recommend you go and seek out, called 'Disabled People aren't allowed to say Fuck' to highlight the hypocrisy of the offending and discriminatory language used against disabled people, while they themselves were expected to be eternally virtuous—patient with ableist society and grateful for any positive treatment, but never angry about the rest. Here's one verse:

> Disabled people are allowed to say
>> help
>> please
>> thank you
>> thank you, thank you
>> thank you very much
>> but they're not allowed to say fuck.

* * *

Art has long played a powerful part in disability politics, as we'll see in this chapter. As the protests raged on in the 1980s and '90s, a new creative wave had emerged, growing up alongside the Direct Action Network, which would bring disabled people's demands to a mainstream audience.

As disability activism grew more widespread, disabled art as activism became an entire sub-movement, inspired by the rights movement, the work of UPIAS and the social model of disability. The National Disability Arts Collection and Archive (NDACA) shows just how important art is in achieving social change. It's an invaluable study space and online resource where you can browse over 3,500 images of the disability arts movement and hear many disabled artist-activists (and their loved ones) discuss their lives and work, which became an intrinsic part of the political movement in the late twentieth century.

The roots of this activist art movement go back pretty much as far as the pan-disability movement. The charity Shape had been launched in 1977 by Gina Levete, who had a dance background, as a disability-led arts organisation working to improve access to culture for disabled people and also by providing opportunities for disabled artists. The founders felt that all disabled people should be able to participate fully in the arts and culture and that the sector should be made accessible and inclusive.

We've already seen how this principle of "nothing about us without us" crossed from political campaigning into art in the 1980s with the prominence of singer-songwriter Ian Dury, reclaiming derogatory words in his lyrics and empowering disabled people with his famous protest song. Vic Finkelstein, who had created UPIAS with Paul Hunt in the 1970s, was another person who shifted his focus in the 1980s towards disability art. In 1986, he helped set up the London Disability Arts Forum with Sian Vasey (also from UPIAS) and Anne Rae to promote and discuss disabled people's shared cultural identity.

Sian Vasey was also instrumental that year in the creation of the magazine *Disability Arts in London* (Elspeth Morrison of Block Telethon fame would go on to be the editor for six years, before becoming a television producer for the BBC's Disability Programme Unit). This was one of two groundbreaking publications to start that year: the songwriter Ian Stanton, a member of the Greater Manchester Coalition of Disabled People, was tapped to become the editor of their journal *Coalition*, which became required reading for disabled people nationwide.

In 1990, Vasey moved on from print media and created the National Disability Arts Forum, and in 1993, she set up Criptic Productions as a partnership, co-producing a three-part series on the disability charities, *Poor Dear*, for the BBC. She then set up her own production company, Circle Pictures, in 1994 and went on to produce and direct documentaries for Channel 4: one on disability and motherhood, and another on disability and technology. Sian continued her work as a campaigner including with Not Dead Yet UK, who led the charge in 2024 against the assisted dying bill, leading a number of high profile protests up until her death in 2020.

In 1996, Baroness Jane Campbell—now a patron of the National Disability Arts Collection and Archive—called the disabled people's movement a "jigsaw". She said that disability art, disability studies and disability campaigning were all needed for the whole picture to emerge.

We can see how true that is in the work of someone like Paddy Masefield OBE, who was a disability activist, playwright and stage director. In the 1980s he'd become a key arts consultant for disability arts for Arts Council England (ACE). Alongside Wendy Harpe, he was uncompromising on the need for cultural and public buildings to be accessible to all. It is mostly thanks to his campaigning that all buildings in receipt of funding from the Arts Council lottery panel are now required to be fully accessible.

Another perfect example is Deborah Williams, the writer, producer and digital composer. She has played a significant role in ensuring that the Disability Discrimination Act 1995—and subsequent disability equality legislation, such as the Equality Act 2010—are implemented in the cultural sector itself.

Activists instrumental in the Disability Discrimination Act were also out there making art about their struggle, from music and poetry to plays, sculptures and even comedy, including regular performances at rallies. It was because of the disability arts movement that the hugely successful 1992 Block Telethon had been more than a protest—it became a celebration of disabled life.

DISABLED ANARCHIST BLUES

Liz Carr was involved in a lot of protests during the 1990s as an activist and an organiser. She tells me about one held in Nottingham, where she lived at the time:

> It was a two or three day action and after the first night we had a "social" in a bar with cabaret performances from disabled artists. At the end of that night, us all still buzzing from blocking buses in the streets and marching powerfully together in protest, we sang the refrain, "proud, angry and strong" and it seemed to go on forever, rising us up, the pride tangible in that room that night. I will never forget that night in Nottingham maybe thirty years ago now.

Not only performing arts but visual arts were also an important part of the growing movement. In 1991, the disabled artist Tony Heaton created the Shaken Not Stirred exhibition, which featured a sculpture made of 1,760 charity collection cans in the shape of a pyramid. A year later, Tony would exhibit the same artwork at the Block Telethon event. He ran into the room and threw a prosthetic leg at the pile to make it topple, to rapturous applause, in the name of rights, not charity.

This was one of the first disability arts events to receive widespread coverage in the media, due to its provocative nature and anti-charity stance. In 1994, he created another iconic sculpture, 'Great Britain from a Wheelchair'. It shows a map of the United Kingdom made out of wheelchair parts and points towards the idea of the country becoming fully accessible, as it very much wasn't at the time and still isn't today.

Finally, disabled people were not only able to organise their own platforms and publicly campaign for their rights, but they could also make space for themselves in the arts. Many of these pioneers left an indelible mark on the British cultural landscape and helped change the outlook from one of pity to one of community, irreversibly changing the way society saw disability rights—and disability itself—in the UK.

Katherine Araniello, who died in 2019, was a London-based live art, performance and video artist, who responded to the negative representation of disability. She used a range of mediums including film, large-scale production and live art performances. With Aaron Williamson, she created the Disabled Avant-Garde, a satirical outfit born in the 2000s that used videos, art and live performances to inspire debate on the way disabled people were stereotyped. They achieved a prestigious national platform for their art, winning commissions from the South Bank Centre and BBC Radio 4 and Tate Modern, praise from internationally famous artists like Yinka Shonibare, and funding from Arts Council England and Arts Council Wales.

Maybe nobody represents the way that disabled art has brought disability politics into the British mainstream more than Liz Carr, one of the UK's best-known disabled actors in the twenty-first century. Liz has been a beloved character in TV hits of the 2010s and 2020s, like *Good Omens* and *Silent Witness*—but, as we'll see in a later chapter, her story has come full circle: maybe the public doesn't remember that she started out chaining herself to buses, but they definitely know her as one of the country's leading commentators on disability rights issues—a platform she earned with her international success as a performer.

As the book goes on, we'll see that in the bleakest times we need art, and disabled art, more than ever.

7

CUTS KILL

1990s–2010s

The issue with disability activists and leaders, and the rights they'd fought for, becoming more visible? They became an easy target for anyone with an interest in creating a political narrative of good and bad Britons.

Alongside the movement of the '90s which fought for disabled people to be taken seriously by society as humans with an equally important set of needs, a more sinister enemy was emerging as the century came to an end—in the post-Thatcher era of neoliberal economics, governments were looking to shrink the state and spend less money, and who better to be the scapegoat than those pesky disabled people demanding their rights?

Lots of people reading this book probably know about benefit changes impacting disabled people in the official era of austerity (the 2010s), and some of you might know that this policy shift actually started in the early 2000s—but it's important to explain that the

Westminster agenda to make benefits claimants public enemy number one goes back even further than that.

In 1992, Peter Lilley, the then Secretary of State for Social Security (the predecessor to the Department for Work and Pensions), gave a speech to the Conservative party conference which infamously became known as his "I've got a little list" speech. It's actually adapted from a song in *The Mikado*, Gilbert and Sullivan's comic opera, in which the Lord High Executioner sings about all the annoying people in society he would kill if he had the chance. Lilley changed it to talk about people on benefits, telling his party, "we're not in the business of subsidising scroungers" and gleefully reading out his little poem:

> Just like in the Mikado, I've got a little list
> of benefit offenders
> who I'll soon be rooting out
> and who never would be missed
> they never would be missed.
> There's those who make up bogus claims
> in half a dozen names
> and counsellors who draw the dole
> to run left-wing campaigns
> they never would be missed
> they never would be missed.
> There's young ladies who get pregnant

just to jump the housing queue
and dads who won't support the kids
of the ladies they have kissed
and I haven't even mentioned
all those sponging socialists
I've got them on my list
and there's none of them be missed
there's none of them be missed!

He ended this disgusting little ditty to rapturous applause and laughter. This would go on to set the blueprint for the way the Conservative governments of 1990–7 treated all benefits claimants, but especially disabled ones. A couple of years later, Lilley would be depicted on the satirical TV show *Spitting Image* as a Nazi commandant at a concentration camp.

To see society's vulnerable spoken about like this by the minister whose job it was to ensure that they are supported was galling enough. But this attitude was supported by the then Prime Minister John Major, who said in Parliament in 1993, "it beggars belief that so many more people have suddenly become invalids," implying that people were all suddenly becoming disabled for benefits as opposed to many realising they needed them.

It's worth noting that this apparent uptick in claims was coming after Major's predecessor Margaret Thatcher as prime minister had closed the majority of shipyards and mines: many men who had been disabled for life by their hard labour in these dangerous industries were realising how unfit they were for other jobs, if they weren't too ill to work at all.

At the time the main benefit for disabled people who couldn't work was called Invalidity Benefit and Peter Lilley vowed to reduce the number of people entitled to it. In 1995, it was changed to Incapacity Benefit—even the wording shift shows the ideology of funds going not to those who needed help or would benefit from help, but only to disabled people who absolutely could not possibly do anything without the help; and this new form of the benefit was subject to taxation.

To determine who qualified for Incapacity Benefit, the All Work Test was introduced, using doctors employed by Social Security to assess who "really" was too unwell to work. Nick Wikeley, Professor of Law at Southampton University, persuasively argues that this created further division between "deserving" and "undeserving" recipients of state support. It felt like the backlash against disabled people coming out of the shadows was just beginning.

This was the start of a steady slope. In the early 1990s, the UK suffered its worst economic recession since the Great Depression of the 1930s, with rioting in communities ripped apart by poverty and millions unemployed nationwide—about twice as many as in late 2024, at a time when the population was smaller.

Even once the national economy started to turn around, the new age of global trade that kicked off as the

Cold War ended meant that quality of life and work opportunities never recovered in large parts of the country, especially post-industrial towns, with labour increasingly outsourced to cheaper countries without as many workers' rights. As life worsened for non-disabled people, it became easier to blame disabled people for these problems.

* * *

The fight for disability rights has never just been with one political party—and the New Labour team that got into power in 1997 had fundamentally the same neoliberal philosophy as the Tory administrations that had come before it. Tony Blair's government continued the project Thatcher had started and Major had continued, to "roll back the state". It was just a different set of faces trying to reform benefits now, and as a disabled person, I know that whenever someone in government is poking the welfare laws, it's never for our benefit. The New Labour reforms spelled one thing: cuts, and new, more hostile criteria and language to justify them.

Looking back on these early years of the Blair government, researchers Linda Piggott and Chris Grover in their landmark paper *Retrenching Incapacity Benefit* (2009) would conclude that "without a discourse vilifying sick and disabled claimants, it was difficult in 1997 for the government to construct a 'convincing story' to justify large-scale cuts in social security and it was forced to acknowledge the political realities of welfare state roll back."

As always, disabled people were there to object and in 1997 DAN protested welfare cuts outside Downing Street and threw red water-based paint at the gates spelling out "Blair's blood". Sue Elsegood later told the BBC, "The cuts were going to make us bleed, make us suffer, as disabled people. We knew there were lots of people who wouldn't be able to afford their heating with the benefit cuts he was proposing." However, this only led Labour to dig in harder and work to create public distrust of disabled people on unemployment benefits. It's the oldest tactic in the playbook, and unfortunately for disabled people, it has worked every single time.

In 2007, the Welfare Reform Act came into law, which meant the Incapacity Benefit was replaced by Employment Support Allowance and with it came the Work Capability Assessment. The Assessment gave more powers to job centre advisors to decide whether claimants were fit for work. This was despite Department for Work and Pensions advisors expressing concern in 2005 that their workload was already too great for them to be able to identify at risk clients.

In the twentieth century, Labour had been the party of progress—so it had to defend its actions making life harder for disabled people. The law brought even more toxic rhetoric from government officials. The then Work and Pensions Secretary Peter Hain told the press, "We must rip up sick-note Britain", entrenching the idea that the country had been overtaken by a culture of laziness and entitlement, with the number of people reliant on state handouts instead of showing up to work growing totally out of control. It was a good thing that "Fifty per cent of those who take the assessment will not pass it"—for Hain, this wasn't a sign that the new legislation was excluding vulnerable people too harshly; it was an affirmation that those previously claiming Incapacity Benefit had been doing so fraudulently.

Sadly, Hain wasn't the only one bringing these ideas to the public from a position of authority: in 2008 David Freud, an investment banker employed as an advisor to the DWP by Hain's successor James Purnell, told *The Daily Telegraph* that only a third of those on disabled unemployment benefits actually needed it. This was despite the data at the time not supporting this claim, and Purnell was later forced to admit that it was a made-up figure. But that wouldn't come out for many years, especially not while this narrative was serving the Labour government.

The lack of disabled representation or interest in disability among the press meant that they weren't doing their job of holding the government to account and fact-checking these claims. Instead we had a slew of negative headlines, including one from the *Daily Express* in 2009 claiming that 75% of those on sickness benefits were "faking" illness—despite the fact that, at that point, no one previously on Incapacity Benefit had been assessed under the Work Capability Assessment system. The figures instead related to new claimants and the article's author Gabriel Milland was later forced to admit that just 36% of them had been found fit for work—this journalist coincidentally would later go on to become a special advisor to Boris Johnson.

Disability activists painstakingly repelled these lies with facts. The apologies came late and quietly but the damage had been done; meanwhile, everyone forgets—until the next time.

* * *

In 2010, the Tories were back in power and with them came not only the Liberal Democrats but a fresh wave of poverty and a snowballing assault on disabled people in the form of austerity. The Conservative-led coalition had won the election with a narrative that Labour spending was to blame for the 2008–9 financial crisis, and that the only way for the UK's economy to recover was to "tighten belts" at the Treasury. Having ousted Labour, hardcore neoliberal ideologues in the Conservative Party now seized on this unprecedented chance to shrink department budgets and withdraw state support, in the name of "fiscal responsibility".

For the true scale of this period's impact, I would recommend checking out the Deaths by Welfare Timeline, which goes all the way from 1942 to the 2020s (see

Bibliography). Seeing the length and scale of the mistreatment and stigmatisation of disabled people isn't easy, but I couldn't be more thankful to China Mills and John Pring, the amazing activists who created this timeline in 2021 and have been updating it ever since.

It's no coincidence that the timeline was first made in response to almost a decade of spending cuts, first under the 2010–15 coalition government and then under further Conservative governments led by David Cameron and Theresa May. Although austerity's reign of terror saw many cruel people heading the Department for Work and Pensions (DWP), perhaps the biggest, best-known villain of the policy's cruelty was Iain Duncan Smith who was Secretary of State from 2010 to 2016. In spreading the disability scrounger narrative whilst trying to frame himself as the "good guy," he's perhaps best known for trying to host an "austerity celebration" week at the DWP.

Austerity saw not only cuts to vital benefits at the DWP, but the tightening of government spending across the board—it meant cuts to many services that disabled people depended on to *survive*, let alone live or thrive, from privatisations and pay freezes in the NHS to the slashing of local council budgets, affecting education, transport, community facilities and social care services.

By the summer and autumn of 2010, just a few months into the coalition, many disability rights groups had already formed in response to the rising threat. John

McArdle and Gail Ward formed the grassroots organisation Black Triangle to "galvanise opposition to the current vicious attack on the fundamental human rights of disabled people by the Government of the United Kingdom." Black Triangle was formed in memory of the Scottish writer and musician Paul Reekie, who suffered from depression and a cardiac condition, and who took his own life in 2010 after his benefits were stopped. He was found with the notification letters from the DWP and his council.

One of the Black Triangle members who attributed his suicide to the "inhumane and unreasonable" reforms was a local GP. The group's campaigns against the Work Capability Assessment, introduced by New Labour and enforced more brutally than ever by the coalition, played and continues to play a vital part in showing the link between welfare reform and disabled people's deaths.

Similarly, the Mental Health Resistance Network, set up by "people who live with mental distress in order to defend ourselves from the assault on us by a cruel government," played an important role against welfare reform, bringing legal action against the government, particularly to do with the Work Capability Assessment.

Marginalised groups of British society were generally quick to recognise how austerity would have an outsized impact on their communities. Around that time Black Activists Rising Against Cuts was formed, bringing together Black activists from all walks of life to campaign about the adverse impact austerity had on Black communities.

Their campaigns intersected with disability rights groups to highlight the impact on Black disabled people, building on Black disability activism of previous decades: in 1990, the Caribbean-born Milliedrette (Millie) Hill had co-founded the Black Disabled People's Association after travelling extensively and setting up in the UK as a researcher on race and disability issues. Following an accident at fourteen which had left her disabled, she had created Bermuda's first organisation of disabled people. She had become involved in the UK movement as she was concerned about the extreme marginalisation of Black disabled people within both mainstream society and the disability activist communities. Now this movement was more important than ever.

On 3 October 2010, in response to the new Conservative Party's benefit cuts plans, a mass protest was held outside the party conference in Birmingham. Disabled organisers coordinated a disabled section of the march in the pouring rain—against the preference of the police, who had wanted to exclude disabled people from the march due to "vulnerabilities". In order to be allowed to take part in the march, organisers of the disabled people's protest had to enlist deaf and disabled people's organisations from all around the world to complain.

In the end, over one hundred disabled people took to the streets, wearing t-shirts emblazoned with "Cuts Kill".

At the time, disabled activist Sam Brackenby told *Disability News Service*, "[The government] may not realise it but this is going to kill people. People don't realise how difficult this is going to be."

Whereas lots of the big, high-profile campaigns of the 1990s had taken place in public spaces to raise awareness of prejudice and call for social change, the earliest activism against the coalition's austerity measures was aimed squarely at blocking political change, speaking directly to the heart of power.

A few weeks after the Tory conference, on 31 October, Mad Pride protested outside Parliament against the effects benefit cuts were having on those with mental health problems. A group of eighty activists took to Speakers' Corner and burned a two-faced effigy of Prime Minister David Cameron and Chancellor George Osborne, the architect of austerity, to express their anger. This was followed by a two-minute scream in memory of those who had died by suicide after having their benefits cut. Denise McKenna, an activist involved in the movement, told *Disability News Service* at the time, "This is throwing a hand grenade into people's lives."

Then, in November, Disabled People Against Cuts was founded by Linda Burnip, Debbie Jolly, Bob Williams-Finlay, Tina Hogg, Eleanor Lisney, Pete Millington, Dave Lupton and Sam Brackenby, with the aim of being a non-violent direct action group who as well as protesting would form links with the government by lobbying MPs and launching campaigns in Parliament.

As well as a national group, local branches sprang up all over the UK—a total of forty exist at the time of writing. The protest group has campaigned extensively for disabled people's right to live independently and two of the co-founders Linda Burnip and Debbie Jolly also campaigned in the 2010s for the UN to launch their investigation into the UK's treatment of disabled people (which we'll discuss in more detail a little further on).

In 2011, the Hardest Hit coalition was launched, bringing together the Disability Benefits Consortium and the UK Disabled People's Council to lobby the government regarding the impact of welfare cuts. The first Hardest Hit campaign gathered close to 8,000 disabled people who marched on Parliament in May 2011. It was considered one of the biggest disability protests in British history—this really was a huge turnout, given how many disabled people aren't able to protest, or struggle to find transport to get to an event like this. But, going up against the combined power of the government and the media, the disability activists' fight was only just beginning.

* * *

The next few years saw an increase in anti-benefits rhetoric from the government—from Iain Duncan Smith's December 2010 *Sun* article calling Britain a "shirkers' paradise", to a campaign to inform on any neighbours you thought were defrauding the benefits system for a reward—all amplified by the tabloids. In 2011, the 'Bad News for Disabled People' report from the University of Glasgow showed a significant rise in news stories about disability from 2004 to 2011. In 2004–5 there had been 713 disability related articles; in the year 2010–11 the number had leapt up to 1,015.

This was not the good kind of visibility: the study also found a significant shift in language. The use of the words "scrounger", "cheat" and "skiver" in articles about disabled people almost trebled from 54 uses in 2004/5 to 142 in 2010/11. There were far fewer stories that viewed disabled people in a sympathetic light, and the gist of the coverage kept moving towards benefit fraud. Stories about benefits and fraud rose from 2.8% in 04/5 to 6.1% in 10/11.

This, of course, meant the public's perception of disabled people changed. The focus groups for the study were asked what they thought the level of benefit fraud was and some overestimated it by 70%, with many pointing to newspaper articles as their source of this disinformation, most of which came from the government itself. Frances Ryan, a disabled journalist who has covered welfare and austerity and author of *Crippled: Austerity and the Demonization of Disabled People*, points out to me that this had a cultural impact on attitudes among disabled people themselves:

> One thing I've been struck by over the years, though, is the impact this had—not simply on how disabled peo-

ple are treated—but how disabled people feel about themselves. How the drip drip of headlines calling someone "workshy" and "costly" inevitably creates a sense of shame and reduced self-worth in them.

She highlights the many people she's met, fifteen years on from the start of austerity, who don't apply for the benefits they desperately need because they're too anxious and those who are scared to stand up out of their wheelchairs in public in case they're reported to the DWP.

This climate gave the coalition political cover to keep making disabled people's lives hell and usher in more major changes and cuts, with the Welfare Reform Act of 2012. This act made the DWP stricter with unemployment benefits—ramping up penalties for fraud and error, introducing Universal Credit as a way of reducing payments under the cover of "simplifying" the benefits system to be more efficient and less confusing for recipients—the Act applied to those who could work too, by changing the main benefit disabled people could get and work, the Disability Living Allowance, to the Personal Independence Payment (PIP).

This new payment was explicitly designed "not to be enough to live on", and the system rested on the idea that how much money people deserved was dependent not on their impairment, but on how badly their impairment was assessed (repeatedly) to be impacting their life.

In the coming years, many would report the same problems they'd had when New Labour introduced the

Work Capability Assessment—that assessors' reports were dishonest, inaccurate or poorly informed about the nature of long-term conditions, all of which led to an increase in people who needed them losing their vital benefits. Part of the problem here was that the austerity agenda didn't only reduce spending by cutting payments and narrowing criteria for payments: it was also about privatising government services. Now, contractors carried out benefits assessments regardless of whether their assessors had any medical knowledge.

Another particularly worrying aspect of the 2012 Act for disabled people was the so-called "bedroom tax", which meant that housing benefit would be cut for anyone judged to be living somewhere with more bedrooms than they "needed"—while exemptions existed for disabled adults who needed their own room, or a separate room for a carer, these were tied to the Personal Independence Payment, and the rules and "proof of need" that was accepted got even more specific in many cases, including that of disabled children.

But disabled people were not going to take this lightly. As a last ditch attempt to halt the bill, over twenty wheelchair-using activists from the Direct Action Network, Disabled People Against Cuts and Uncut UK blocked traffic across Oxford Circus by locking themselves in chains. Another main aim of this protest was to show disabled people who were feeling desperate after being worn down by the constant toxic narrative from politics and the press that there were still people fighting for them. DAN activist John Smith told *Disability News Service* at the time that the protest was "about disabled people getting angry again, like in the 1990s, and that is a good thing."

In 2012, another national moment struck disabled communities and their allies with both positivity and rage: the London Olympics and Paralympics. It's startling to look back on now and see the juxtaposition of scroungers and fakers with the "heroic" and "inspirational" light in which the paralympians were portrayed. Disabled people were apparently unworthy of positive coverage if they weren't superhuman patriots winning the country medals. The link between this idea of a "right" sort of disabled person and the cold, cruel spirit of the welfare reforms is obvious in the context of comments like Prime Minister David Cameron saying in 2013 that benefits had become a "lifestyle choice for some".

During this time disability rights groups were not silent. Disabled People Against Cuts organised a lot of mini protests around Atos, which was not only the government's main contractor for benefits assessments but was also, ironically, sponsoring the Paralympics. The campaign group sent a coffin full of letters to their main headquarters in London from disabled people, the culmination of a week of very public action against Atos.

Looking back on it today, Ellen Clifford from DPAC says: "whilst we'd been doing a lot I think this week changed public awareness about the Work Capability Assessment, because it was there for them to see during the Paralympics."

Ellen tells me DPAC also did a lot to link the disability rights movement to other anti-capitalist movements during the austerity era, such as creating links with unions and working with politicians. Under the incredible pressure of the cuts and hostile welfare reforms, the disability rights movement was proving itself more creative and wide-ranging than ever in its efforts to stop the policies, or at least stop the public forgetting about their impact.

In October 2013, disability campaigners organised the 10,000 Cuts and Counting event, to remember those who had died within six weeks of their benefits claim ending after a Work Capability Assessment between January and November 2011. Parliament Square, where the protest took place, was partially covered with white flowers, each representing a disabled person who had died.

This was an act of resistance against the deaths being brushed under the carpet—and there was no question that government policies were making a difference and doing serious harm. The Work Capability Assessment had prevailed and was being touted as a good thing. But medical professionals saw the danger in it and after successful lobbying from disabled people, the British Medical Association (BMA) belatedly voted at their annual conference to call for the DWP to end the assessments.

In the same period, two key tactics started to emerge as vital weapons in the fight to show the public that the coalition was being criminally neglectful of and harmful toward disabled people: legal activism, and online campaigning.

In 2012, two claimants backed by the Mental Health Resistance Network were granted permission from the high court to bring a judicial review against Iain Duncan Smith for the Work Capability Assessment citing the mental distress it had caused. The case was ruled in the claimants' favour in 2013, with the upper tribunal finding that by making claimants collect their own evidence the Department for Work and Pensions failed to make reasonable adjustments under the Equality Act (one of the last pieces of legislation brought in by Labour before the coalition came to power). The DWP were ordered to investigate ways to make sure the necessary evidence was obtained without added stress on the claimants.

In January that year, disabled campaigners published the Spartacus Report, a piece of research written to respond to the government's consultation on the introduction of Personal Independence Payments (which would go ahead a few months later under the Welfare Reform Act). The report claimed that the government's consultation of changes to Disability Living Allowance failed to meet its own code of practice and was presenting a highly misleading view of the responses it received.

A small group of disabled activists circulated the report widely on Twitter with the hashtag #spartacusreport and it started trending immediately. That people were actually discussing a serious policy report regarding disability felt practically unheard of, and the fact that it had taken a handful of disabled people to do the work of scrutinising the government that Parliament and the media had failed to do was a story in itself. The DWP had to go on Twitter themselves, using the hashtag, to try to justify their work.

Finally, the mainstream was discussing disability issues on disability activists' own terms. In spite of the defeat in the Lords, the success of the Spartacus campaign changed the tide of support on welfare reform. Suddenly journalists were looking critically at disability benefits and people were supporting the disabled cause. One of the writers of the report, Sue Marsh, was even invited on *Newsnight* to face the Cabinet minister Chris Grayling to discuss the reform.

This heralded a new form of disability activism where disabled people could operate outside of charities and conventional media channels and still have an impact even without strength of numbers. (Since then, the resulting Spartacus Network has also worked on areas relating to Employment and Support Allowance, the Work Capability Assessment, social care, the "bedroom tax" and more.) The public and the press couldn't look away anymore.

* * *

CUTS KILL

In November 2012, Iain Duncan Smith appeared on the BBC's *Question Time* and was, of course, asked many questions about benefit cuts. During this PR nightmare for the coalition government, the real, deadly stakes of the welfare reforms were laid bare. Journalist Owen Jones, who also featured on the panel, rightly said,

> the reason this debate has become so toxic is because of a cynical demonisation campaign of people on benefits by this government, what they are doing—and you can shake your head as much as you want, Iain—what they're trying to do is redirect people's justifiable anger at the ever-declining living standards, from those at the top, who caused this crisis to people's neighbours down the street.

Despite the host David Dimbleby's attempts to stop him, Jones asked Duncan Smith about the deaths of two disabled people, Brian McArdle, who had died a day after being found fit for work, and Karen Sherlock, who had died after her Employment and Support Allowance was stopped thanks to the introduction of the Work Capability Assessment.

Duncan Smith's reply, attacking Jones as a hypocrite and boasting—"We are changing their lives; I'm proud of doing that. Getting them off benefit is what we're going to do"—did not go down well with the audience. Throughout the discussion a female audience member could be heard shouting, "the government has got disabled people's blood on their hands!"

She wasn't exaggerating. Research by the University of York found that cuts to healthcare, public health and social care were linked to over 57,550 deaths between 2010 and 2014, with many more tens of thousands dying as a result of being deemed fit for work. Often, these tragedies became a call to action: Errol Graham was found dead in his flat in 2018, eight months after his benefits had been cut. His body was found by bailiffs who had come to evict him. His daughter-in-law Alison Turner is now still campaigning for justice for Errol.

Alison is of course not the only family member of a disabled person who has died due to the treatment they received from the DWP. There's Joy Dove, the mother of Jodey Whiting, Anne-Marie and Declan O'Sullivan, the children of Michael O'Sullivan, Gill Thompson, sister of David Clapson, and so many more. I could write so many books to remember the people who have had their lives cut short and the courageous campaigners they've left behind, fighting to make their loved ones matter in death in the way their lives didn't matter to the state. This more than anything is why I wanted to write this book and encourage a new generation of disability activists to take the mantle.

In 2013, after years of lobbying, Disabled People Against Cuts and other organisations persuaded the UN to look into the way the UK government was treating disabled people under the 2008 UN Convention on the Rights of Persons with Disabilities—they fought for us every step of the way. The UN's eventual report, its first ever on violations of the Convention, would condemn the UK government in 2016, finding it guilty of "grave and systemic violations".

When the report was released, the Cameron government (no longer in coalition with the Lib Dems) attempted to discredit it by leaking it to the *Mail on Sunday* the day before it was due to publish. The piece was clearly meant to discredit the report's findings, branding the committee "controversial" and mentioning that one of its authors had once suggested his homeland of Denmark pay for disabled people to visit prostitutes for their wellbeing, which had absolutely nothing to do with the report. This leak and personal attack shocked committee members, who perhaps were not as used to British tabloids as the country's disabled people are.

After the report came out, DPAC told the press that the actions of the Conservative government were "obviously based on a deliberate intention to cause harm without any regard to the horrendous consequences for disabled people". Most of the breaches related to independent living, work and employment, adequate standard of living and social protection would have been caused by policies introduced between 2010 and 2015 by the DWP.

The true scale of deaths as a result of these grave violations of basic human rights, especially in terms of disabled people, may never be known, as successive governments have refused to release their reports into benefits-related deaths. Despite having been forced to admit that they do keep these records, ministers have been passing the buck and systematically refuse to answer questions. Many court cases, freedom of information requests and appeals by victims' families have been brought against the government to attempt to expose the DWP, with no result.

Dialogue doesn't seem to work either: Alison Turner, Errol Graham's daughter-in-law, tells me that government officials have always blatantly disregarded disabled people throughout the many hearings she's had with them.

In 2014, the War on Welfare petition reached 100,000 signatures and meant that disabled people secured a debate in the House of Commons for the first time to discuss the impact of benefit cuts. The discussion was led by Labour backbencher and longtime ally John McDonnell. Despite this, the coalition still refused to carry out an assessment on deaths caused by benefits cuts. This was a huge blow to disability activists but one win in 2015 was that Atos pulled out of their contract with the DWP early. This came after six years of regular protests involving placards with the infamous slogan "ATOS KILLS".

According to journalist Amelia Gentleman writing in *The Guardian*, the company was more preoccupied with the damage to their public image than the plight of disabled people: Atos senior vice-president Lisa Coleman told a Commons select committee, "I have shareholders and stakeholders who would not let me bid for a contract that would give rise to both the reputational and profitability issues we are facing now." This was a bittersweet victory for the movement.

* * *

By the time the coalition government ended in 2015, so much damage had been done—and Cameron and Osborne's Conservatives came out of that year's election with more power to continue the same policies. Long gone was the hope that disabled people could live independently, helped by their local community to thrive. This wasn't helped by the fact that the Independent Living Fund was scrapped in 2015, something the government worked hard to make happen and which further eroded disabled people's rights to live full lives without the need for residential care.

A couple of years later, there were more cuts made to benefits with the Welfare Reform and Work Act becoming law in 2016. It froze some benefits for four years and Iain Duncan Smith faced calls to be prosecuted for his involvement in disabled people's deaths.

Also in 2016, the DWP and the Department of Health published 'Improving Lives: The Work, Health and Disability Green Paper', which only talked about ill health as a problem in relation to missing work and the cost to the economy. In the paper, the DWP claimed that only 10% of those moving to Employment Support Allowance under the Universal Credit reforms would go into the support group—the real figure being 50% of people—despite the fact that the 10% figure had already been disproven back in 2013.

Meanwhile, activists were still not done fighting. Disabled people pooled their resources: Recovery in the Bin, a mental health collective set up in 2016 to oppose the emphasis on a need to return to work and productivity, ran Benefits Defence workshops where experts taught disabled people to better defend themselves and others from the DWP system.

In 2019, disabled artist Vince Laws created 'DWP Deaths Make Me Sick' shrouds. The giant sheets were spray painted with the deaths of people who died after being cut off from benefits. There are twenty-five shrouds in total. Vince is also the author of *A Very Nazi Queer Faust*, a theatre piece written "to protest the slaughter of sick and disabled people."

Between 2015 and 2020 the rate of disability benefits-related deaths is truly staggering to behold, and the Conservative governments responsible refused to admit any wrongdoing. David Cameron, Prime Minister until 2016, even spoke ill of disabled people who had died on live TV in 2015, insinuating that any deaths were deserved because (he insisted) the system was helping everyone who needed it—anyone who was refused help obviously just wasn't trying hard enough to succeed. When he was asked about the death of David Clapson, who had been found on his floor surrounded by a pile of CVs after having his benefits cut, Cameron's response was:

> The people watching this programme who pay their taxes and work very hard, they don't have taxes so people can sign on and show no effort getting a job. As I put it, on the steps of Downing Street, those who can should, those who can't, we will always help. That's the principle that should always underline the compassionate benefit system.

This response, Deaths by Welfare timeline co-creator John Pring tells me, was "sick-makingly vile." John spent over a decade collating evidence that DWP policies were killing disabled people, which he wrote up in his book *The Department: How a Violent Government Bureaucracy Killed Hundreds and Hid the Evidence*. The title says it all really. John tells me the timeline is important because "it was so violent that you can't see it but when you step back you can see it all laid out through time and how systemic it was ... it suddenly all makes sense. It's suddenly very real and terrifying."

This chapter was earth-shatteringly upsetting to write, and is probably a very hard read for many people. My main takeaway though is that, although the governments of the 2000s and 2010s aimed to turn the public and the media against disabled people (and succeeded in many ways), at every cruel turn disabled people were there to fight back and show that they would not go quietly. We didn't have Parliament's support, we didn't have the media's support, we relied on each other and doggedly and inventively fought the system despite everything being thrown at us to persuade us to give up.

When I spoke to Barbara Lisicki she urged disabled people to come together again: "we need people to step up and be leaders, fight this until the end."

Unfortunately, however, the British state would soon find another way to let disabled people die.

8

WE SHALL NOT BE REMOVED
COVID, 2020–2

After decades of relentless media and government narratives determined to belittle and dehumanise disabled people, when a deadly virus took over the world it was almost too easy for the UK to turn its back on the people it should've been protecting the most.

When the Covid-19 pandemic struck in March 2020, it devastated the whole world. Everything had to shut down, and everyone scrambled for the right response to this terrifying disease that seemingly came from nowhere and was killing so many (thousands in the UK in that first month alone).

When Covid hit, the country was being run (and I use that term loosely) by Boris Johnson, an incompetent media personality turned politician who used his power as cover for him and his equally over-privileged mates to get away with whatever they wanted. In fact when the pandemic took hold Johnson had not long won the general election by a landslide, meaning disabled people were already reeling, feeling defeated and isolated by the scale of this party's renewed popularity after so many years of cruel policies they'd fought hard to expose.

Then the deadly pandemic struck, throwing us all into disarray. The novel coronavirus that causes Covid-19 is a disease spread by breathing in particles, but it took weeks for the UK to take national action limiting chances for those particles to be breathed in. Johnson, like many other world leaders, refused to take the virus seriously at first; by the time the country was ordered to lock down on 23 March, it had been two weeks since the government had estimated that as many as 10,000 were infected.

If effective measures had been found earlier to better contain or slow the spread, this might have both saved lives and spared the country the extreme policy of a full lockdown, with all of its harms for vulnerable people. But by the 23rd, the virus had spread all over the UK, and there was now no choice but to lock down.

Even at this early stage, campaigners and the community were worried about what Covid and Covid policy might mean for disabled people. For one thing, the Johnson government had been slow to act partly because it was inclined to pursue "herd immunity"—a strategy involving enough of the population developing natural antibodies to the virus for everyone to be "protected", i.e. deliberately letting people get infected (the focus being on healthy people, at a low risk of death)—

but it didn't occur to the people favouring this policy that the initial mass wave of infection might bring in a mass disabling situation, even if most people survived the virus. Lack of representation in the corridors of power meant that none of them ever thought of post-viral fatigues: no one predicted what many disabled people saw coming.

We'd had experience of how conditions could arise from big viruses, such as the swine flu triggering things such as narcolepsy or even how viruses like meningitis could be disabling long term. This was also something disabled people were warning about from the very beginning. This is why it's also important that we get more disabled people into politics, as more disabled parliamentarians would've meant this could've been voiced.

The second problem with lockdown was that, while it was supposed to be the best way to protect disabled people, and was sold as a noble sacrifice made by the non-disabled—accepting a situation painted by many as a huge infringement on people's rights, in order to save those labelled "vulnerable" by the government—the thoughtless way it was implemented amounted to shutting many disabled people back behind closed doors like in the 1950s.

By the time lockdown started, many disabled people (those with weak immune systems, labeled Clinically Extremely Vulnerable) had already been instructed by their doctors' surgeries over a week earlier to "shield": to stay at home no matter what, while those who could "afford" to get infected carried on with business as usual.

You'd think with this there would have been government support for those that couldn't leave their houses at all—especially given the discrimination aspect, at a time when the rest of the country still wasn't being asked to follow more than partial, flimsy Covid rules—but this wasn't the case. While many people talked of being "trapped" in their houses, this truly wasn't the case unless you were disabled and vulnerable.

In my opinion, Boris Johnson's intentions were evident from his very first press conference on 12 March, almost two weeks before he eventually declared a national lockdown. I'll never forget the chill that ran through me when he declared with a sense of complacent inevitability that "we will lose many loved ones". This attitude made it all too believable for many when reports later came out of him allegedly wanting to "let the bodies pile high" in pursuit of herd immunity (comments Johnson has always denied).

Even if you don't believe that it was policy to throw vulnerable people under the bus in order to "get Covid over with", once that strategy was abandoned, the government's lack of consideration for disabled needs—as if "giving them a lockdown" was more than enough—was on show in its comms.

To give just one example: while there were near constant press conferences and briefings coming out of

Downing Street during the UK's first lockdown (spring 2020), Number 10 flat-out refused to provide a British Sign Language (BSL) interpreter so that deaf people could also receive the information. BSL consultant and deaf campaigner Lynn Stewart-Taylor founded the Twitter campaign #WhereIsTheInterpreter after the first nine briefings did not include an interpreter.

In July 2021, a deaf woman, Katie Rowley, took the government to court over two televised Covid briefings, and won: a judge ordered damages to be paid, declaring that the lack of BSL had "served to disempower, to frustrate and to marginalise" deaf people and constituted discrimination. In September 2022, a much bigger case was brought when 276 campaigners headed up by Lynn took the government to court for excluding deaf people. Devastatingly, this case was struck out of court after the judge ruled that the claim had not been filed within sufficient time limits.

As well as this, whilst policies were (belatedly) being created to protect people in care homes and other residential homes, disabled people who lived independently were left to fend for themselves, quite literally in some cases, as it took weeks of lockdown for the government to produce any guidelines on what disabled people who employed their own carers were supposed to do to protect themselves and their carers whilst there were strict rules about visiting others' homes. Again it's hard to imagine this happening in a cabinet including a decent number of disabled people.

Organisations with expertise and the authority of representation weren't consulted in any policies around supposedly protecting clinically vulnerable people. Mark Harrison of Reclaiming Our Futures Alliance told *Disability News Service* in March 2020, at the very beginning of lockdown: "If you don't involve the objects of policy in developing policy then you get bad policy." Fazilet Hadi, policy manager at Disability Rights UK, also told DNS,

> There has been no consultation before laws or guidance is produced and to some extent this is understandable given the pace of change. However, mistakes are being made. We fully understand that government and health and social care bodies need to act quickly during the crisis but as required by [the UN Convention on the Rights of Persons with Disabilities] it is essential that they consult with organisations led by disabled people when shaping new laws, guidance and emergency schemes. New forms of rapid consultation should be developed.

Despite this, Disability Minister Justin Tomlinson pretty much disappeared off the face of the earth during the pandemic—pretty strange, when the public was repeatedly being told that they had to put up with restrictions for the sake of disabled people—and there were no focus groups or briefings on the impact on disabled people until May 2020.

* * *

When the lockdown happened, as well as panic and fear, many disabled people felt a lot of anger. After years of being told we couldn't work from home, as this was deemed unfair to other staff members and costly to companies, it was frustrating to see just how quickly almost every office made that happen when it meant profits—and the health of non-disabled people—were at risk.

Unfortunately, the culture of double standards on the right to life and dignity wasn't only outrageously unjust: it was becoming directly lethal. As the cases ramped up, disabled people could see a pattern of those who were previously fit and healthy being given priority in hospitals. There were rumours emerging of Do Not Resuscitate orders being placed on disabled people as early as April 2020, forcing the NHS to rush out guidance that month clarifying that this should never be done—though this is something the press wouldn't pay attention to until much later, after the healthcare regulator found in December 2020 that the practice had caused potentially avoidable deaths in care homes.

During the height of the pandemic that spring, reports emerged that these orders were being given either by GP surgeries or when disabled people were admitted to hospital. The reported justification for this was that these patients were less likely to survive and therefore, given limited hospital resources, those healthier (non-disabled) had to be made a priority.

This idea, and how easy the media and the public found it to believe, was so vile that it makes me cry just writing about it. But this horrendous explanation wasn't actually true. Instead, DNRs were put on learning disabled people, autistic people, and people with Down's syndrome, who were no more or less "clinically vulnerable" and likely to die of Covid than a non-disabled person. Imagine a society so dismissive of your humanity and your equal right to live that they will let you die because they don't even care enough to understand whether you're actually vulnerable. Out of sight out of mind, I guess.

You can trace this mindset back to the very use of the label "vulnerable" (which applied generically to all disabled people, and put the emphasis on their essential "weakness") instead of "susceptible" (which would have said something meaningful about who was at greater risk of serious illness with Covid, as not all disabled people were). It implied that there was nothing that could be done to save us, when in truth the government just didn't try hard enough. Somehow it was presented to the public as more "natural" for disabled people to die in the pandemic, somehow less of a loss—what other oppressed group in society could this have been said about, without an outcry against throwbacks to fascism?

I can't begin to tell you how much the first few months of the pandemic were fraught with constant panic for disabled people, worried that if we were to become infected we would not be saved. I remember feeling the most ill I ever had in my life when I believe I caught Covid in April 2020 and begging my then husband not to call an ambulance no matter what. I was so scared that if I went into hospital I might be left to die when they saw my medical history.

Even while living with this terror, disabled people were already organising for the world after lockdown. In May 2020, the We Shall Not Be Removed campaign started to provide a voice for disabled creatives during the pandemic and to fight for an inclusive recovery. It was done in partnership with Disability Arts Online and over 700 people joined in discussions on how to make sure that disabled people in the arts wouldn't be forgotten, after so many had had to withdraw from the public space and shield. Activists knew that neither the government or the media would fight for them, and yet again they worked together so that disabled people's voices were heard.

During the summer of 2020, the government ended the national lockdown and changed the rules, allowing people who weren't designated "clinically vulnerable" to meet up outdoors as long as they pinky promised not to touch each other.

All the while, vulnerable people remained shut in their houses full-time with no support, disabled and elderly people were left without proper PPE in care homes, where infection kept running riot as hospitals discharged patients who were still sick back into care to free up NHS beds. Those in homes weren't allowed to see family members, based on ableist assumptions that people live in either a state of emergency crisis where survival must come first, or else in the "normal" state of health and freedom—when disabled people know that every day living with impairments is a compromise, requiring an imperfect, sometimes almost impossible balance between physical, mental and emotional costs and benefits.

It's Saturday night and I'm sitting on Zoom with the Disabled People Against Cuts activist Ellen Clifford. Even in 2024, the subject of Covid is as traumatic for her as it is for me, but Ellen and I still think it's important for us to reflect on how different the experiences of lockdown could be for disabled people like us: "Right from the beginning," she tells me,

> people were going on about how dreadful it was, when really they were living like a lot of my friends have been forced to live for years, and nobody's given a shit. [Non-disabled people] might feel confined in their own homes, but they can use the toilet when they can, get a drink when they want, whereas most of my friends can't do that. So I think I felt a lot of anger and bitterness about that.

Ellen also reminds me of the small number of disabled people who said we should see lockdown as an opportunity for non-disabled people to live in disabled people's shoes. "But that never happened, because as soon as they could they got out by keeping us indoors."

In that summer period, it felt to both of us like disabled people wanting a bit of help to enable them to live was "spoiling the fun" for everyone else. How dare we ask for everyone to wear a mask? How dare we want to continue working from home? How did the UK accept so easily that ordering people not to stand uncomfortably close to me, or to wear a bit of cloth on their mouth in public indoor spaces, was a more serious infringement of rights than our right to live?

But whilst everyone outside of residential care was abandoned by the government, in 2020 disabled people banded together to help each other (non-disabled people of course were involved in this too through helping their relatives and neighbours). Those who could and were safe to still go out ran errands and got people shopping or cooked each other meals. As Ellen points out, "we already had that kind of infrastructure in place, because we already had to have peer solidarity, otherwise we wouldn't have survived austerity and welfare reform." These structures as Ellen calls them helped disabled people respond quickly to the ever changing situation.

New forms of organising and activism also sprang up within the disabled community during lockdown. During the early years of the pandemic, Twitter became a refuge for disabled people who felt abandoned in their homes—many of us alone or with unsupportive families. It was the place we connected with others, shared our frustrations or gained support.

Many online calls and groups were set up by and for disabled people during this time, including The Staying Inn, hosted by Dr Amy Kavanagh, which provided a space for us to come together and socialise while isolating, through activities from pub quizzes to "stitch and bitch". The Staying Inn website puts it best: "We can create stronger connections even when we are socially distant."

Social media was also a powerful place for disabled organisers and individuals to dispel misinformation and disinformation about both Covid itself and about the implications of Covid plans, which was vital for disabled people to understand a fuller picture than the national narrative was offering.

Whilst the death toll rose over August and September, the economy had taken a hit—and guess which issue Johnson and his then chancellor Rishi Sunak seemed to care about the most? Ending the lockdown wasn't enough, so Sunak launched Eat Out to Help Out which offered vouchers to get people back to bars and restaurants.

Just months later, public policy and economics researchers concluded that this initiative led directly to infections and deaths; in 2023, during the Covid inquiry, the government's own chief scientific advisor during the pandemic testified that the scheme was "highly likely" to have increased Covid deaths, and government scientists testified repeatedly that they were never even asked to model or advise on the public health impact. The autumn wave of Covid would be so substantial as to force the UK back into total lockdown from late December 2020 (in Wales and Northern Ireland) and very early January 2021 (in England and Scotland).

In November it was confirmed that 59% of all Covid-related deaths in England had been people with disabilities. That's six out of every ten people. In Wales, it was higher at seven in ten. When you consider that disabled people only make up 24% of the population, this is absolutely horrific, and a spectacular dereliction of duty not only in government, but in Parliament and the media, which should have held the government to account over the discriminatory nature of its policy and the fact that it was failing.

That same month, restrictions once again changed to mean more people would be forced into work: the "clinically vulnerable" (confusingly not the same as clinically extremely vulnerable, which was very high risk, this was "just" high risk) were no longer required to shield. This meant that disabled people who couldn't work from home had to make the terrifying choice between their health or being able to afford to live. The guidance said nothing more about this than "If you cannot work from home, you are advised not to go to work and may be eligible for Statutory Sick Pay (SSP) or Employment Support Allowance (ESA)."

* * *

Inevitably the death and infection rates continued rising, and Christmas was cancelled for millions around the UK, prompting a belated reintroduction of lockdown. As the shutdowns ground on into a second year, disabled people were increasingly suffering from almost all hospital appointments being cancelled, both to redeploy healthcare staff to Covid wards and ICUs and to limit the spread of the virus. Hospitals ceased to exist for everyone but cancer patients in treatment and emergency patients, like those giving birth or who'd suffered a traumatic injury—that's millions of people, about half the population, with a long-standing health problem who lost access to specialist care overnight.

When the UK first began to open up again in that risky summer of 2020, many disabled people had expected some provision for healthcare to come back when bars and restaurants started opening up. But no such luck: while those who weren't shielding were urged to eat out to help out, anyone whose conditions required regular monitoring or specialist care were left to suffer with no alternatives given for their care, and soon lockdown was back.

At the time, I was going through a chemical menopause for endometriosis, something I was warned I could only do for three months before a follow-up gynaecology appointment due to my risk of blood clots. However, I went almost a year between consultations, and my appointments to receive the drug keeping me menopausal were constantly cancelled or delayed.

I wasn't the only one, of course. Campaigner Ellen Morrison told me in an interview for *Stylist* magazine that, before Covid, she would typically have eight specialist hospital appointments over a six month period—but during the pandemic this ended up being two phone appointments in all of 2020.

Ellen told me in September that year, "I feel like the pandemic has made accessing the healthcare I need almost impossible. I have no idea when I'll get back to where I was pre-pandemic." Many who had battled for years to have diagnoses and treatment plans were left in limbo, and many will never be able to recover the lost progress of 2020–1.

When vaccination became available in the UK, with a "priority order" rollout beginning at the very end of December, a first jab was offered to "vulnerable" people first, including anyone over a certain age regardless of their state of health—it's thought this is why disabled people continued to represent a disproportionate number of Covid deaths in 2021, because the priority had been given to all elderly people regardless of conditions, rather than all disabled people regardless of age.

From the end of the universal lockdown in spring 2021 and, in some parts of the country, on into 2022, the UK saw further chaotic loosening and tightening of restrictions, including a nonsensical tier system that was criticised as disadvantaging poorer and more northern cities in favour of keeping London open.

At every turn, the focus was on the goal of reopening and going back to organising society like it had been before, rather than in a way that would have allowed disabled people, too, to come out of lockdown. The Johnson government proudly plugged the end of restrictions in mid-July 2021 as "freedom day", without any thought as to how unfree disabled life could be in the UK with no adjustments made to include everyone in post-lockdown life.

When people were forced back to the office again it was seen as "getting back to normal", while many disabled people were still too scared to leave their homes, now that nobody had to wear masks or keep their distance. The test and trace app was widely discussed as a nuisance for people whose health permitted them not to care about catching Covid, dubbed the "pingdemic" and portrayed as an unreasonable, indefinite demand for "people" (always a default norm of non-disabled) having to put their lives on hold, with little awareness in many quarters that disabled people were already stuck in that situation, thanks to opening up policies racing ahead of protection policies.

The pingdemic happened less than a week after "freedom day"—at a time when vulnerable adolescents, for example, had not yet been vaccinated, the rollout only being extended to them on freedom day itself. This included children with cancer and other teens who were severely immunocompromised.

Despite facing horrendous amounts of abuse online, in the 'Covid wind-down' period of 2021–2, disabled campaigners fought tooth and nail to draw attention to details like this that were escaping mainstream attention, and to push for protections and for disabled people to be kept safe. Whilst many were, understandably, in survival mode (and that's perfectly okay, I don't want anyone to worry that focusing on themselves wasn't enough), activists were working hard to ensure disabled people weren't forgotten.

But, similar to the way that LGBTQ+ movements were hit hard by the losses of the AIDS pandemic in the 1980s, disabled campaigners in 2021–2 were fighting a losing battle, at the same time as watching their friends and colleagues fade around them, either forced out of public roles by the risk of Covid after restrictions ended, or else dying of Covid and related complications. "We worked out that we lost as many disabled activists during the first couple of years of the pandemic as we did in the decade or more before that," Ellen Clifford tells me.

These included Manjeet Kaur, the chair of Refugee and Asylum Participatory Action Research, an organisation based in Manchester which campaigned for the rights of displaced people. As a disabled person, she had a particular interest in ensuring disabled asylum seekers had adequate housing. Manjeet died in April 2020.

Seán McGovern was a prominent campaigner and in his time was head of the TUC disabled workers' committee and disability officer for the London Labour Party. Alongside protesting against things such as the closure of Remploy, Seán also wrote poetry, speeches and blog posts about austerity, cuts and activism. One poignant post ended with the battle cry, "I cannot sit by and let the few destroy my class! I will not stand by and see my welfare state destroyed and sold off for short-term profit! I will resist these thieves in our midst!" Seán died suddenly in May 2020, just a day after his beloved mother, Delia.

Roger Lewis' death is one Ellen describes as "being a direct impact of lockdown." Whilst Roger died of stomach cancer in 2022, it was left undetected and untreated for a long time due to the Covid restrictions. Roger was part of the DPAC steering committee and as a member of Unison fought for disabled people's employment rights.

* * *

The absolutely worst thing about the national Covid narrative—the thing that made disabled people feel most alone—was how desperate everyone was to return to the "normal" from before the pandemic, which of course had never worked for disabled people in the first place. And now the medical impacts of the virus itself were set to make life harder than ever.

The pandemic killed hundreds of thousands of disabled people in England alone, just between January 2020 and February 2021; but the myriad symptoms, and the way Covid attacked the body, led to many more becoming disabled. For many it activated existing disabilities, particularly those who had ME and Fibromyalgia, and for others a new disability was born. Long Covid was the name given to the condition many had to live with after being infected with Covid.

In a nutshell, Long Covid is when people don't recover and still have symptoms months or years later. It is usually talked about as post-viral fatigue but it's not necessarily just fatigue. The most common symptoms are extreme fatigue, brain fog, dizziness and shortness of breath as well as muscle and joint pain. The emergence of Long Covid was baffling to doctors in 2020—as far as they were concerned, there was no reason why these symptoms should hang around from a respiratory infection. But somehow Covid was creating impairments in a whole new set of people who had previously had no long-term health problems.

For many disabled people, some of the tone or emphasis in this discussion made for quite a frustrating time. Long Covid and its debilitating impact was often treated by politicians and media as more deserving of coverage than other impairments, because of the type of people (formerly non-disabled) that it was affecting—whilst people who'd been disabled were still fighting to be heard on their existing struggles (despite the fact that Long Covid presented very similarly to the symptoms of a lot of chronic illnesses).

But due to existing strains on healthcare, those with Long Covid ended up also struggling to be believed.

Dr Elisa Perego, PhD, is an Honorary Research Fellow at University College London whose research paper 'How and why patients made Long Covid' laid out how sufferers fought, mainly through a single social media platform, to establish that Long Covid was a real condition. Her report details that "Long Covid has a strong claim to be the first illness created through patients finding one another on Twitter: it moved from patients, through various media, to formal clinical and policy channels in just a few months."

When I interviewed her for *Verywell Health*, Dr Perego told me, "I fear no healthcare system in the world is currently able to keep up with the monstrous wave of acute Covid and Long Covid cases"—and yet it wouldn't even have been recognised as a condition without these online campaigners, who simply started by sharing their experience then moved on to creating a survey of symptoms. The condition started out as "Covid long haulers" in the US but it was shortened to Long Covid by British campaigners, used first by Dr Perego on Twitter. Perego and other medical experts who had also been struck by Long Covid fought hard to get the term into public consciousness, using the hashtag #LongCovid.

Their fight for their due doesn't stop with Long Covid being accepted in healthcare as "a thing", either: "Stigma against chronic diseases in medicine will also contribute to poor care for Long Covid patients in addition to many other chronically ill people."

While the existence of Long Covid eventually gained a lot of attention, those actually living with it report feeling abandoned by doctors and society. Sam Williams, who has Long Covid, wrote in the *Canary* in November 2024:

> There are two parts to my disability experience. The first part is the disability itself. That's really bad. The second part is how society treats me and people like me. That's much worse. The UK is in deep denial about Long Covid and about all disabilities. Society both ignores and shames me. My feeling of social abandonment is total.

This is a sentiment echoed by many, as people continue to deny that Covid ever existed or indeed that it still does. It's like Paul Hunt and Vic Finkelstein's social model of disability, which separated "impairment" and "disability", never happened.

People with Long Covid and other disabled people came out of the pandemic made to feel worthless by the government and, in the words of its former chief adviser Dominic Cummings, "The incompetence, the constant lies, the obsession with media bullshit." But disabled people and their loved ones seemed to be the only ones left dealing with the consequences.

Former Health Secretary Matt Hancock—responsible for sending sick people back to care homes, for the department behind the Do Not Resuscitate notices, for schools remaining open while Covid raged in children and, of course, for forcing disabled people to shield for almost nine months instead of calling for stricter restrictions; the man who allegedly covered up (per WhatsApps shared with the Covid inquiry) "lots of feedback that eat our [sic] to help out is causing problems in our intervention areas. I've kept it out of the news but it's serious"; the man who enforced social distancing and isolating shortly before being caught breaking Covid rules with his own workplace affair—was invited in 2022 onto ITV's *I'm A Celebrity Get Me Out of Here* to rehabilitate his image.

Apparently he'd become a campaigner for neurodivergent rights too (he himself is dyslexic), a huge slap in the face to all the disabled people whose lives have been destroyed by policies he oversaw. However, one bit of comeuppance he did face was that his wife very publicly kicked him out of their house following his affair (if you've never seen the photos of this featuring the most judgemental sausage dog in the world, I cannot recommend it enough).

If only disabled people could have escaped the pandemic with nothing more than a slap on the wrist and a fine, like the Conservative ministers and staff who attended the infamous lockdown parties at the height of Covid restrictions, including the Prime Minister, his wife and Rishi Sunak. After Boris Johnson unceremoniously resigned—brought down by a completely unrelated scandal, not by any pandemic policy or rule-breaking—we finally saw calls for a Covid inquiry answered. The inquiry itself continues at the time of writing. With every hearing, we hear fresh evidence of how the government not only failed disabled people, but actively endangered them.

Meanwhile, Rishi Sunak—the Chancellor who had rushed to get everyone back into pubs, then offices, who jointly ended the shielding programme—was made Prime Minister by his party, representing the UK on the world stage for the next two years.

And now, while Covid still rages on, those at particular risk from the virus are being given no more help than they were when the government first abandoned lockdown, despite the huge weight of evidence now available about the effects of Long Covid. Vaccines, whilst still available to those at risk, are no longer available on the NHS to most of the population, including most disabled people who were recognised as in greater need during the initial rollout (except chemo patients); and they've only been made available privately (for those who can afford it) since spring 2024.

It's also costly to get Covid tests—only people with a limited set of very serious conditions such as cancer are potentially eligible for lateral flows on prescription; this isn't the default even for the clinically vulnerable. If you do buy a test they're seen as decreasing in effectiveness, due to lack of state investment in seeing them upgraded to include many of the new variants.

And, despite the medical knowledge that frequent infections can lead to long-term health issues, we have stopped recording, publishing and reporting on the figures. The official worldwide death toll is still stuck at 7 million from the end of 2022, but *The Economist* estimated in October 2022 that the real figure now was more likely to be between 27 and 36 million. In April 2023, just three years after the start of the pandemic, the NHS Covid app shut down, meaning there was no longer any way to record that you had caught the virus.

The true scale of how many disabled people have died from Covid may never be known, but activists and others are still processing the trauma of that time. At the end of the day, Covid showed how disposable disabled people really were—and this was only made possible after decades of eroding public trust in us.

As the rest of society moves on from the pandemic, in their lifestyles and their minds, there's been nothing left for disabled campaigners to do but seek recognition and justice for what took place. For example, many disabled groups were involved in the fight to get an inquiry in the first place. Long Covid groups which were founded in the wake of the pandemic including Long Covid Kids and Long Covid Support stressed the need for ongoing support for those with Long Covid.

A collection of families whose loved ones died due to Covid realised how silenced they felt by the government, so banded together to create Covid-19 Bereaved Families for Justice. CBF4J along with the political campaign group Led By Donkeys decided to create something which would cause an immediate reaction and highlight the true scale of Covid deaths. The Covid memorial wall was a series of hearts that listed every single Covid death, which continued to be added to over the next few years. It ended up stretching over 500 metres and includes the deaths of over 240,000 people.

The 2020s weren't done battering disabled people, though: the often individual hardships of the lockdown era would soon be replaced with a national economic crisis. And of course the hardest times always fall on those who are already struggling to live.

9

HEATING OR EATING

2022–4

Not content with letting disabled people die during a deadly pandemic unprecedented in modern times, the state also decided to bring back tried and tested methods of killing us—not giving us enough money to feed ourselves and heat our homes.

If I'm being honest, it feels a bit silly putting the cost of living crisis that exploded in 2022 in the "past" section. But, even though it's still very much happening, it's important to include it in this connected narrative of recent British history: we keep facing the same issues in different guises and the fights we face today still involve receiving the appropriate support to live and thrive.

It's more expensive to live if you're disabled than non-disabled, even without a nationwide economic crisis. The charity Scope estimated in 2024 that households with a disabled person had to spend an extra £1,067 per month compared with non-disabled households. This is because of the added cost of adjustments and access needs. Additionally, disabled people often require more energy or water, specialist food, equipment, prescriptions and private vehicles and parking, due to the inaccessibility of public transport.

The 2023 Costly Differences report by the Resolution Foundation analysed YouGov data and found that, in 2020–1, disabled people had on average 44% less disposable income annually than non-disabled people (£19,397 as opposed to £27,792). The report also found that 34% of disabled people fell into the lowest household income category, compared to 13% of non-disabled people. The last thing they needed was for the UK economy to go into freefall in 2022.

The Institute for Government defines the UK's cost-of-living crisis as "the fall in real disposable incomes (that is, adjusted for inflation and after taxes and benefits) that the UK has experienced since late 2021". In other words, prices for goods and services have become more expensive than incomes, and people are struggling.

Some of this economic downturn had been a long time coming, due to trade difficulties caused by the UK leaving the EU's single market after Brexit, and the Ukraine war, which hiked up gas prices due to Russia cutting off supplies to the West—coupled with the challenges of the pandemic, this was all a perfect storm. But life also got a lot more expensive for many people in Britain during Liz Truss's fifty days as Prime Minister that autumn, which saw a mini-budget so financially disastrous that it temporarily trashed the pound and turned the markets against her, and left millions of people with exponentially higher mortgage rates long after she'd been forced out of office.

The Costly Differences report also found that almost half (48%) of disabled adults surveyed said that they'd had to cut back on energy use in their homes that November. This is compared to 32% of non-disabled people—which, considering disabled people often need more energy to charge and run equipment, is scary. 41% of disabled people also said they couldn't afford to heat their homes, close to double the figure for non-disabled people (23%.) And finally, almost one in three (31%) of disabled people surveyed said they had less money to spend on food, compared to 18% of non-disabled people. And this survey was of just 8,000 people, with 2,000 participants being disabled.

The Office for National Statistics (ONS) report on the increased cost of living from June to September 2022 surveyed over 13,000 people, and it painted an even bleaker picture for disabled people. That report found that over half (55%) of disabled adults said they were struggling to afford energy bills—and this was during the months when British people don't even have their heating on—while over a third (36%) were finding it difficult to afford their rent or mortgage payments compared with 40% and 27% of non-disabled people, respectively.

As disabled people struggle to afford food they increasingly turn to food banks. The Trussell Trust estimated in 2023 that the majority of people (69%) accessing their food banks are disabled, while an even higher proportion, 75%, have at least one disabled person in their household. And, unfortunately, the increased health risks for disabled people haven't been limited to poorer nutrition or the choice between heating and eating.

In February 2023, the Royal Pharmaceutical Society revealed that the crisis was impacting disabled people's ability to afford their vital medication. This is due to the fact that despite NHS healthcare being free, prescriptions are not, costing £9.90 per item unless you're on means tested benefits, are over sixty years old, a new parent or fit a very limited medical criteria (that many disabled people don't). While pre-paid certificates are available, allowing patients an unlimited number of prescriptions for a fixed charge per year or per quarter, many can't afford to pay for months of medication upfront.

The Pharmaceutical Society's survey of its members, conducted in late 2022, found that half of all pharmacists had reported an increase in patients asking them which medicines on their prescription they could "do without" due to the cost. The same proportion of pharmacists also saw a rise in prescriptions not being collected, and two out of three pharmacists had seen an increase in being asked if there was a cheaper, over-the-counter substitute for the medicine they had been prescribed.

The Chair of the Pharmaceutical Society in England, Thorrun Govind, called for prescription charges to be scrapped, telling me in *The Big Issue*, "We are deeply concerned that people are having to make choices about their health based on their ability to pay. No one should have to make choices about rationing their medicines and no one should be faced with a financial barrier to getting the medicines they need." At the time of writing in January 2025, there has been no policy change.

Despite the worsening situation, very little was done to actually help disabled people in 2023. There were of course the cost of living payments, but these disproportionately benefited some disabled people over others. Those on Employment and Support Allowance or Universal Credit received £900 across eighteen months (still not enough to live on, as the government itself recognised by setting the 2023/4 minimum wage at almost double this monthly rate), while those on Personal Independence Payments received just £150; as it was, the ESA and Universal Credit rates had been uplifted from £400, whilst PIP recipients saw no such uplift.

This was despite research from the Joseph Rowntree Foundation in 2022 which found that in the poorest fifth of the population, four in ten households do not receive means-tested benefits.

Disability rights campaigners of course fought back. They released two online petitions demanding that all disabled people in receipt of benefits received extra support. The first, by disabled student Abigail Broomfield, asked that disabled people and carers who had been left out of the support packages in 2022 were not ignored in 2023. The second, by disabled mum and carer Rachel Curtis, asked for help with energy bills, which are higher for disabled people.

Collectively the petitions got over forty thousand signatures between them and a survey was launched as a result which got over eleven thousand responses. 93% of respondents said that they or a disabled person they cared for had been forced to cut back on essential items. Disabled MP Marsha de Cordova called the minuscule support "woefully insufficient and the very definition of what we would call sticking-plaster politics."

However, despite the cross-party works and pensions committee recommending that payments were increased and made to all disabled people in receipt of benefits, the DWP refused to help. The then chair of the committee, Sir Stephen Timms, told Disability News Service: "Support payments provided to groups such as disabled people which have been disproportionately impacted during the cost-of-living crisis fell short of what was needed."

It's worth pointing out here that Timms is the current minister for disabled people, who at the time of writing has not yet announced any further support for disabled people in the cost of living crisis.

Whilst many in Labour were supportive of disabled people getting more support, the then works and pensions shadow secretary Jonathan Ashcroft said that it was actually benefit fraud that was to blame for the lack of cost of living support. Ashcroft claimed the amount of benefit fraud and error could've "funded an extra £300 cost-of-living payment", putting the blame on those most vulnerable in the crisis instead of those who were supposed to help them.

Sadly, matching disability benefits to the rise in inflation has never been the UK government's strong suit. You only have to look at the DWP Christmas "bonus" to know that. If you're not the super lucky beneficiary of the DWP Christmas bonus, don't worry, it's only a tenner. When it was introduced over fifty years ago, £10 was seen as enough to buy a full Christmas dinner with all the trimmings—but in December 2023, I priced up what I could get by way of a Christmas meal from Asda: a full festive dinner came in at £37.01, with the cheapest turkey being £8.50. If the bonus had risen in line with inflation, each disabled person would be looking at £168 extra, and the Trussell Trust would have to hand out far fewer emergency food parcels. They gave out approximately one million in the winter of 2023–4.

Not only did disabled people see very little support to meet their additional and particular costs in 2023, and not only did politicians from both parties seem to be pitting us against each other in their latest blame game and their inconsistent policies for different benefits—the Sunak government was also following in the footsteps of every other since the 1990s, and trying to make it harder for people to qualify for unemployment benefits via changes to the already historically cruel Work Capability Assessment.

In 2023, Stride unveiled plans to overhaul the Work Capability Assessment—not to scrap it or make it a less traumatising process for disabled people—to actually make it harder for those unable to work to be declared as having Low Capability for Work Related Activity (LCWRA).

The government's rationale for this was that 20% of people in the Support Group for the LCWRA group said they "would like to work at some point in the future". However, this is ignoring the glaringly obvious fact that 80% said they wouldn't or couldn't, and that the future is not the present: just 4% of people said they felt they would be able to work now, and only if the right job and the right support were available.

Stride's reasoning for pushing disabled people into work was that, in the post-lockdown world, we could all work from home now, which is untrue for a variety of reasons. Firstly, many jobs that provide work from home opportunities are in sectors which require higher education or senior roles, which those on Universal Credit tend not to qualify for, whereas lower skilled and lower paid work tends to be in shops and cafés.

There's also the fact that many disabled and lower-income people can't use or don't have access to computers. In 2022, one in five households in England earning under £25k had no internet access at all, rising to almost one in three for disabled people and then, according to Lloyd's Bank research from 2021, 32% of people with an impairment don't have basic digital literacy.

There is currently no specific government help to get disabled people access to a computer or training to use it. Whilst the Access to Work grant is supposed to help disabled people get equipment they need for their jobs, the backlog means many can't take on work (see Chapter 12). You also can't actually access "access to work" until you have a job offer—an opportunity made far less likely by a lack of computer skills. It was also a bit rich for the government to be pushing benefits reform based on a landscape of remote working on the one hand, while also pushing for people to get back to their offices.

When the consultation was launched in September 2023, disability rights groups utilised social media to get as many people as possible to respond, but respondents reported struggling to understand what they were being asked and that the timeframe to complete the consultation was too short (the government had already issued its response to the consultation by November).

This is something the veteran campaigner Ellen Clifford realised was illegal, as consultations typically have to last twelve weeks and we were given just eight.

She took the DWP to court, where they were forced to admit that they'd launched the consultation with no real idea of how many people they would actually be able to help into work if the reforms went ahead.

The Office for Budget Responsibility later revealed that, despite the proposed cuts potentially affecting around 453,000 new applicants, just 15,400 or 3% of those would be able to find paid work. Yet the changes would mean around 93% of those affected would be recategorised, and would lose around £416 per month—or £4,990 per year. Around 290,000 of these people would be subject to conditionality, expected to engage in work search activity or risk having their DWP benefits stopped.

In March 2024, ahead of the spring budget, disability rights activists from Disabled People Against Cuts and many other organisations blocked roads outside Parliament and demonstrated in cities around the UK to protest the proposed cuts. The protests took place in Newcastle, Edinburgh, Cardiff, Norwich and London, where the group initially blocked the road to DWP headquarters and then moved along to block traffic outside of Parliament for over an hour. "We are calling for active resistance across the UK to these brutal attacks on disabled people," DPAC announced at the London protest.

DPAC chose to end the protest after members became distressed by police attempts to move them on. Ellen Clifford explained to me that the reason police surrounded disabled people and attempted to "kettle" them (when police surround protestors in one area and refuse to let them move on) is because much like in the Direct Action Network's day, police still find it impossible to actually arrest disabled people due to how inaccessible vehicles and stations are.

Meanwhile in Newcastle, DPAC North East surrounded the historic Grey's Monument in the centre of the city. Francesca, a DPACNE organiser, told me in an interview for the *Big Issue*:

> The North East is already part of a pilot which sees disabled people's welfare payments go down even further as part of universal credit reforms, when so many are having to choose between not just heating or eating but forgoing food so we can afford to power our wheelchairs and ventilators.

"It was never a legitimate attempt to hear the voices of deaf and disabled people or support them into work," Ellen Clifford told Chaminda Jayanetti of the *Big Issue* later in the year. "In reality, a lot of people will struggle to pay everyday bills if these proposed changes go ahead."

Although the Tories were voted out in July, at the time of writing in January 2025, the new Labour government has not yet announced whether they will be upholding the changes. This is something campaigners have urged them to reconsider. In October 2024, twenty-four disabled people's organisations signed an open letter to new chancellor Rachel Reeves and Secretary of State for Work and Pensions Liz Kendall urging them to rethink the "dangerous" plans.

The letter, signed by people and organisations including John McDonnell, DPAC, Disability Wales and Unite, states, "The consequences of these measures will be devastating for the disabled people affected. They will also add to already unreasonable workloads and working conditions for frontline [Department for Work and Pensions] staff."

Meanwhile, the cost of living crisis rages on. The latest figures from the Joseph Rowntree Foundation cost of living tracker found that, in October 2024, 82% of low-income renters on housing benefit were going without essentials. Further data from the JRF shared by iNews showed that 62% were spending more than 40% of their income on rent, while 37% of low-income households, some 4.3 million people, were in rent arrears. This was while Chancellor Reeves announced that Local Housing Allowance would not be going up in the Autumn Statement.

In other words, disabled people and their allies have as much injustice to campaign about as ever. The cost of living crisis has shone a light on some of the acute pressures facing disabled households, but the late 2020s is also a world of slower-burning crises and questions for disability rights. It's time to look at those now, in Part Two.

PART TWO

TODAY AND TOMORROW

10

DON'T MAKE ME THE PROBLEM
ABLEIST MEDIA NARRATIVES

As we've seen throughout the disability rights movement's journey, the media has always played a part in upholding the disablist and ableist narratives put forward by the government about disabled people. Part of the reason this is happening is of course that very few people in the media are disabled.

Whether streaming on a phone or watching live on a big flatscreen, television is still the UK's favourite entertainment, with 97% of households owning a set. This makes it a real problem that the Creative Diversity Network's yearly Diamond report consistently shows poor representation of disabled people in the TV industry. In the year 2022/3, when 24% of the UK population was estimated to be disabled, just 9.6% of writers, 6.5% of directors and only 7.8% of producer directors were disabled. Across the board, only 6.7% of senior roles behind the camera were held by disabled people.

On screen, disabled people make up just 8.7% of all actors, presenters and contributors. This is the level of representation deciding what gets written, programmed and made. Whilst stories about us are being told, they're not being told by people with lived experience of what it's like to be disabled, but through a lens that makes sense to non-disabled people.

You've seen the usual stories millions of times: disabled characters presented not as individuals in their own right, but serving as plot devices in the "real" characters' arcs—usually as burdens to their loved ones, with a non-disabled character coming to terms with, or being somehow motivated by, their child or partner's disability. Hardly ever including the nuances of disabled life, the tone very often portrays us as super inspiring for "overcoming" disabilities, or else plays out our deepest trauma in excruciating detail for clicks while ignoring all of our less extreme experiences.

To be fair to TV creators, since the overwhelming majority of them are not disabled, we have to assume that most are getting their info from how disability is covered in the press—which also has a huge representation problem. While the NCTJ found that 22% of journalists had a work-limiting health problem or disability in 2022, up massively from just 10% in 2015, it's been pointed out that working in the industry is not enough to ensure you have the power to shape narratives.

Natasha Hirst, the first disabled president of the National Union of Journalists, told the 2023 Disability

Wales conference that there were many barriers preventing disabled journalists from getting into newsroom roles:

> Disabled journalists experience many barriers in their careers, and although there are schemes to get disabled people into journalism, there's very little support for them to progress their careers in getting to those senior roles where they are able to influence change. There are not enough disabled role models, workplaces are not accessible enough, and many disabled journalists tell the union that they experience terrible discrimination at work.

There are so many problems with the UK's journalism and small-screen drama being heavily dominated by the non-disabled. Firstly, the 24-hour media's quest for the most attention-grabbing headlines means that our authentic stories told authentically by us are not seen as newsworthy enough. But when the media frames disability as either tragic or superhuman, the end result doesn't reflect society or help any disabled people.

Many paralympians have spoken up about how even their own lives outside of the games don't live up to what the media portrays. In January 2023, the British wheelchair racer Hannah Cockroft told BBC Sport, "The segregation between paralympians and every other disabled person is damaging. Britain is an incredibly scary place for every disabled person right now. You feel targeted with every announcement that comes out, you feel unsupported."

I can definitely think of times I've felt that way, whether it's the pervasive language used around benefits claimants or the new suggestions in the 2020s that conditions such as ADHD and autism have been caught from TikTok. This chapter will look in more detail at actively hostile media narratives, and at journalists' failure to challenge hostile narratives from government.

Secondly, the "ableist default" perspective in both "factual" and creative TV leads to misinformation about disability, which causes real harm. I'll give just two examples of something catastrophic that was broadcast to millions, but that would never have got through if there had been a disabled person in the room with the power to stop it.

At the start of 2024, thousands of people took to Twitter and Instagram and coordinated official complaints to Ofcom after Giselle Boxer claimed on the BBC's entrepreneurs' competition show *Dragons' Den* that a combination of acupuncture, Chinese herbs and ear seeds had cured her ME (myalgic encephalomyelitis or chronic fatigue syndrome—ME/CFS). As activist and journalist Hollie-Anne Brooks wrote on *Digital Spy*, "Editorially, the BBC has made a grave decision in allowing a product to seem that, coupled with various wellness practices, it could somehow cure an illness, without scientific backing."

Following the pushback from the ME community, the episode was pulled from BBC iPlayer, then later reinstated with a disclaimer. By then, it will have been too late to correct this narrative for the 4 million viewers who watched the episode when it originally aired, BBC One's thirteenth most popular broadcast of the week.

That was a situation damaging to public understanding of chronic conditions, and of one particular condition. My second example is a less concrete harm, where pervasive cultural attitudes have fed back between the TV screen and the real lives of disabled people. There's one storyline in particular that comes to mind whenever I think of the portrayals of disability I saw in TV dramas growing up—Honey Mitchell in *EastEnders* finding out that her daughter Janet had Down's syndrome. The storyline focused on poor Honey's feelings about having a disabled child—how she couldn't possibly be expected to look after her "defective" offspring; at one point the audience was even expected to sympathise with her when she considered killing her own child.

As someone who had recently been diagnosed with a debilitating condition that made me reliant on my family, this story made me feel like a huge burden to my parents. It also cemented the dehumanising idea that disability was only relevant for how it made non-disabled people feel. It was only as an adult journalist, whilst I was talking to John Pring of Disability News Service, that I realised this was the reason I, and probably so many of my generation, had grown so ashamed of being disabled: these are the sorts of stories that were hammered down our throats as kids.

One of the worst things about the Honey storyline was the way it normalised abuse (or at least the temptation to abuse) in a disabled household. These narratives of a non-disabled person feeling all the feelings and making all the decisions about your disability weren't just seen by disabled viewers like me, but also by the people entrusted with our care.

And, unfortunately, there are horrific, all-too-real stories such as that of Kaylea Titford, a teenage wheelchair-user born with spina bifida who died in October 2020 due to gross neglect by her parents. The media seemed to spend as much time on how hard parenting Kaylea must have been as on the awful crime they'd committed, often focusing on her weight or even calling her "revolting", despite her parents being jailed for manslaughter.

According to the Office for National Statistics Crime Survey, in 2019 disabled women were more than twice as likely as non-disabled women to experience domestic abuse. Data from SafeLives published in 2017 found that disabled people typically experience abuse for an average of 3.3 years before accessing support, compared to 2.3 years for non-disabled people. Even after getting help, disabled victims were 8% more likely than non-disabled victims to continue to experience abuse. This is because it's harder for disabled people to find support and they're often isolated in situations where they know society makes saints of their abusers for trapping them in the first place. So, the way journalists and TV writers handle this topic matters.

Finally, if disability isn't present on the team putting together the content, then it's likely to feel ignorable. Way too often, disability just isn't acknowledged or depicted by media at all. As a disabled journalist working during the pandemic, I found it almost impossible to get stories that encapsulated how disabled people felt and were living out into the world.

When the ONS reported that six in ten of those who died of Covid in England and seven in ten in Wales were disabled people, this should've been front page news, but the media was too busy covering (mostly positively) the Eat Out to Help Out scheme, and was swept up in a "post-Covid" mood that saw our calls for continued testing and masking as trying to control people. The "back to normal" narrative prevailed, ignoring the fact that many disabled people weren't alive to return to normal. Even journalism that did include the disabled perspective on something like mask-wearing framed the whole thing as disabled people's preferences, weighed against the inherent value of freedom and convenience.

When preventable suffering resulting from Covid policy *was* covered by the media, it was very rarely about disabled people. Journalism preferred to focus on victims seen as closer to the hearts or lives of the average non-disabled Briton. At a time when the media was obsessed with the weekly clap for NHS workers and the struggles they faced in frontline services, they chose to ignore the strain that lockdown and the terrifying case rate were putting on the very kinds of disabled people many NHS staff were working so hard to save. Huge swathes of the media focused on how hard this time was to be "locked up" indoors for those who were used to freedom of mobility, while the truly devastating parts of the pandemic mishandling, such as the Do Not Resuscitate orders placed on disabled people in the first wave, weren't even covered in the press until months later when disabled people's family members and charities like Mencap started kicking up a fuss.

However, out of this unacceptable approach to coverage has come the same fierceness we always see from the disabled community: a determination to have our voices heard and to fight for the representation we deserve. It has led to disabled creators fighting back, creating their own content without compromise, and bringing the rest of the community on this journey with them.

Similar to how the Spartacus Report used disabled activists' own channels to challenge austerity reforms, we are bypassing traditional media to talk to the country directly, without a go-between—and those of us who've made it onto the establishment platforms are pushing for big structural changes to make sure that we're not the last ones in.

* * *

As we saw in Chapter 7, particularly since the early 2000s, governments have been going hard on "benefit fraudster" crackdowns and turning disabled people into villains, amplified by the media. Together, politicians and journalists have been feeding the public a constant diet of disablist notions—if you're on disability unemployment benefits but can do something like your own shopping, are you really disabled? Surely if there are pictures of a wheelchair user standing up or walking, they're lying about needing a wheelchair?—and while the British public has turned its back on austerity politics, the fight against toxic disability narratives in the press has got harder in the latest economic squeeze.

Any disabled person knows that you can't have a big TV and enjoy the odd takeaway if you're also being supported by the state—the 2020s backlash against austerity and the public mood in favour of big government spending hasn't changed that. A YouGov Poll carried out in early 2023 found that just 28% of respondents thought that those on unemployment benefits (which disabled people often are) should be able to afford a takeaway once a month. In the same survey, 24% thought those on unemployment benefits shouldn't be able to afford a balanced diet.

It's no secret that this attitude has been fed down through the press from the mouth of government itself. Whilst disabled people struggled in the cost of living crisis to afford food or their gas bills, the Sunak government was orchestrating a campaign of "cracking down" on benefit fraud. This was launched on social media in

April 2023 with then Minister for Disabled People Tom Pursglove pulling the worst Liam Neeson impression ever, threatening to "track you down" if you were committing benefit fraud and gleefully attending a dawn benefit raid in a publicity stunt.

While the DWP claimed this was about benefit fraud as a whole, the involvement of the disability minister obviously put the focus on disabled people. The video was rightly ripped to shreds on social media but it didn't stop the dehumanising narratives. The following month, May 2023, the Jeremy Vine Show put out a tweet (since deleted) reading "is it time to crackdown on jobless benefits? Nearly 4 million people in the UK are being supported by the state without ever having to look for a job. That's because they've been deemed too sick to work. Is it wrong for taxpayers to fund them indefinitely?"

The disability charity Scope was one of many accounts to respond in disgust: "The rhetoric around disability benefits is getting nastier and nastier. Almost half of people in poverty are disabled. Meanwhile, daytime TV paints disabled people as a drain on taxpayers, and questions their right to support." Neither Jeremy Vine nor the show's producers apologised, but since the backlash they have tried to cover more disability related topics, inviting disability activists, including myself, to discuss news items. I appeared alongside a right-wing outrage merchant given the same platform—my view is that you can't really "debate" or "both sides" basic human rights and decency, but that's just me.

DON'T MAKE ME THE PROBLEM

The media trope that unemployed disabled people were costing the taxpayer too much came straight from the government itself. In October 2023, the then Chancellor of the Exchequer Jeremy Hunt declared "war on the workshy" at the Conservative party conference. In his keynote speech he called people on benefits "workshy shirkers" who were "coasting on benefits".

As I said at the time in my *Daily Mirror* column, this was a desperate attempt from the Conservatives to stay in power. It wasn't about facts—like ministers' extortionate salaries; or £42 billion a year lost to tax evasion; or the untold expansion of the disabled population thanks to three years of Covid; or the public money lost to the Conservatives' donor pals who'd been awarded private contracts in the pandemic, and more generally allowed to carve up the health, transport and care sectors, making them inaccessible to working-class people. But most of the press, instead of scrutinising or fact-checking Hunt's narrative, republished it happily.

After fourteen years of Conservative government presiding over austerity, economic upheaval in the form of Brexit, the dangerous handling of a pandemic and the biggest cost of living crisis most generations have ever seen, there's still much work to do to ensure Labour treats us any differently. The press has a key role to play in that, and if it won't do it willingly, disabled campaigners are here to challenge it.

Part of the work is holding the traditional media to account. In October 2023, I hosted a panel at the

Disability Wales Conference which featured executives from media companies including BBC, ITV and Reach (owners of *The Daily Mirror*, *Express*, *Star* and many local news outlets including *Wales Online*). During the panel, the audience made up of disabled campaigners, held the media to account over many things, but mainly over the way the media ignored how disabled people were impacted by the pandemic (again, a Welsh death rate for disabled people of seven in ten).

Rhian Davies from Disability Wales told the conference that the media had been "complicit in accepting the UK government's narrative that the deaths of disabled people during the Covid pandemic were inevitable, unavoidable and expendable." Broadcasters were left speechless and vowed to change. We will be here to remind them of that promise.

Then there's the work that we can do outside of the journalism establishment. Authentic representation in the media is often only possible through those of us who have managed to get a seat at the table, and in turn created opportunities for the rest of our community. My now former online platform *The Unwritten* (2020–3) was born out of my frustration and exhaustion with the media's lack of nuance in its disability coverage; I decided to create that space for disabled people to tell all our stories—be it success, struggle, life, love, loss and everything in between.

We published everything from first person diagnosis stories to political analysis with a deep focus on how disability intersects with the rest of our identities—sexuality, gender, race, religion, class, education, family and relationships among others. We got an incredible number of pitches about sex and relationships and had a regular column on this written by disabled journalist Hannah Shewan Stevens.

The Unwritten gave a starting point to those who were struggling to get their pieces out there in an ableist media landscape. It was a starting point to many who never thought their work would have a place in the media because they're disabled. Thanks to all of our work, I think the industry is changing slowly. I see more editors reaching out to disabled writers now, and making an effort to get their language right.

* * *

There's also been a real hunger for change in today's TV landscape, for an end to the "inspo porn vs trauma porn" narrative binary. Whenever disabled people are portrayed in the media, these are usually the two possible ways their stories might get told.

The late great activist Stella Young coined the term "Inspiration Porn" to describe the way non-disabled people will applaud disabled people just for going to school or leaving the house. While the praise might seem positive, the problem is what this says about everybody who's not managing X achievement: when those who don't have the means to strive or are let down by governments or institutions are seen as not trying hard enough, not being brave enough, or maybe even faking disability.

The flipside of inspiration porn is trauma porn: our deepest and often very private medical history is used as fodder to shock and appal non-disabled people consumers in an entirely negative narrative, with the emphasis often on carers, rather than disabled people, fighting this tragedy.

The two porns, inspo and trauma, sometimes even come together in one story. We saw this in the May 2023 coverage of rugby player Rob Burrow raising money for charities which support his condition motor neurone disease. The press praised him as a saint and focused on how much his loved ones were doing for him. Burrow's wife was portrayed as a kind of "white knight", and the front pages were plastered with images of his good friend Kevin Sinfield carrying him over the finish line at the Leeds Marathon. The message to disabled people is clear—our stories only matter, whether as art or journalism, if they can be exploited.

As Hannah Shewan Stevens told me, "For disabled people to thrive, we need to move on from this toxic ricocheting between inspiration porn and tragedy porn ... it keeps us trapped in these metaphorical boxes. We need to diversify people's perspectives of our lives." This is as much about challenging stereotypes in drama as it is about challenging media coverage. As we know from

Chapter 6, disability art is disability activism. Increasingly, disabled creatives in the UK's TV world are making their own art, fed up of non-disabled people writing disabled characters incapable of having jobs, romantic relationships or sex.

Autistic people have typically been infantilised or treated like human computers in their depiction on screen—and portrayals have nearly always been of young boys or men. That's where Elle McNicoll came in. McNicoll is the author of *A Kind of Spark*, which centres on Addie, an autistic girl who fights to get a memorial to the women who were killed during the witch trials in her village. Elle also wrote for the CBBC TV adaptation which explored the fact that many women accused of witchcraft were probably actually neurodivergent.

The series, which aired in 2023, was the first UK production about neurodivergent characters to have a majority cast and crew made up of neurodivergent and disabled people. McNicoll told me it was important that autistic girls could see themselves in both her characters and real people. "We have to teach this new generation of autistic women that being autistic is fabulous. It's not something to be tolerated but celebrated."

As Ella Maisy Purvis, who played Elinor Fraser in the show, told me when I interviewed them for *Digital Spy*, it was important to show that "autism isn't a thing that's just been created in the modern world. It's not created by vaccines or it's not a buzzword or like this cool new trend. We're here and we've always been here."

Ella also returned to play the character of Bonnie Bridges in season 2 of the show, a character who, like them, has ADHD and autism. In contrast with the show's other characters, Bonnie wasn't raised to be proud of her conditions, which causes her to lash out. Ella told me that this was important to show too—because "why can't disabled people be angry with the way they've been treated?"

It's not enough for disabled creators to be at the wheel, though. We need everyone working in TV to be on board with authentic and diverse stories about disability, not turn it into a segregated art form.

One of our biggest allies in the industry has been the acclaimed screenwriter Jack Thorne. He wrote BBC Three's 2016 factual drama *Don't Take My Baby*, starring disabled actor Ruth Madeley—a drama about a disabled couple's struggle to keep their newborn baby and how societal and media narratives paint disabled people as being incapable of parenting—and BBC Two's 2022 film *Then Barbara Met Alan*, about the lives of Barbara Lisicki and Alan Holdsworth and the activism that led to the creation of the Disability Discrimination Act. Ruth Madeley starred here too, as Barbara. She is a one-woman showcase of how much light we can shine when TV representations of disabled people are done right.

My personal favourite of Ruth's recent roles is as Shirley Anne Bingham in *Doctor Who*. First appearing in 2023, and slated to return in 2025, Shirley is a tough talking hilariously witty science officer—who also happens to have a wheelchair packed to the teeth with weapons. When a target is identified as being located upstairs by a UNIT officer (if you don't watch the show, they're like the army and CIA but for aliens), there's an awkward pause when he realises Shirley can't get up there in her chair, but she quickly cuts him off with "don't make me the problem."

When I interviewed Ruth about this role for *Digital Spy* she told me "it was so important to show that the problem isn't us, it's actually all the stuff around us."

Another pivotal moment actually happened by accident. Whilst chatting to the Doctor in one scene, we saw Shirley cross her legs. The reaction to this tiny moment was huge. In a small vile corner of the internet, some thought she wasn't really disabled—this was a sentiment we actually saw echoed from another character in a later episode who had been infected with a hate bomb where she screams at Shirley, "I've seen you stand!" However for disabled fans, this was a crucial moment to show that disability isn't "one size fits all".

When I asked her about it, Ruth was perplexed by the reaction. "I was just getting comfy, to be honest! I was just existing in my body, but that was clearly such an important thing for other disabled people to see."

Another way in which disabled people have broken through is via comedy. Although not without trolling, comedians such as Rosie Jones and Francesca Martinez have gained popularity in the mainstream media. After opening up about their experiences as disabled women they have been asked on chat shows and even invited onto political debate shows to shed light on issues affecting disabled people.

When Francesca appeared on *Question Time* in 2019 she particularly took aim at Boris Johnson's support of austerity, highlighting the number of disabled people who had died due to being found fit for work. In a now famous speech she said, "I think whatever your politics, you can agree that punishing disabled people for falling on hard times is absolutely morally wrong and they have blood on their hands."

Another vehicle through which disabled comedians have worked to break through and represent disabled rights, as well as other issues, is the show *The Last Leg*. What originally started as a companion to Channel 4's paralympic coverage has evolved over the years to become one of the biggest late night chat shows, covering all manner of news affecting the British public. What sets *The Last Leg* apart from other shows is that two of its hosts, Adam Hills and Alex Brooker, are disabled. The show has played a vital part in explaining issues such as the cost of living crisis and even dating with a disability to the general public.

Whilst we've seen more representation of disabled people in drama, soaps, sport and even sci-fi, sitcoms were an area where we were lacking. This is seen as a harder area to crack due to biases from commissioners. It's similar to how female comedians have often said they've had ideas turned down because the channel already has "one of those" (meaning a sitcom written by and about a woman).

One show that has managed to break through and worked to change perceptions of disabled women is *We Might Regret This*. This ballsy comedy gives viewers an insight into what life is like for Freya (played by Kyla Harris, one of the co-creators) a disabled women who relies on carers, and in particular how this impacts her sex life. The programme shocked some viewers because many non-disabled people don't expect disabled people to be able to have sex, but it also worked to normalise parts of our lives that others treat as "not for us".

Thankfully since the 'poor Honey' storyline, soaps have improved their disability representation greatly and have become one of the most inclusive parts of British television. In recent years, soaps have woven storylines for a whole range of disabled characters that don't just focus on their disabilities.

When the *EastEnders* character Frankie Lewis (Rose Ayling-Ellis) was assaulted in a 2022 episode, viewers learnt how much harder it is for disabled (especially deaf) people to be believed as victims, but they also saw her behaving like any other resident of Albert Square by fighting with the Mitchells. When *Emmerdale*'s character Ryan Stocks (played by James Moore), who has cerebral palsy, lost his adoptive mother, again in 2022 we saw his true raw reaction in a world that often delegitimises or sanitises disabled people's feelings.

Izzy Armstrong (Cherylee Houston) has been a fixture on *Coronation Street* for many years, suffering heartache and elation just like anyone else, but during the early years of the Covid pandemic, the character—who uses a wheelchair and is immunocompromised—was able to show the harsh realities of opening up too soon for disabled people.

By the time of writing in 2025, it's now the case that nearly all disabled characters in soaps are played by disabled people, something which still doesn't happen enough in other areas of media and entertainment programmes.

There is still a long way to go, and representation in the scripts doesn't automatically mean justice for disabled people working in front of and behind the camera. We still need campaigners, as the stats at the top of this chapter make clear. In 2021, Jack Thorne accused the TV industry of "utterly and totally failing disabled people", and launched a pressure group called Underlying Health Condition with Genevieve Barr, Holly Lubran and Katie Player aiming to elevate disabled voices in the industry and collaborate with other organisations to fix the accessibility problem in the film and TV industry.

The fight for the guarantee of TV representation—and empowered, accurately varied representation—is far from over, and the more disabled people are allowed to participate in the industry, the more the representation will be authentic. People watching at home can be part of the fight too: opposition to media ableism that's already out there has predominantly been over social media, such as the backlash to Giselle Boxer's Acuseeds being backed by *Dragons' Den*.

* * *

The battle's still going in journalism too, because it can't all be on disabled journalists. As is the way with much independent media, *The Unwritten* wasn't something I could sustain, and while parts of the press have got much better at platforming disabled voices and covering disabled lives with sensitivity, there are still unfortunately far too many media organisations that don't want to change.

In the UK, most major print and online media outlets are regulated by the Independent Press Standards Organisation, better known as IPSO (members include the *Daily Mail*, *The Sun*, *The Times*, *The Telegraph*, *Metro* and the *Daily Mirror*). It was first established in 2014 in the wake of the Leveson Inquiry into press ethics and culture. It replaced the Press Complaints Commission and is responsible for ensuring the press adhere to the Editors' Code of Practice, which sets out the rules on accuracy, the right to privacy and protection from harassment and apparently, discrimination.

However, there are many things wrong with both IPSO and its code. Firstly, it's a voluntary organisation, meaning that some major organisations such as the *Financial Times*, *The Independent* and the *Guardian* have refused to join. It is therefore not a universal body controlling the legality of what the mainstream press is allowed to publish. IPSO also refused to seek approval from the Press Recognition Panel, which oversees press regulators.

The Independent Monitor for the Press (IMPRESS) by comparison has a much more eclectic membership such as local press, *Novara Media*, *Bellingcat* and *The Canary* and is recognised as the only regulator which is fully compliant with the recommendations of the Leveson Inquiry. IPSO is much criticised for its ineffectiveness, with the National Union of Journalists saying member outlets "continue to fail to take their responsibilities seriously by hiding their failings behind another pointless so-called regulator."

In January 2023, sick of seeing constant ableism in the media, I contacted the Head of Standards and Regulation Jane Debois offering to help them create guidelines on reporting disability. I had experience in this area as I'd been part of updating the *Daily Mirror*'s disability guidelines during my stint as guest editor of the week-long series *Disabled Britain*.

Guidance already exists for reporting on other protected characteristics such as race, sexuality, religion and gender, and I naively went into the meeting believing the people I'd be seeing wanted to work with me. Instead, I was told that they had no remit to create guidance for reporting on disability as "nobody complains about ableist stories." I couldn't believe what I was hearing. It was explained to me that IPSO needs a specific number of complaints about one story to set a precedent. But unlike other movements, there hasn't been a catalyst as media ableism has been happening for decades and is far too accepted in society.

I left the meeting to find that two of the outlets regulated by IPSO had published stories claiming that ADHD (attention deficit hyperactivity disorder) wasn't real. I decided to give IPSO some complaints by mobilising my Twitter and Instagram following, creating templates and easy-to-follow guides on how to complain. Over 300 times, to be precise.

Our campaign made the national press, but the result was a disappointment. IPSO staff seemed taken aback that I'd actually supplied complaints, and insinuated I had misunderstood. It turned out that despite these sorts of articles clearly being discriminatory, the code allows them to happen because the discrimination clause only applies if it's against individuals. What else could be done?

A few weeks later it was rumoured that Sophie Morgan would be *Strictly Come Dancing*'s first wheelchair-using contestant and *The Sun* ran the headline "cha cha chair" and called Sophie "a wheelchair" as opposed to a wheelchair user. This was clearly one person being discriminated against so surely we had a case here. After yet another round of campaigning, IPSO came back to us and said it had to be a complaint from the individual themselves. When Sophie did complain, she didn't get a response. Surprise, surprise.

Never one to take no for an answer, I was made aware that there was a consultation on the IPSO code, so I coordinated over a thousand people to ask that the regulator broaden its discrimination clause to include groups of people. If this were to happen, it would mean the media industry as a whole wouldn't be able to attack any minority. They couldn't be disablist, racist, xenophobic, sexist, homophobic or transphobic.

Nine months later, I was informed there would not be a change to the code. The regulator claimed the reason was that it would "inhibit debate on important matters." I don't know about you, but I don't think a minority community's right to not be targeted by the press should be up for debate.

In its report following the consultation, IPSO also claimed that they don't need to create provisions prohibiting the incitement of hatred against anyone with protected characteristics because this is already prohibited by law—essentially admitting that, in the current system, the press can in fact break discrimination law without consequences from the industry. We will keep fighting IPSO on their decision not to extend the discrimination clause, with campaign groups planning to lobby the Starmer government.

The campaign for change at IPSO has also been working on a case-by-case basis, targeting the spate of opinion pieces in the 2020s claiming everyone is making up having ADHD because it's trendy due to TikTok or because their favourite celebrity is getting a diagnosis.

Over the last couple of years, ADHD diagnosis rates have soared, especially in adult women, because the traits are easier to miss in girls. The ADHD Foundation estimates girls in the UK are three times less likely than boys to be diagnosed and supported with ADHD, and on average are diagnosed nine years later than boys. The charity also estimates that 50 to 75% of the one million UK women with ADHD are undiagnosed. A big reason for the increase in diagnoses is that ADHD is clinically underdiagnosed in girls.

In other words, as more women have been talking about their experiences online, more of us have been realising that what we considered to be personality faults are actually ADHD traits. Of course, this is not how the right wing press sees this. Instead of a community that enables disabled women who were missed by the system to feel seen and get support, they have reported the rise in diagnosis rates as something created by social media fashions. But content creators with ADHD are standing up to the press, calling them out in videos and demanding change.

In its code review report, IPSO said that journalists had simply been asking why there had been an increase in ADHD diagnosis. This isn't strictly true as they were jumping to their own conclusions as to why and making light of a chronic condition.

So far, complaints to IPSO have gone nowhere: one against *The Telegraph* over an online calculator showing how much of your tax went to benefits; one about a *Times* column that repeatedly conflated two very different benefits to insinuate that everyone on disability benefits were "scroungers"—after filing a complaint using the accuracy clause I was told that the piece didn't break rules because the code doesn't apply to opinion pieces about what the writer believed to be true. You couldn't make it up. As a journalist, I'm now of the opinion that IPSO protects the media as opposed to the public.

* * *

Stricter regulation is definitely one way forward. However, when I'm asked how we make the media less ableist, my answer is always the same: by getting more disabled people into the media.

So many disabled journalists are put off the industry after they enter it, but many struggle to even get that far, due to how inaccessible an industry it is. It's all well and good for editors and publishers to talk about how important they think disabled talent is, but the culture of their organisations needs to reflect that. Far too many newsrooms still require people to work in offices for a good chunk of the week, in loud, often physically inaccessible spaces, in chairs and at desks that can be painful for many disabled people. Newsroom shifts are long and deadline-based, and don't have the flexibility to allow those with conditions that cause fatigue to take breaks.

And then there's the fact that, more often than not, newsrooms are based in London, the UK's least affordable city, and one that still doesn't have a fully accessible transport network.

Most outlets also still require journalism degrees which can be another obstacle for disabled journalists who find education inaccessible and unsupportive. While it's great that more outlets are hiring disabled staff writers to write about disabled topics, there's still a feeling that there's only so much room at the table. I've been told on more than one occasion that the disabled staff writer will be covering a story that I pitched as a freelancer. One publication even told me that they wouldn't be taking me on as a columnist, despite writing regularly for them, because they "already had one" disabled columnist. News outlets need to remember that disabled people are not a monolith and we need a host of disabled experiences to get a true picture.

And it's still the case that disabled writers are often contacted for freelance pieces instead of given staff contracts, meaning they miss out on many employment benefits such as private health, counselling and holiday or sick pay. By only employing us for one or two pieces outlets get to say they've had a disabled writer on board but without committing to change by investing in it long-term.

It's also not enough to have disabled journalists filing copy to your newsroom. In order for the media to be representative we need disabled editors, CEOs, section editors, sub-editors, columnists, photographers and everyone in between. This needs to be intersectional too—disabled queer journalists, disabled Black journalists, disabled nonbinary journalists, disabled journalists from low-income backgrounds. Disabled people in these roles can help to further challenge the diversity of the company they work for.

My main goal in tearing down media ableism is to bring other disabled people with me. I never want to hear "Oh, we already have Rachel Charlton-Dailey." I want it to be "Rachel Charlton-Dailey recommended you."

11

A DECENT LIFE

INDEPENDENT LIVING AND EQUAL ACCESS

Toxic media narratives have made it easier not only for the state to discriminate against us without much backlash, but companies too. From transport, accommodation and workplaces to the world of culture and leisure, lack of access to public life is still making today's disabled people second class citizens in the UK. How can disabled people participate in public life if they can't access public spaces, or jobs, or help in any way?

While so much of the scrounger rhetoric focuses on disabled people's lack of agency, it's society that has made it unnecessarily difficult to participate in our economy and civil society—or just to live with dignity like everyone else, going shopping, visiting museums, getting a bus to meet friends, visiting a new area or having fun in a bar or club.

We've seen the work of disabled activists to get the 1995 Disability Discrimination Act into law so that disabled people had an equal right to access goods and services. When all discrimination acts were mashed together to form the Equality Act of 2010, those laws were weakened.

Many believe that instead of providing greater coverage, the Equality Act was not specific enough on different kinds of discrimination. For example, the DDA made it illegal for service providers such as cafés and shops to discriminate against disabled people (though only in some cases, not all) and amendments in 2004 meant steps had to be taken to remove barriers to access, but the Equality Act actually undid this work. The legal duty on companies providing goods, services and facilities has been replaced with a much flimsier duty to make "reasonable adjustments" in order to prevent a disabled person being placed at a "substantial disadvantage" to non-disabled people who would have no problem with access.

The Equality Act doesn't actually state what a reasonable adjustment could be—it just gives examples, like installing ramps, larger signage or information, an induction loop and disability awareness training for staff. It also points out that "What is considered a reasonable adjustment for a large organisation like a bank, may be different from what is a reasonable adjustment for a small local shop. It is about what is practical in the service provider's individual situation and what resources the business may have." Given the lack of funding to support smaller companies in including disabled people, this is a loophole for disabled employees or service users to fall right through.

The wooliness of the law means that accessibility is not built in, but seen as an afterthought and something often included only once a disabled person complains. This is despite the act saying "You should not wait until a disabled person experiences difficulties using a service, as this may make it too late to make the necessary adjustment."

At best, many places offer temporary accessibility that can be rolled out as and when a disabled person decides to appear and "make a fuss". Think of a ramp that can be moved so as to not spoil the aesthetic of an old building, or cafés and shops that have buttons disabled people can press for assistance in entering buildings. The onus is always on the disabled person warning people in advance they will be visiting and have access needs, or asking for adjustments. This means that many non-disabled people have negative reactions to these requests, as if the disabled person is asking for extras or favourable treatment (as opposed to the bare minimum required by equality law).

It's not just the private sector failing disabled people in this way. We'll cover the crisis of funding and attitudes in education more in Chapter 12. An even more shocking example of discriminatory state provision is healthcare. Whilst you'd think that this at least would be accessible, it's often anything but. Many struggle to attend appointments in (still inaccessibly designed) older hospitals, and guide dog users are often treated like they're doing something wrong by bringing them to their appointments.

Even more scarily, emergency services can also be inaccessible to those who struggle to use the phone due to being deaf or not being able to communicate. The only alternative is a 999 video British Sign Language (BSL) service or a text relay service. Unbelievably for an emergency service, you have to preregister for this. It's also badly publicised so disabled people may not even know it exists. There's no doubt that the UK's access crisis kills.

* * *

One area of the public sector that massively discriminates against disabled people is independent living. Society has moved past institutionalising disabled people, but older homes can be difficult to adapt, and there aren't enough new accessible or adaptable homes being built for current demand, let alone future generations.

According to the English Housing Survey, it's estimated that a wheelchair user can visit fewer than one in ten homes in England. Meanwhile Habinteg Housing and the Papworth Trust found that around 1.8 million households in England are in need of accessible housing. It's particularly bad if you're a wheelchair user, with over 400,000 people currently living in unsuitable and inaccessible homes.

Your home is the one place that should be safe and easy for you to get around. However, due to funding, councils are overwhelmed with calls for support. There are currently around 104,000 disabled people on council waiting lists up and down England for accessible or adaptable homes. At the current rate, it's estimated that a disabled person may have to wait a staggering forty-seven years to get a new build fully-wheelchair-accessible home.

On 29 July 2024 disabled activists led by Inclusion London marched on Downing Street to demand that the new Labour government pledge to provide more accessible housing, and at affordable rates, as many disabled people can't afford sky high rents or mortgages. Laura Vicinanza from Inclusion London told protestors, "Housing is the cornerstone of independent living. Yet, hundreds of thousands of Disabled [people] in this country are living in homes that are inaccessible, unsafe and unaffordable. This is unacceptable."

The protest also shed important light on how the lack of accessible social housing traps disabled survivors of domestic abuse. Angie Airlie from Stay Safe East, a charity which supports disabled survivors of abuse across London, highlighted that disabled people escaping abusive living situations often end up in local authority temporary accommodation, which is usually unsuited to disabled people's needs.

Angie told protestors, "When the home is no longer a safe place, due to abuse, harassment, or crime, there is often no place for the victim to go. Victims are trapped—unable to escape from the torture of hate crime and/or abuse." The protest culminated in activists hand-delivering a letter signed by over forty disabled people's organisations to Number 10 Downing Street calling on Prime Minister Keir Starmer and Deputy Prime Minister Angela Rayner (who is also housing minister) to commit to "immediate and decisive action" to end the shortage of affordable accessible homes. This fight is ongoing.

A vital reason so many disabled people with more complex needs can live their lives is because of care and carers, through a package mostly provided by local authorities. With councils ravaged by funding cuts, once again disabled people are suffering. The great disability rights journalist Frances Ryan brought to light a horrendous case that was due to be implemented in Bristol in early 2024.

Due to a huge deficit, the council was trying to come up with ways to save money. Bristol had proposed that anyone whose at-home care was not seen as "best value" could see that care withdrawn and be told to live in a care home instead. This was to be called the Fair and Affordable Care Policy, though it doesn't sound very fair to the disabled people whose independence would be severely limited by its introduction. Fortunately, disabled people were ready to fight the proposals.

Bristol Reclaiming Independent Living responded to the public consultation saying it was "fundamentally flawed, likely unlawful, and would cause misery to many disabled people and their family and friends in Bristol." This response was the final nail in the coffin for the policy, after almost a year of campaigning from BRIL and of course Frances' journalism. As Frances wrote in her *Guardian* column,

> At its heart, this is a story of savage public funding cuts and growing need, of what happens when more than a decade of Westminster austerity collides with already bruised communities and squeezed local services. But it is also a story of who exactly in society matters: who gets to have a decent life, with a safe home and loving family, and who doesn't.

Disabled people were brutally reminded of this fact in one of the most horrific man-made disasters to strike British people in their homes this century.

On 14 June 2017, a fire broke out in the high rise Grenfell Tower block of council flats in North Kensington in London. The fire was started by an electrical fault with a fridge on the fourth floor, but it has since been proven that the fire spread so quickly due to the building, owned by Kensington and Chelsea Borough Council, being clad in highly combustible aluminium panels bonded together by a plastic filler. The fire burned for sixty hours and claimed the lives of seventy-two people. At least fifteen were disabled, and those fifteen who died represented 41% of the block's thirty-seven disabled residents.

Subsequent inquiries heard how disabled residents had raised concerns about the safety of the building and about not having any Personal Emergency Evacuation Plans (PEEPs) in place for them, but they had been "bullied" or "stigmatised" by management. Emma O'Connor, a disabled survivor of the fire, reported having been placed in high-up flats despite assessments from the council finding that she needed to live on the ground floor.

Claddag, a national campaign group of disabled residents living in homes with unsafe cladding, was founded by disability rights campaigners Sarah Rennie and Georgia Hulme after the fire. Claddag took the government to the high court to ensure that it was a legal requirement that all disabled people living in high-rise buildings had PEEPs, on the recommendation of the chairman of the Grenfell Inquiry. The government had launched a consultation on this recommendation, but in 2022 had said it wouldn't be doing that—it didn't want to save disabled people in fires, apparently.

That's where Claddag stepped in and launched its high court challenge that summer. Unfortunately, they lost the case, and emergency evacuation plans are still not a requirement, but disabled activists continue to fight for this.

At time of writing in January 2025, the Labour government still deems emergency plans too costly, despite the party having said while campaigning that they would work on this. Instead the Starmer government appears to be implementing what John Pring called a "watered down" version of PEEPS called Emergency Evacuation Information Sharing Plus, rebranded by Labour as "residential PEEPS", which will mean one person in the building must be in charge of identifying at-risk people. This has sparked criticism not only from disabled campaigners but also the very people whose job it is to keep everyone safe in the event of a fire—the National Fire Chiefs Council (NFCC).

They had told the Home Office during the 2022 consultation that such proposals were only "a first step in laying out how to identify residents who may be in need of assistance to evacuate their building in the event of a fire." The fire chiefs insisted: "more must be done to ensure that [those in charge of high-rise buildings] undertake their responsibilities in a more suitable and sufficient manner than simply providing a toolkit to guide them."

There has been anger among disabled people's organisations at the 2024 proposals. Adam Gabsi, chair of Inclusion London, and himself a wheelchair user living on the sixth floor of a high-rise building, told *Disability News Service*,

> Instead of introducing real PEEPs, they have proposed fire risk assessments for high-rise blocks and misleadingly rebranded them as 'residential PEEPs'. This is not only a misrepresentation of the original recommendations but also an insult to those who lost their lives at

Grenfell and to all disabled people still waiting for meaningful action.

Grenfell was such a high-profile case that there can be no excuse for those running accommodation not to consider the safety of disabled people in the event of a fire. Or so we thought. In March 2023, Dr Hannah Barham-Brown, a GP who uses a wheelchair, was staying at a Premier Inn in Central London when the fire alarm went off. Hannah had been assured on check-in that someone would come and get her should the fire alarm sound, but when it did, she says there was nobody to be found and no way for her to contact the front desk, as her room didn't have a phone.

Ironically, Hannah was in London to attend a Motability event at the House of Lords, as she is a governor for the accessibility charity. In an exclusive with the *Daily Mirror* she told me, "The door of my room had evacuation instructions but even though it was an accessible room, the instructions were for non-disabled people." After fifteen minutes of the alarm going off, she realised nobody was coming to get her, so she got in her chair and went to the top of a staircase. "I know from previous training, that's the safest place to be."

Luckily, she was found by her Motability colleagues who were also staying at the hotel. They helped her get down the four flights of stairs to the basement exit. They also had to help her back up fifteen steps at the entrance (which she hadn't been told about prior to her stay), where she had to wait while they brought her chair downstairs.

According to Hannah, staff told her that although roles were handed out ahead of the drill, no one had been allocated to collect her. "A member of staff came and said 'We're really sorry, but we divided all the roles between us and there wasn't anyone left to come and get you', to which I said, 'You're telling me you would have left me there'. And they said 'well yes, I suppose so.'"

When asked for a comment, Premier Inn said they had dispatched a member of staff "within minutes" and had found that Hannah (who didn't know, of course, that it was a drill) "had already chosen to leave" her room. The hotel chain insisted that "We have robust fire evacuation procedures and are confident these were followed correctly", but also felt the need to defend itself by saying that the listed status of the building where Hannah was staying "places constraints on the way we can operate." Not much comfort for Hannah, who told me the incident had left her feeling unsafe travelling independently.

By all accounts Hannah was lucky that it wasn't a real emergency like Grenfell Tower. Sadly, the UK's service sector is filled with examples of staff discrimination against disabled people, including being denied entry or service, from eateries to shops—this is despite it being literally written in the Equality Act that we have the right to access all services and that it's illegal to refuse us.

In many cases there's a lack of knowledge, training or education about this, that is, outside of the annual "awareness day" Purple Tuesday, which revolves around "improving the customer experience for disabled people and their families"—encouraging businesses to set this goal not because the law and the principles of democracy demand it, but because of the spending power of the "purple pound" (especially foul-tasting in the mouth when disabled people have even less money than everyone else).

Hannah's ordeal wasn't even the first time this decade that Premier Inn has been hauled over the coals over accessibility. In November 2022, disability rights campaigner Angharad Paget-Jones was staying in a different London Premier Inn with her partner and her guide dog Tudor when she was suddenly woken by staff banging on her door. They burst into her room while she was half dressed, claiming there were reports she had an animal in her room.

When Angharad showed them Tudor's documentation, a yellow booklet which outlined her rights and what Tudor's job was, which was given to her by Guide Dogs UK, she claims the hotel staff told her she didn't look blind and that the guide dog ID could be fake. Despite her asking them to leave and asking to speak with a manager, Angharad told me for an interview in the *Daily Mirror* that staff then used a master key to enter her room without her consent and demanded that she be the one to leave—despite their whole party, Tudor included, having checked in with absolutely no problems.

Angharad told me that she suffered a panic attack as a result of her treatment. "It was terrifying to be outside in a place I didn't know. It really made me realise how vulnerable I am."

As a result of Angharad's story coming to the attention of the press, Premier Inn reviewed their policies and ensured all staff received training. The charity Guide Dogs UK also works with blind and visually-impaired people to highlight how common guide dog refusals are, despite service animals being exempt from any bans as they are doing a job.

* * *

Illegal intolerance of guide dogs is just one part of how hard society makes it for disabled people to move around on their own. We actually often face discrimination when we *don't* have any particular needs, because of staff assumptions—not being served alcohol, being ignored while servers address our non-disabled companions, staff insisting on helping us when we didn't ask, then being offended if we resist or refuse. But sometimes disabled people do require assistance to be out and about, and in no area is this more true than public transport.

The Access for All programme aims to ensure that train stations across the UK are accessible. Founded by the Disabled Person's Transport Committee, it provides state funding for improvement works in the name of equality. However, there's still a long way to go. At the time of writing, 61% of train stations have step-free access, but worryingly only 20% of new builds incorporate step-free access into their plans, fewer than 2% have level boarding and only 73% have a train ramp. Just 53% of all stations have ticket machines that are accessible while just 21% have accessible ticket offices. Just 38% of stations have any kind of toilets at all while only 35% have accessible toilets and, even worse, just 0.2% have a Changing Places toilet.

Due to British railways' lack of accessibility, disabled people can easily be left stranded—whether they're denied assistance outright, or whether the assistance simply doesn't work the way it should—the assistance staff being rude, or simply not turning up, even when it's been booked.

Paralympian Tanni Grey-Thompson regularly documents on her Twitter/X account the many times when she is left stranded on trains. She made headline news in summer 2024 when, ironically on her way to the Paralympics in France, she was forced to crawl off a train at London's Kings Cross station. This wasn't the first time, and Tanni is of course not the only one—a quick scroll of the hashtag #DisabledByTheRailway will show you just how many disabled people struggle to use trains. This is why disabled people were such a big part of the summer 2023 Save Our Ticket Offices campaign against government plans to close over 1,000 railway ticket offices in England.

Without the refuge and assistance that ticket offices provide, many disabled people would struggle to travel by rail for a number of reasons. Ticket machines are inaccessible to many disabled people; the office is where we know without a doubt we can find a member of staff; and some of us prefer to use cash to help us budget, whereas self-service machines are increasingly card-only.

They also don't cover all ticket types: Caroline Stickland, CEO of the campaigning charity Transport for All, told me in the *Daily Mirror* that disabled people weren't able to buy discounted tickets such as the 50% wheelchair discount on machines: "When we factor in the fact that disabled people will face almost £1,000 a month higher costs, we're adding an extra financial burden on disabled people."

The government tried to claim that a tiny amount of tickets were bought in ticket offices, but it was quickly revealed that this figure was actually one in eight or, to show the true scale, around 118 million journeys a year.

In order to pass this into law the Department for Transport first had to hold a public consultation. Not only did the disabled community come together to fight this, but prominent rail unions, the RMT and the Association of British Commuters, rallied with us. As well as in-person events, online rallies were held to get to as many people as possible, with speakers including the RMT boss Mick Lynch, Tanni Grey-Thompson and the Greater Manchester mayor Andy Burnham. August saw a national week of campaigning against the closures, including disabled groups holding protests outside stations threatened with losing their ticket office. The real magic ingredient was the hashtag #SaveTicketOffices, which spread around the country.

Campaigners were able to ensure that a staggering 750,000 people responded to the consultation and the Sunak government was forced to u-turn, scrapping their plans a few months later. Katie Pennick, formerly of Transport for All, remarked on the day that the decision came in, "It is appalling that disabled people's concerns were dismissed for so long. We can't help but wonder what we could achieve if disabled people were listened to and accessibility was prioritised."

The activists and protests of the past and present are the reason disabled people can use public transport at all. But as well as national network issues, most urban transport is also still massively inaccessible. For example, only 60 of the 272 tube stations across London have step-free access. 195 of the stations do not have level boarding access (so you need a ramp to get onto a train), and while 92 stations have some form of step-free access within the station, only 32 of them are accessible all the way from street to platform (but then don't have level boarding!).

That means that even though Transport for London advertises 92 accessible stations, they are not actually fully accessible. The worst performing in the survey is the Bakerloo Line, of which only 6.7% of stations are accessible. Caroline Stickland said, "Currently, only one in three London Underground stations has step-free access. This shuts disabled people out of vast swathes of the network, forcing us to take long and convoluted routes, and even preventing us from travelling entirely."

It is incredibly important to take stock of all these transport statistics. Each one is a barrier to disabled people being able to live their lives fully. How can public narratives focus so heavily on disabled people supposedly cheating the system for benefits when so many physically aren't able to commute or go to appointments safely or comfortably?

It's not just public transport that disabled people struggle to use in order to get around. With towns attempting to appear "greener" and opening up more outside spaces for restaurants and cafés, disabled people who rely on cars to get around, and pavements to walk, are facing barriers once again. Blue Badges were first introduced in 1970 (as Orange badges) by the Chronically Sick and Disabled Act, as discussed in Chapter 3. Since 2010, they have been delivered by local councils.

When the Covid pandemic hit in 2020, many local authorities banned parking in city centres to allow people to social distance, but also so that businesses such as cafés, restaurants and bars could open up and use the outside space. In 2021, the city of York went even further and made the town centre a no-parking zone. When disability rights campaigners expressed concern that this would stop disabled people from getting into the city centre, and asked for Blue Badge holders to be the exception, York council ignored them and brought in a full ban on Blue Badge parking in "pedestrianised areas"— not too dissimilar to what we saw in the late 1980s when disabled people had to take a stand against Chesterfield Council, as we discussed in Chapter 5.

Campaigners including Labour councillor Katie Lomas and the groups York Accessibility Action and York Disability Rights Forum fought to stop this and in 2024 the council pledged to bring back Blue Badge parking in the city centre. It hadn't been an easy road to get to this as two councillors, including Katie, were told they would be excluded from the council debate because, as Blue Badge holders, they would apparently have a prejudicial interest.

Katie wrote about her experience for the York Disability Rights Forum blog, and shared that "I believe my interest, as a disabled person who has a Blue Badge, in the matter of disabled access to the city centre was not more prejudicial than for example someone who cycles participating in a debate on cycling infrastructure." She felt this was discriminatory and should not have been allowed as disability is a protected characteristic.

During the meeting, several councillors and members of the public expressed outrage that Katie wasn't allowed to participate: "compounded the feelings that the Council was just not listening to disabled people about access to the city centre." Following the outcry, the decision to exclude her and her colleague was changed; but this was presented as the councillors being granted "special dispensation". Katie argues that this means they still agreed the councillors had a prejudicial interest and that it felt worse than being silenced as it "retains the direct discrimination." Campaigners allege that York Council refused to engage with them on the issue.

In January 2024, York city centre reopened to Blue Badge holders, however in order to access areas with moveable barriers they must present the badge to staff between 10 a.m. and 5 p.m. And it's a bittersweet outcome given how the council handled things: it is a consistent problem in British society that minorities and women are deemed unable to have a neutral or level-headed position on issues that concern them. Anyone who doesn't go with the status quo is seen as not being able to handle their emotions, as if access needs are a matter of feeling or opinion rather than human rights—something we should all be passionate about.

* * *

The most frustrating thing about disabled people's exclusion from policymaking is that their expertise could have been used to make buildings, infrastructure and rules accessible in a way that would benefit everyone, not just disabled people. But where we're shut out of official halls of power, we can still put forward our own proposals and take action in our communities.

Part of being an activist is having to stay vigilant about new developments in society and law which will inevitably exclude disabled people, and the growing movement to tackle the climate crisis has led to more and more people joining the environmental discussion.

While there is no consensus on solutions, one thing keeps cropping up and it's the exclusion of disabled activist voices from the debate. There can be no climate justice without disability justice, yet so many green initiatives from the individual to the local exclude or even ostracise disabled people, making the existing access issues even worse. This is especially problematic as climate breakdown disproportionately affects disabled people—research from the United Nations Economic and Social Commission for Asia and the Pacific shows that disabled people are up to four times more likely to be injured or die in climate disasters compared to non-disabled people.

In the UK, there's often been an obvious "default non-disabled" perspective driving green policy. While there was such a huge furore about banning single-use plastic straws in 2020, disabled people who needed them to drink and eat safely were ignored and derided, even though the ban has been proved to make very little difference to plastic waste quantities. When Clean Air Zones and Low Emission Zones were introduced in cities across the UK in 2020–3, they came without an exemption for Blue Badge holders, which prohibited disabled people who can't walk far from accessing city centres.

In July 2023, disabled activists took the Department for Environment, Food and Rural Affairs to court over their decision not to include consideration of disabled people in climate disaster plans. Campaigners Doug Paulley and Kevin Jordan joined up with Friends of the Earth to argue that the government's National Adaptation Programme breached both the Climate Change Act and the Human Rights Act and failed to protect property, infrastructure or vulnerable people (not just disabled people, but also young children and the elderly) from climate change. Kevin Jordan was made homeless over Christmas 2023 due to his Norfolk home being destroyed by coastal erosion caused by the rising sea levels and climate crisis-related storms; Doug Paulley's health conditions are exacerbated by severe heat.

The Labour government that came to power in July 2024 continued the case and upheld the policy, which was found lawful in October. (The campaign group is planning to appeal against this ruling.) This is why the work of people like Emma Geen is so important. She is the Climate and Disability Programme associate for Bristol Climate and Nature Partnership, which works directly with local disabled people to create climate actions. She also co-produced the world's first community climate action plan by and for disabled people in 2021. She is an advisor on the Sensing Climate research project and a Personal to the Planetary fellow. In a 2024 article in Bristol 24/7, she explains that "centring the needs of Disabled people in climate issues is essential because we face unique risks and have unique skills and insights to offer."

One of the measures in the plan for Bristol is to make roads accessible by making them smooth and with no obstacles. The plan also states that the Clean Air Zone to have an exemption for Blue Badge owners and that of public transport should be made accessible and affordable, which would reduce road pollution. Additionally, working for all people to have affordable and environmentally friendly energy will have an impact on disabled people whose usage needs are higher than average—according to Scope, just over two fifths of disabled people (43%).

Too often in British society, everyone else gets to live their lives while disabled people are expected to put up with having our rights stripped away and our access denied. But disabled climate action shows how much richer public life could be for everyone, if we had an equal place at the table.

12

DOES THE MINISTER REALLY THINK THIS IS SUPPORTING PEOPLE?

WORK AND EDUCATION

Disabled people should be valued for more than their ability to have a job and make money, but many disabled people have no choice but to work—and many disabled people want to be able to work more than anything, but can't. Like everything else in the UK, the worlds of work and study weren't made for us.

Firstly, there are the obvious barriers that stop disabled people from literally getting into these establishments—many old buildings especially that are used for offices or schools are just not accessible. If the Disability Discrimination Act hadn't been watered down by the Equality Act, disabled people could have required organisations to take more steps towards accessibility. But as things are, small businesses can claim financial reasons why they can't afford to change their set-up.

Then there are the cultural attitudes discriminating against disabled people in education and in work, on an individual and an institutional level. A government study published in 2014 showed that in 2008, 19% of disabled people experienced unfair treatment at work compared to 13% of non-disabled people. Many young disabled people sadly have experiences of prejudice and inflexibility too: educators treating them like they don't want to learn or refusing to give them extensions, the awful experience of your first bully being a teacher who was supposed to protect you.

The overwhelming barriers in the education system and in the world of work have predictable results for the life chances of disabled people. Each year the TUC hold Disability Pay Gap Day to highlight just how much less disabled people make than their non-disabled colleagues in the same roles.

The pay gap is so bad that from 7 November each year disabled people essentially work for free until the end of the year. In 2024 disabled people earned on average £4,300 less than non-disabled people. The TUC's annual Disability Pay Gap Day report revealed that non-disabled people earn 17.2% more than disabled employees, which adds up to around £2.35 more an hour. This is an average of £82.25 per week for 35-hour workers. The gap has widened by £700 since just 2022.

If you're a disabled woman it's even worse, naturally. The TUC found we earn on average £4.05 an hour less than non-disabled men, which is £141.75 less a week and over £7,300 less a year than a non-disabled man in the same job—let's all pretend to be shocked there.

The TUC also highlighted how much more disabled people were struggling to afford food. A food shop for an average household is approximately £63.50, about three quarters the size of the disability pay gap. The Joseph Rowntree Foundation found in 2023 that 57% of households with a disabled person had experienced food insecurity and seven in ten went without essentials.

There's also a progression gap, which itself partly explains the pay gap: data from the DWP's Employment of Disabled People report in 2024 showed that working disabled people were less likely to work as managers, directors and senior officials or in professional occupations than working non-disabled people.

Inequality of opportunity at work is also affected by unequal educational outcomes, of course. According to the Office for National Statistics, just 24.9% of disabled people aged 21 to 64 have a university degree, compared to 42.7% of non-disabled people.

On top of this, disabled people are almost three times more likely than non-disabled people to have no qualifications at all. 13.3% of disabled people had no qualifications, compared with 4.6% of non-disabled people. Disabled people report that universities routinely refuse to give them specialist equipment and provide extensions and just 40% of eligible students are accessing their disabled students allowance which funds specialist equipment.

It's even worse for primary age children. In 2017, the Department for Education found that only 14% of SEND children at Key Stage 2 had reached their expected level for reading, writing and maths. This contrasts with 62% of non-disabled children.

* * *

It all starts at school. With neurodivergence diagnoses exploding in the UK since the pandemic (see Chapter 10), there's a growing awareness that the inflexible culture of the education system puts many children at a disadvantage. Pupils with neurodivergent or learning disabilities are often seen as naughty, lazy or disruptive so, instead of support, they are punished. While disabled students make up only 15% of the school population they account for nearly half of all school exclusions. A 2022 Disability Policy Centre report, 'The State of the Nation in SEND Education: England', found that in some local authorities nearly 100% of all pupils sent to Pupil Referral Units were disabled.

But the problem that needs fixing—and that can be fixed—isn't student behaviour. It's funding and training. There are currently 1.5 million disabled school age children in the UK who require support in order to be able to stay in school. Unfortunately, as the *Guardian* reported in 2022, local governments are struggling with a £2.4 billion "funding black hole" for Special Educational Needs and Disabilities (SEND—a very long-winded way to say disabled but nevertheless...). Once again, lack of funding and understanding means disabled children suffer, and their equal right to an education can't be provided for.

In order to gain any support in school, children need to get an Education, Health and Care Plan (EHCP), but this can involve a lengthy cycle of disappointment and fights with local authorities before accessing any support. Parents resource centre Special Needs Jungle reported in December 2021 that, since the introduction of ECHPs in 2014, councils had spent over £253 million fighting parents at SEND tribunals. Yet research in 2020 found that 95% of all appeals ruled in the parents' favour. This means that nearly every single tribunal ultimately found that local authorities had acted unlawfully by refusing to support disabled children.

This wasn't an extreme experience for SEND families, either. The Disability Policy Centre's 2022 report stated that 65% of parents, carers and guardians "had to fight" for their child's Education, Health and Care Plan. Meanwhile 46% of disabled people had their disability undiagnosed throughout school.

In the absence of necessary educational and clinical support for SEND students to stay in mainstream schooling, Pupil Referral Units are just one place that they can end up. While disabled people aren't technically put in asylums anymore, young autistic people are spending time in Child and Adolescent Mental Health Service (CAMHS) units, either because their meltdowns are misdiagnosed as mental health problems, or because there isn't a better or safer place for them to be given the state of funding.

The National Autistic Society estimated in October 2024 that over 2,020 autistic people and people with learning disabilities were in inpatient mental health hospitals in England, including 200 minors in inpatient units (98% of these kids being autistic). Many of these people are held there when they don't need to be, and in many cases the settings are inappropriate. An average stay on one of these wards is 4.8 years.

In an article for *The Canary*, the writer and activist Charli Clement said, "Many reach crisis point because they have been consistently failed and unsupported, and [it] feels like there are no moves being made to change these inequalities in the home, in schools, or in communities."

Neurodivergent students especially are up against the very recent nature of public awareness, and the ignorance this has created among those running classrooms and campuses. But even disabled communities with a longer-standing activist presence, and more widely accepted impairments, are still fighting for their right to education. Since the 2010s there has been a campaign to make British Sign Language a recognised language, and therefore one taught in schools.

SUPPORTING PEOPLE?

The British Deaf Association estimates about 151,000 people use BSL in the UK, with 87,000 of those being deaf. In 2018, twelve-year-old Daniel Jillings, who is deaf, started calling for BSL to become a GCSE subject as he felt that it was unfair for him and other deaf pupils not to be able to do an exam in their own first language. While there are many foreign language GCSEs available, deaf BSL users cannot achieve a GCSE in any of them because of the speaking and listening parts of the exam, so not only are deaf people refused the right to learn and gain a qualification in their own language, but they're shut out of learning additional languages too.

Daniel also felt that the BSL GCSE would give hearing children the opportunity to learn BSL in school so they can communicate with deaf people both in school and adult life. In the longer term, this could encourage many more people to pursue a career in BSL interpreting, which will further benefit the deaf community. In December 2023 the Department for Education confirmed that, as a result of Daniel's campaigning, BSL would be taught as a GCSE from September 2025.

The British Deaf Association (the contemporary version of the BDDA created in 1890, see Chapter 1) asserts that "Deaf children in the United Kingdom have a human right to linguistic and cultural enrichment through the acquisition of BSL (and Irish Sign Language in Northern Ireland). BSL is a rich and dynamic language that is an integral part of our cultural identity." It's important to foster a positive linguistic and cultural environment from a young age for all children—evidence shows that children with inadequate access to any form of language experience "language deprivation" which has lifelong consequences on a deaf child's language, emotional and cognitive development and wellbeing.

The British Deaf Association points out that "parents are told to 'choose' between speech and signing, a binary choice that removes richness, inclusivity and diversity from our lives." It maintains that "Immediate support with learning BSL is a proven clear marker of later success in life academically, personally and socially, and supports improved mental health and reduces risk of self-harm. Yet our families have to pay [outside of state education] to learn their child's natural language, our natural language."

There is also currently no national programme of early years BSL provision for young deaf children in the UK. While some progress has been made, very few of these laws have had involvement from deaf charities, meaning provisions often don't match the needs of deaf people.

A similar issue is being raised by blind and visually-impaired charities. The Royal National Institute for Blind People (RNIB) state that too many blind and partially sighted people are still being deprived of a proper education, unable to secure employment and denied their democratic right to vote independently.

SUPPORTING PEOPLE?

Around two million people live with sight loss in the UK today. RNIB highlights that from difficulty accessing treatment and services to a lack of emotional and practical support, blind and partially sighted people each face their own set of challenges every day. Only one in four blind, or partially sighted, people of working age have a job and their feelings of loneliness are high.

Educational attainment is also unacceptably worse for blind and partially sighted people. In October 2023, RNIB publicised the Department for Education's annual report on this, which showed that vision-impaired pupils' lower school results are consistent from "Early Years Foundation Stage" all the way "through to GCSEs."

When we aren't even given an equal chance to learn, how are we supposed to thrive in the world after education?

* * *

When Covid happened, many disabled people expressed anger at how quickly the world was suddenly able to make working and studying from home possible. I'll never forget the heartache I felt when a disabled friend told me their university, which had pushed them so hard to study in-person at the expense of their health and hadn't let them study from home, had instantly implemented home-schooling when lockdown hit in March 2020. They'd been forced to drop out in February.

When being able to work from home suddenly became the norm and therefore acceptable, disabled people finally felt like they were on an almost level playing field. If anything, they were thriving, as many of us were able to give tips to our non-disabled colleagues unused to working from home and feeling isolated. We finally felt like we were all living in the same situation.

Speaking from personal experience, between summer 2020 and summer 2022 my career flourished. Working as a journalist meant that it was expected of me that I work in an office, but this wasn't an accessible setting. A bright newsroom, full of people on uncomfortable chairs working long shifts would never have worked for me—not to mention the fact that I live in the North East of England and so many media jobs require you to work and live in London. The lockdown period meant it became okay to hold meetings and run a whole series for a national newspaper from my sofa and even speak at a national conference—the Student Publication Association National Conference (yes they know what it spells)—from my bed.

However, the end of restrictions meant gradually forcing people back into offices. Unless you could do hybrid working you weren't getting jobs you could've been offered months before. And employers' panic about worker disengagement and the loss of office culture (or really of presenteeist culture) meant that even disabled people who'd had more flexibility before suddenly had to fight to do a job at work that they could do perfectly well from home, because of a one-size-fits-all approach.

So much pressure was put on employees to compromise their health if they were immunocompromised but not on the official list of vulnerable people. One of my friends even had to go through months of bullying and scrutiny from the CEO and the entire board of their company, ridiculed on the office internal server, because they were the only one still keen to shield and the office was lax in enforcing social distancing. They ended up quitting to work for themselves.

The government has been no help, gaslighting disabled people about how much of a barrier they faced from this office culture now back with a vengeance. Laura Trott, a DWP minister and then Treasury minister under Rishi Sunak, said it was disabled people's "duty" to work from home, while Trott's boss Mel Stride told the Commons "The Work Capability Assessment doesn't reflect how someone with a disability or health condition might be able to work from home, yet we know many disabled people do just that."

Both Sunak and Starmer have echoed this idea. But it's untrue for several reasons. Firstly, there are so few jobs that are actually work from home full-time and open to disabled people who need this setup. In October 2023, I covered for the *Mirror* the story of Claire, a member of one of my own local disability rights organisations, Difference North East. The same morning the government was running its consultation in her area on the proposed changes to the Work Capability Assessment,

Claire did a job search for work-from-home jobs on the DWP website.

She found 6,188 "home working" jobs nationwide, but when she filtered this by disability-confident employers it went down almost sixfold to 1,531. She then set the location to the North East, anticipating that many of the jobs would actually be hybrid, requiring days in an office—it went down to 78 jobs. Claire then selected part-time, as that's all she can do, and was left with just 14 jobs. Nine of them were personal assistant roles—working in someone's home—and the rest were working in care homes.

It's laughable that governments have been pushing "home working" on disabled people yet can't even accurately define it as a job allowing you to work in your own home. This meant there were zero suitable jobs for Claire and other disabled people in the North East who required part-time home-working.

There's also the fact that many aren't able to work even from home. As we saw in Chapter 9, many disabled and lower-income people don't have access to a computer or the internet. There's also the elephant in the room that many disabled people aren't qualified to work in sectors where working from home is an option. As we saw at the start of the chapter, disabled people tend to have a lower level of education and less job experience so end up in what is considered "low-skilled" work, whereas remote working is mostly limited to sectors where jobs require higher education, seniority, or digital literacy.

Of course this comes at a time when the DWP is trying to once again move the goal posts of disability benefits and kick over 400,000 disabled people off Universal Credit and force them into work with little support, with the changes to the Work Capability Assessment proposed by Sunak's government and upheld by Starmer's (see Chapter 9).

Then there are the barriers facing disabled people who are actually able to work outside of their home—or should be able to. One employer that has faced criticism is the very government department whose mission is supposedly to Get Britain Working. In 2020, the BBC's *Panorama* programme discovered that the department of work and pensions had lost more tribunal cases for disability discrimination than any other employer in the UK. I certainly receive a lot of complaints about it from disabled people hoping that I'll cover their allegations.

To give just one example, I was contacted by someone who claimed she had been offered a job, but then given sick leave immediately, as the building she was supposed to work in—a job centre, by the way—didn't have a hoist in the bathroom to enable disabled people who need it to transfer safely onto the toilet.

The problem isn't unique to the DWP, obviously. In the 2023 Civil Service People Survey, civil servants were asked if they'd been discriminated against. Just 5.9% of non-disabled civil servants said yes, against 17.9% of civil servants with a long-term limiting condition (or y'know, disability). 16.02% of disabled civil servants said they had been bullied or harassed compared with just 6.4% of non-disabled workers. 40.3% of disabled employees who'd been discriminated against said it was because of their disability.

If we zoom into the Department for Work and Pensions, however, it gets bleaker. There are 15,669 civil servants who declared they have a long-term limiting condition working across the DWP and 18.9% of them said they had been discriminated against, compared with 5.5% of non-disabled staff. 16.3% said they'd been bullied or harassed, compared to 5.887% of non-disabled people. The survey found that disabled civil servants working at the DWP had higher stress levels and were less likely to be flourishing in their jobs.

Taken together, all these stats really tell you everything you need to know about the institution deciding which (or whether) disabled people "deserve" state support, don't they?

* * *

So, participating in the world of work, at least as it's currently organised, is much harder for disabled people. Aren't there supposed to be solutions in place for this, helping disabled people who want and are able to work to do so? Well, yes and no.

The main offer from government is the Access to Work fund—there, according to the DWP, to "help you get or stay in work if you have a physical or mental health condition or disability", by making adjustments more affordable. In theory, grants are available to cover things like specialist equipment or assistive technology, support workers, BSL interpreters or a job coach (such as an ADHD coach), commuting costs, adapting your vehicle to get you to work, and any physical changes that your boss may need to make to your workplace such as chairs or desks. However, as with most things involving the DWP, there's a backlog.

One politician who has always fought for disabled people's rights, including in opposition as shadow minister for disabled people, is Vicky Foxcroft. The Labour whip revealed whilst campaigning for the 2024 election that she's disabled herself. During an Access to Work debate in May that year, Vicky provided one of my favourite moments of the dying Sunak era, which really highlighted just how badly the situation was being managed. Vicky asked Mims Davies, Minister for Disabled People, Health and Work, about the backlog, and quoted some damning stats:

> On 1 April, 32,445 [people were awaiting an Access to Work decision]. Every month, the figure keeps increasing, so since the beginning of 2024 the Access to Work backlog has risen by more than 7,500. Does the Minister really think this is supporting more disabled people back into work?

Mims' response was actually flabbergasting: "If we are trading figures, at the close of business on 7 May 2024, there were 36,721 applications awaiting decision."

That's right, she freely admitted that the backlog had increased by a further 4,276 people in the space of five weeks. As I said at the time in my *Canary* column, the shadow minister had gone, "Access to Work is a bit shit" and the minister had replied, "Actually you're wrong, it's even shitter than you thought."

Since this very weird exchange, the situation has grown even worse. At the time of writing, the backlog is over two years. There's also been a battle just to get the DWP to admit how many applicants that two-year wait represents. In October 2024, the new Labour Minister for Work, Alison McGovern, finally admitted that 55,000 disabled people were waiting to access support.

One massive problem with Access to Work is that you can't apply for it until you have a job offer. Anecdotally, campaigner Ellen Jones has remarked on LinkedIn that the backlog is now so bad, it's essentially quicker to get support if you quit your job and get a new one—because the DWP are focusing more on new claims than existing ones, hoping to stop the uncontrollable rise of total cases pending. So, those already in work risk losing their jobs due to lack of Access to Work funds. You couldn't make it up if you tried.

Jess Thom, campaigner, comedian and founder of the comedy and creativity platform Touretteshero, tells me that Access to Work was a "vital equalising scheme", including for her: Jess requires 24-hour care whilst also working a 40-hour week. For this, Access to Work provides 45 hours of support work (her working hours, plus a half-hour commute at the start and end of each day); it will also cover a PA when she tours and their accommodation as well as specialist equipment and accessible transport. As Jess points out, "it means essentially that it doesn't cost more to employ me as a disabled person." But she also says the fund is being mismanaged due to staff cuts and cost-cutting schemes. The most disastrous was the 2015 Cameron government's introduction of a cap on how much disabled people are entitled to receive.

> It used to be that there wasn't a limit ... it was based on actual needs instead of a fairly arbitrary amount. The cap is one and half times the average national salary, which isn't a lot considering that it often has to cover things like the salary of several support workers. This particularly affected disabled people who had higher support needs or specialist support such as needing British Sign Language interpreters who can cover very specific things.

Jess points out that the cap has affected her personally. Her company Touretteshero employs a number of disabled people who use Access to Work to varying degrees—but she is the only one in her company that has their funding capped.

> The idea was, when they introduced the cap, that they said it would give people more control, like with a personal budget, but because it's almost an acknowledge-

ment that they're not going to meet all of your support that means that you have to be able to prioritise [how you use] it.

For her, this meant putting more of her own money into a support worker, meaning she can travel less. Not ideal for a comedian.

These caps are also reviewed every year, but according to Jess, this conflicts with the DWP's cost cutting, which requires applicants to make claims annually. "Every year we have to start fresh with a different person ... explaining my support, which is quite complex," Jess said. However, with the current backlog it's getting harder and harder for people like Jess to have their cases reviewed in time without losing their support. As it currently takes six months to process existing claims, people like Jess who have their claim capped at a year are having to apply right after their current claim has been accepted.

There's also no system these days to help reallocate money that has already been approved. For instance, when Jess's wheelchair broke she was told she'd have to start a new application as opposed to just using the money she'd already been granted for something else that was now lower priority.

On top of this, many disabled people also have to try and get their support backdated or reimbursed, which forces them to front costs they shouldn't have to pay, and puts a huge administrative burden on them. All in all, the Access to Work system is not functioning: if the state is so intent on pushing tens of thousands more disabled people into the jobs market, they must do more to ensure that we actually *can* access work.

While we wait for Access to Work to be fixed so that it's fit for purpose, where does that leave us? According to the latest ONS release in 2021, there were more disabled people who were self-employed (13.8%) than non-disabled people (12.5%). This is consistent with 2020. Given the choice between facing lower pay and fewer job opportunities at best, discrimination at worst, or else having to move outside the structures imposed by employers, it is unsurprising that many disabled people would choose to work for themselves entirely.

Despite the obvious dangers of not being able to control their working conditions, disabled people are also more likely to be on zero-hour contracts than non-disabled people. The Trades Union Congress found in November 2024 that 4% of disabled people are working this way, compared with 2.9% of non-disabled people. Black and minority ethnic disabled women are three times more likely than non-disabled white men to get stuck in them, due to all the barriers they face in getting and staying in secure long-term employment.

This means disabled people are more likely to get trapped in a cycle of poverty as they can't plan for the future; more likely to have to work any hours they can despite the effect it will have on their conditions; and less likely to challenge unacceptable behaviour by bosses as they have the constant threat of not getting shifts that they need to feed themselves. Labour campaigned on a commitment to ending zero-hour contracts, but we will have to wait and see on that one. The Employment Rights Bill was only introduced in October 2024, and still has to make its way through Parliament.

It is obvious that making work and education accessible for all is a major fight disabled activists have been having for over a century. The barriers to equitable life chances have never been tackled fully in consultation with disabled people and charities and it is long overdue. You can't be annoyed at someone for not being involved in the running of a household if they can't even set foot inside the house.

13

ASSIST US TO LIVE

BIRTH, DEATH, GENETICS AND ASSISTED DYING

Disabled lives in the UK are either worth less, or worthless; businesses, the medical world and governments kill us, and embrace policies based on a social consensus that it would be better, even for us, if we didn't exist. This is something many non-disabled people will truly never understand no matter how sympathetic to the cause they are; because they've never attempted to buy milk while hungover, only to be stopped and told "I'd kill myself if that happened to me" and you know they don't mean the hangover.

While government policies have long made life for disabled people unliveable, it's actually society as a whole—including people who don't think we're fraudsters or scroungers, and who would consider themselves compassionate towards us—that sees "disabled" as the worst thing a person can be. This prejudice results in British institutions, from the legal system to medical and scientific communities, seeing it as legitimate to find ways for us not to exist—from sterilising disabled people in care into the twentieth century, to the use of Do Not Resuscitate orders during the Covid pandemic, to the assumptions often underlying public arguments around questions like genetic screening or assisted dying. For disabled people, these debates aren't just 'ethical'; they're existential.

Eugenics is the idea that undesirable traits can and should be bred out of the human race. At the beginning of the eugenics movement—in the late nineteenth century, the same moment when the disability rights movement first emerged—getting rid of these elements was considered not just a kindness towards disabled people, but important for the moral and economic health of the nation.

While disabled people are often still viewed as burdens on families and state finances, we've generally moved away from an idea that disability represents moral weakness that risks infecting society if we don't stamp it out. But what British society *hasn't* shaken off is the flipside of the eugenicist moral universe: the assumption that quality of life is so low for disabled people, especially learning disabled people, that they must also consider their traits undesirable. Surely they wouldn't wish their suffering and their struggles on anyone?

At its worst, eugenics was used as an excuse to round up and murder millions of disabled adults, children and babies during the Nazi Holocaust, on the grounds that incurable illness was 'life unworthy of life'. The regime gassed or gave lethal injections to people with mental health diagnoses, people with dementia, people severely injured in bombings, people with chronic and congenital conditions, people with impaired hearing or vision, older people living in nursing homes.

But that's just the most extreme outcome of the eugenicist worldview. Eugenics is also wanting to find a "cure" for conditions such as autism and Down's syndrome, instead of wanting to reorganise society so that it includes everyone across a spectrum of difference. Eugenics gets away with pursuing cures as a good cause by casually ignoring the fact that there are people with those conditions who live full and happy lives. Eugenics promotes the non-existence of a disabled child as the solution to parents' understandable anxieties about being able to care for that child, rather than the solution being a state that supports parent carers.

A given person's answer to these questions isn't some kind of sealed off, individualised "ethics"; it's politics. We need to confront the fact that our society is currently set up as if we'd rather fund the Prime Minister's travel by private jet than give disabled children and their families a good quality of life.

Quite often, disabled campaigners raise concerns around eugenicist ideas when faced with research billed not as seeking a cure, but seeking vaguely to find out more about certain conditions. In August 2021, the University of Cambridge announced an ambitious project called Spectrum 10K that aimed to be the largest study of autism in the UK. It included 10,000 autistic people and their families and was supported by many famous parents of autistic children. Researchers planned to assess autistic people's lifestyles and wellbeing via a survey that would look both at factors that contributed to autism and the likelihood and range of co-occurring conditions. Most of this was not of much concern to disabled people. But the study's interest in "factors contributing to autism" included harvesting and storing disabled people's DNA.

Spectrum 10K explicitly stated that *they* would not look to prevent or eradicate autism, however the data samples would be stored in an academic database and made available to other researchers. There was a fear of what would happen if the study showed that genetic factors did play a big part in the condition.

Another concern was about the ideas underpinning the study. It was led by Dr Simon Baron-Cohen, Director of the Autism Research Centre at the University of Cambridge. Baron-Cohen has come under fire from autistic communities due to his work which influenced testing autism in children for decades. The Empathy Quotient has been debated among psychologists because of its reliance on a theory of sex difference, associating how autism presents with the idea of a "male brain". As such, it has been linked to the lower rate of diagnosis in autistic women and girls.

I was one of the first disabled UK journalists to cover the study and (to my knowledge) the only disabled journalist to interview Simon Baron-Cohen about it, during my time at *Verywell Health*. When I asked him whether the study would drop the DNA collection if feedback supported this, his response was simply: "Is the autism community saying no genetic research should *ever* happen?"

The American arm of Spectrum 10K was headed up by Daniel Geschwind, a Professor of Human Genetics, Neurology, and Psychiatry at UCLA who guided the development of the Autism Genetic Resource Exchange—a programme funded by the not-at-all threateningly named Cure Autism Now. It merged with Autism Speaks in 2007, another divisive organisation for the neurodivergent community, which likewise had "cure" in its mission statement for a decade and had a history of emphasising the suffering and agency of caregivers over autistic people.

"Family can be much stronger than autism ever anticipated, and we will not be intimidated by you," says one video by the non-profit still available on YouTube as of January 2025; the campaign ad champions "this community of parents and grandparents", rather than of people with autism, and—weirdly addressing parents as the voice of autism itself—warns "If you are happily married, I will make sure that your marriage fails." Autism is somehow both an evil supervillain ("I know ... no morality") and a disease (comparable with, and actually worse than, "paediatric AIDs, cancer and diabetes"). The organisation may well have moved on from this mentality, but you can see why activists felt worried enough to demand closer scrutiny of the study.

The campaign Boycott Spectrum 10K organised a joint statement signed by many autistic activists that expressed "grave concerns" for autistic people's capacity to consent to this level of DNA storing and the lack of safeguards in the future. They demanded "we insist on the full publication of the full application as it was approved for funding, in order for full transparency of this study to be reached. We also insist on the re-evaluation of the study by the ethics awarding body."

The study was subsequently paused whilst Spectrum 10K assessed where to go next, as campaigners protested for hours outside the Cambridge Autism Research Centre. After the Centre's gates were locked, they were forced to protest on a main road, and use the accessible facilities at a nearby golf club.

Priscilla Eyles told fellow protestors, "They've locked the gate, they don't even want to speak to us and yet they claim they're friends to autistic people. How?" The campaign did lead to action—three independent consultations were carried out with the autistic community into the study—however the third and final report was never published.

The fate of the study was left unclear, with the website going down in July 2024 due to "technical issues affecting the University of Cambridge's School of Clinical Medicine." Then finally on 30 January 2025 the Spectrum 10K research team issued a statement announcing the official closure of the programme.

Yet again an example of a project "meant for disabled people" and "done with respect" but which immediately shut down as soon as disabled people spoke up about the way it had been handled. The whole thing reminded me of Block Telethon.

* * *

Another eugenics issue to draw campaigners' attention in the twenty-first century has been interventions to stop disabled babies from being born. In the UK, abortion is only legal up until the twenty-fourth week of pregnancy, that is unless, per the Abortion Act 1967, "there is a substantial risk that if the child were born, it would suffer from such physical or mental abnormalities as to be seriously handicapped." This means that it's completely legal to terminate disabled foetuses right up until full term.

In 2019, over 3,000 abortions were carried out because the baby was likely to have a severe disability, with 275 of those taking place after the 24-week general limit on abortion. Heidi Crowter is an activist with Down's syndrome who took the Department of Health and Social Care to the high court over the Abortion Act 1967 in 2021 and lost. She was granted an appeal, but lost this too in November 2022. When she brought her case, she'd said: "The judges might not think it discriminates against me, the government might not think it discriminates against me, but I'm telling you that I do feel discriminated against and the verdict doesn't change how I and thousands in the Down's syndrome community feel."

However as with most things surrounding a pregnant person's body, this isn't a black and white subject. Many make the argument that all pregnant people should have the right to choose. This is a question that disability rights activists struggle with, as many of us are women, assigned female at birth, and/or pro-choice. Ruth Madeley who hosted the 2022 Channel 4 documentary *Disability & Abortion: The Hardest Choice*, told me in an interview with *Stylist* magazine, "I constantly felt like I was being pulled in two different directions; it was tough to make these two parts of myself try to coexist in such a difficult conversation."

Ruth was at the high court the day Heidi's ruling came and she spoke to a parent who highlighted the real issue fuelling this conundrum: the lack of support for disabled families. The woman told Ruth,

> A week before my daughter was born, the message was 'your daughter is so disabled that you could legally terminate her now and it'd be [morally] fine'. But a week

after she's born, your daughter is not disabled enough to get the benefits and the things that she needs to live well and independently.

When the funds and infrastructure to assist parents to look after disabled children isn't there, it's understandable why so many do terminate.

My own feelings about this mean that I can't support the Crowter case. While aborting babies because they're disabled amounts to eugenics, nobody should be forced to give birth to a baby they don't want. In my opinion, if those putting their energy into the campaign had truly cared about the wellbeing of disabled children, they would've been advocating for better education, housing, care and benefits, so that disability wasn't seen as a catastrophe and parents felt they could actually raise a disabled child if they wanted to.

But this is where it gets murky. Whilst Heidi and other disabled people fighting to have the UK's abortion law recognised as discriminatory have been doing it for the right reasons, many involved in the campaign haven't. As I revealed in *The i Paper* in November 2024, the case was hijacked by the Christian far right who want to ban all abortion.

As Heidi herself is a proud Christian, her case gained coverage and support from organisations including the Christian Institute. Her legal team was led by a barrister known for supporting the Institute on their stance on conversion therapy being used on LGBTQ+ people.

Against this background, the Crowter case didn't end up being a nuanced discussion about disability rights. When the Institute highlighted the lawsuit on their site, they focused very little on the specific disability aspect, featuring a video of Heidi alongside an alleged 24-week ultrasound scan (of a non-disabled foetus). The Institute website as a whole is obviously not only concerned with abortion that discriminates against disability: it quotes not only the total number of abortions in Great Britain since the Abortion Act was passed (not the total involving "handicaps"), but also the Sixth Commandment in the Bible—the one about murder.

At the end of the day, the fight here should've been with the fact that the law hadn't been updated in fifty-five years and, as such, the language was terribly outdated. The fight should be with how disabled lives are seen in society, and how "foetal abnormality" is associated with loss of freedom for parents.

The Crowter case struck a nerve with Ruth, whose own mother was told in 1987 she could terminate if she wanted—if that had happened the world would be poorer without the incredible wit and talent of Ruth Madeley. "There needs to be so much more put into our world to accommodate and welcome disabled people as equals so people feel they can raise disabled children in it."

* * *

While debates continue to rage about disabled children coming into the world, the UK has also seen a huge campaign and public conversation around the "right to die". In 2024, MP Kim Leadbeater brought a Private Members' Bill that would legalise assisted dying for the terminally ill, allowing anyone with less than six months to live to end their life by prescribed injection.

Many welcomed the bill, and of course nobody wishes terminally ill people to suffer in pain. But many, if not most, disabled people were opposed to the legislation, warning that it could become a slippery slope to disabled people being forced by coercion or circumstance into ending their own lives, and that it would enshrine in law a cultural assumption that disabled lives aren't worth living.

To summarise the criticism: killing us is cheaper and easier than reforming social care, paying benefits people can live off and funding the NHS properly—we can't protest about the social model if we're dead.

One of the most passionate and high profile activists on the topic is Liz Carr. Her 2024 documentary *Better Off Dead?* highlighted how complex the issue is and why disabled people want it taken seriously:

> I oppose assisted suicide along with many other disability rights groups and activists because I believe it is ultimately a socially approved medical solution to the perceived problems of "disability". Those who say they're pro assisted suicide talk about how if they ever

get to the point where they are incontinent or someone else has to wipe their arse or they have to use a wheelchair, they would want to die—that it's about choice, autonomy and dignity. Many of those realities belong to us, to disabled people's lives—and we know that with the right support systems, being able to do or not do certain things does not [determine] dignity or autonomy. People often say they want assisted suicide for reasons that are really all about the disability experience.

Wherever you stand on the assisted dying legislation, it's obvious that disabled people are at the heart of the whole argument. Liz told me about the time she appeared on *Newsnight* with Debbie Purdy, who was a disabled journalist: "We were discussing how a young man had become disabled in a rugby accident, paralysed and wanted to die. Two disabled women discussing a disabled man's assisted suicide but still the pro-reform side is far too quick to insist that the morality here has nothing to do with disability."

Whilst some of the main faces of the campaign have been disabled, on the whole it's been non-disabled people speaking for us. Others say they are suffering and choose to die—to live as they are is unacceptable. The public, the MPs, the courts and the medical profession are all dominated by non-disabled people, who tend to see "health" as the default, natural state of human existence, and find it reasonable to see incurable ill health as a situation to be escaped. Liz Carr tells me,

The persistent negativity of "disability" and of disabled people, the idea that our lives are tragic, painful, full of suffering is so pervasive that even those of us who define as a disabled person can believe this about ourselves. We believe the negativity and we experience the lack of opportunities and support as an individual problem when in fact it is because of the socially created institutional, environmental and attitudinal barriers imposed upon us. But believing our lives are tragic could lead us to want to die and to access medical assisted suicide. It would take little "convincing" that your medical condition was the reason you wanted to die, the press and public would understand that, in fact everyone would understand your so-called choice as rational and understandable.

But if it's rational and understandable, that's not because of an impairment or illness; it's because of the state of our welfare and healthcare systems. As Liz says,

> That is when we start to use the law as the solution to the social problems that cause us suffering: the lack of social care, the absence of pain management, lack of accessible housing, poverty, benefit bureaucracy etc. That is what is happening in Canada where the most recent 2023 figures show that the disabled people who have used that law to die have increasingly listed loneliness and feeling like a burden as their reasons.

Medical Assistance in Dying (MAiD) is legal in Canada, and there have been reports of it being offered by care providers and medical practitioners as a substitute for, you know, medical attention and care. In both Canada and the Netherlands, where MAiD is legal without restrictions, assisted dying accounts for 5% of all deaths. Using these figures, *The Canary* estimated that around 30,000 people could be legally euthanised a year in the UK under the Leadbeater legislation, despite it saying that it would only apply to 1,000 a year.

Although the bill states that assisted dying would only be offered to those with six months to live, there's cause for concern that this will be quickly changed and expanded. All assisted dying requests have to go through legal courts. For one thing, with the backlog in the UK justice system, the state could be forced to expand the timeframe just to allow the rights already legalised to be exercised in practice. For another, changes to the law and its application in the UK often come not through fresh legislation passed by Parliament, but through common law: individual rulings in court about how existing legislation should be interpreted, which then set a precedent with legal power for future cases.

We've seen throughout this book how frequently activists bring test cases to try to shift policy in a whole range of areas—this is likely to happen to test the limits of the assisted dying law too, and then it won't matter how meticulous MPs were in scrutinising, wording or safeguarding the original act. How it operates will be down to legal judgements.

We already know that some powerful voices want to see the legislation expanded. A number of MPs, prior to the bill text being published, called for it to cover all disabilities and conditions. Whether it's about cost-cutting or well-intentioned "compassion", this terrifying outlook is the reason why Paula Peters said in the UNCRDP UK Monitoring Coalition's press release on the subject, "After 15 years of austerity where poverty and homelessness are rising, there's deep concern about disabled people being coerced and pressurised into ending their own lives prematurely. That we will be a burden on the state and too expensive to keep."

For all of the above reasons, many disabled activists are against legally sanctioned assisted dying full stop. In the 2010s, long-time campaigner Baroness Jane Campbell founded Not Dead Yet UK, a network of disabled people inspired by the American organisation of the same name founded in the mid-1990s. The organisation has opposed Parliament's attempts to make laws on assisted dying as they think it would lead to the legal of euthanisation of disabled people.

In 2014 and '15, the group successful lobbied against several bills to legalise assisted dying. The first was introduced and passed in the Lords then went through to the House of Commons where it was debated by MPs. It was eventually thrown out at committee stage. An almost identical bill was proposed in the Commons, and this time in the debate stage the house voted against it

330 to 118. The prevailing slogan throughout these campaigns was "assist us to live, not to die".

Not Dead Yet UK's activism has also included battles in court and participating in the international campaign Me Before Euthanasia, which protested the 2016 film adaptation of Jojo Moyes' book *Me Before You*, released to much backlash. The film and book paint a romanticised version of assisted dying from the point of view of a non-disabled woman who falls in love with a tetraplegic man when she's hired to be his carer. At the UK premiere of the film, Not Dead Yet activists caused a stir by unfurling a banner on the red carpet which read "Me Before You is little more than a disability snuff movie, giving audiences the message that if you're disabled, you're better off dead."

The campaign against the 2024 bill, backed by all 350 Deaf and Disabled People's Organisations (DDPOs) in the UK, wasn't just about the overarching principles at stake. The movement against it—a coalition including Disabled People Against Cuts, Disability Wales, Disability Rights UK, Black Triangle and many other organisations, and individual activists from Liz Carr to Ellen Clifford—had specific arguments and criticisms to make about details of the new proposals. Backers claimed the bill was safe, but it has been scrutinised for its lack of safeguards—mainly that it doesn't go far enough to stop coercion or even really highlight how to spot it, and that, worryingly, doctors would be allowed to suggest euthanasia to patients.

Another major concern has been the way the legislation made its way into Parliament. Whilst most major bills like this, which would affect the whole country, have to go through a huge process to be legalised, this was legislation introduced not by the government, but by a backbench MP as a Private Members' Bill, meaning the public don't get to voice their opinions on the matter through consultation.

Yet again, society is bringing changes to our lives without listening to us. As we've seen throughout this book, disability rights have often been protected because of formal responses to public consultations, but here there was no official channel for disabled people to mobilise and express their concerns.

Another problem with the legislation being a Private Members' Bill (as opposed to government business) is that such bills, automatically deemed less important, are scheduled completely separately in the Commons. Votes take place on a Friday, when many MPs don't go into Parliament, because it's the day they're traditionally expected to spend back in their constituencies around the country.

As Ellen Clifford warned ahead of the debate, "a lot of them are planning to just not go and abstain, because they're undecided ... by not voting they are taking a stance and they're still complicit in what will happen afterwards."

There's also concern that the bill has been rushed through—the prime minister Keir Starmer has even said this is because he promised TV personality Esther Rantzen, who is dying, that he would make time for it in Parliament. The full bill of the text was finally published less than three weeks before it was due to be debated and the debate itself lasted just five hours. Campaigners had said this would not give adequate time to fully scrutinise the bill or for MPs to be properly informed.

It also gave activists very little time to raise awareness of the stakes. The strategy was to get their message to as many MPs as possible, with both Disabled People Against Cuts and Not Dead Yet UK urging people to email their MPs, sending them their comprehensive guides and explaining to them what this debate means for the disabled community. But, as Ellen Clifford told me, "I emailed my MP and the automatic reply came back saying replies typically take four to six weeks, which is double what we've got."

There have also been allegations from the "against" side that the "for" side has contributed to negative public views of disabled people, emphasising the very painful slow deaths in a way that suggests opponents of the bill were monsters unwilling to end people's suffering, or painting all those opposing the bill as religious zealots trying to control people's bodies.

When it comes to ideological agendas and institutional ties, though, the camp supporting the legislation has come under plenty of scrutiny. In the final weeks ahead of the late November vote, the campaign group

Dignity in Dying had huge posters around the London Tube (those aren't cheap). Hannah Sharland's reporting for *The Canary* has highlighted the fact that Dignity in Dying was co-founded in the 1930s by Eugenics Society members, including one who was open to the idea of "applying euthanasia ... to young children with mental or emotional deficiencies". She also found that significant funding in the twenty-first century has come from a trust which also backs right-wing think tanks and political parties that support shrinking the welfare state.

Shadowy conservative and disablist organisations aren't the only ones who got organised, though. Activists may have been denied the chance to write to their MPs, but they rallied to make videos about their fears and tag their representative in social media posts using the hashtag #AssistUsToLive. Disabled journalist and campaigner Melissa Parker was a big part of this campaign in the week before the debate, asking Twitter and Bluesky users to "tell them why it's personal".

On the day of the Terminally Ill Adults (End of Life) Bill's debate, hundreds of disability rights campaigners and their allies took part in a protest outside Downing Street. The bill may have passed, but they were there all day to make the voices of disabled people heard.

One weird thing to note is that whilst the 2015 bill was thrown out when 330 MPs voted against it, just nine years later this bill passed through the Commons with the exact same number voting for it. This just shows the seismic shift in opinion over such a short space of time. I asked Liz Carr how it felt for the issue to have come back to Parliament:

> Ten years ago in 2015 [when the proposed legislation was defeated], elated. This time, on 29 November 2024? Gutted, absolutely gutted and let down by our politicians. Not surprised but still disappointed. When the vote was announced, I was separate from my "gang" of other disabled activists; I had a microphone and camera in my face to get my reaction. But I have heard that in the group of activists from Not Dead Yet, Disabled People Against Cuts, Black Triangle, Changing Perspectives, Inclusion London, WinVisible, DRUK and others, there were tears like there has never been before. This matters to so many of us. This is personal. This is terrifying.

In a world where disabled perspectives have been erased, and where society's trust in us and our trust in society has been eroded by successive governments, it can be easy to become overwhelmed by our awareness that swathes of politics, business, media, the medical world and the general public think disabled people shouldn't exist; but I prefer to look at it another way, in fact I have to or it'll consume me. In a world that actively wants to silence us, we still have a voice and for as long as I can I plan to use mine. As I write this, the assisted dying bill hasn't been put into law—there's a long battle for our rights still to come.

ASSIST US TO LIVE

I, of course, don't exist in a vacuum. I know how terrifying the world is for disabled people and how isolated you can feel. Please know that I and so many others have your back and want you to live. As this book has hopefully shown, disabled people have never, and will never, let this happen without a fight.

CONCLUSION
JUST ASK

One thing I was acutely aware of whilst writing a book about history as it happens was that parts of it could be out of date by the time it reaches readers. By the time you are reading this, there may have been changes to welfare, the assisted dying bill could have progressed and evolved in Parliament, and God knows what else might've happened. But as this book has hopefully shown, the fight for disability rights has been a long hard slog, and it's still far from over. As the UK marks the thirtieth anniversary of the Disability Discrimination Act, disabled people are still nowhere near having equal access, opportunity and rights.

Sure, buses and trains are better than they were, but disabled people are still reporting being left on trains or train platforms, discriminated against by staff, or not given the space to get to where they need to go. Sure, employers aren't technically supposed to discriminate against current and potential employees because of their disability, but they still do—from the government down—and state support for disabled workers is not fit for purpose. Yes, we can live independently, but there's not enough accessible housing or at-home care provision, and care homes sometimes fail disabled people too.

Sure, disabled kids are educated in mainstream schools, but these schools lack funding for their needs, and children and young people still experience discrimination.

Yes, disabled people are more visible in national arts and media than ever before, but there's still too much insistence that you can only work a news desk if you are physically at the desk.

Yes, more disabled journalists are covering our stories, but they should be free to cover politics, sport, culture, lifestyle and entertainment as a whole—interviewing the stars of our favourite TV shows *even when they're not disabled*, being sent out for fluffy travel pieces, and all manner of things that have nothing to do with disability.

I've tried to think of a sentence starting with "yes" relating to welfare too, but there are no positives there.

Where do we start? Here are just a few areas of empowerment that would make a big difference in our ability to tackle the rest. Emma Lewell-Buck is MP for South Shields, and she's also one of the few openly disabled MPs in Parliament (see the Introduction).

Emma spoke to Grace Quantock as part of the *Mirror*'s Disabled Britain series, explaining how the issues disabled people face carry over into a political career: "You're always made to feel that you have to fit

CONCLUSION

into stuff, not stuff fits around you." She discussed how, as a dyspraxic woman, the process of applying to run as an MP and actually carrying out the campaign to get elected was really inaccessible to her, as her brain worked a different way to neurotypical candidates. "Campaigning was taking me twice as long because the format just didn't function in the way that I do."

Before 2015, disabled people could access extra support when running for Parliament through the Access to Elected Office Fund; the Tories promised to reopen this in their (now dead) Disability Action Plan, conveniently forgetting they had been the ones to close it in the first place. Something like this coming back would help to get better representation for disabled people at the top of our democracy.

Not only should more disabled people be able to get into politics but we all deserve the chance to scrutinise policy to protect our interests—not just as activists, but as regular citizens. Too often, public consultations are long, energy-zapping and hard to decipher. Governments need to work with disabled activists to ensure that we're at the heart of all policymaking, instead of just including a few "token" disabled people who never rock the boat and won't put up a fight.

The government should see the consultation as a chance to get it right and serve people, not a hurdle to get over in the most inefficient and obtuse way. Each time a consultation is launched, it's a box ticking rather than an information gathering exercise. Why wouldn't they want people to offer an opinion or specialised input when the government itself doesn't have the skilled and knowledgeable staff to do it for them?

Those who already have a platform need to be using it to lift more people up to join them. Part of this is about straight, white, middle class and cisgendered disabled activists and allies making sure that their movements work with disabled people of the global majority and LGBTQ+ disabled people, to understand the intersection at which they live and how that affects their lives.

Another part of it is people with a following making sure that they're intervening for real change. As the media scrambles to fix underrepresentation, more often than not they'll go not to campaigners and organisers, but to the new wave of influencers who, although they want to raise awareness and build community, have no ties to activism, no specific demands to challenge the status quo, and no mention of the work so many have done to allow them this position.

It's important, I feel, that influencers recognise the privilege their built-in audience and "unthreatening" reputation affords them. Whilst it's important to share personal stories and experiences of your community, influencers need to do more to liaise with Deaf and Disabled People's Organisations and try their best to put forward the talking points of the community as a whole, and in some cases (I say this affectionately) be

CONCLUSION

more scared to take risks whether or not it'll affect your brand deals.

All online advocacy work should include specific calls to action: linking to petitions, signposting protests and online actions and encouraging others to take their anger to those in power to fix it. And more than anything, it should involve not being afraid to turn down opportunities on TV if you think someone else less famous is more suited to talk about the politics. Take the chance to connect media organisers with others who know more than you.

That said, here's a piece of advice I would give absolutely everyone within the movement: You can't be expected to carry the whole movement on your shoulders. We're a community at the end of the day. The media itself needs to do better, to invite a comprehensive list of disabled people with a wide range of experiences and life experience onto their shows and into their pages.

* * *

If we work, and are supported, to build our political bloc; to offer our stories and expertise to policymakers; and to put forward an inclusive, focused movement—then we'll be in a better position to confront the many, many fights to be had to ensure disabled people can live their lives to the fullest.

And how can you help with them? Well, the only way is through active resistance and that comes in many ways. Learning is a big part of that, including massively unlearning some opinions you perhaps have about disability and disabled people (even if you are disabled yourself). This starts by consuming more media written by disabled people and I can recommend a whole raft of incredible disabled journalists.

Aside from myself, obviously, there's Frances Ryan at the *Guardian*, James Moore at the *Independent*, Sam Renke and Eleanor Noyce at *Metro*, Penny Pepper at *Byline* and the incredible Isabella McRae at the *Big Issue*. At my current home, *The Canary*, many of us are disabled and scrutinise the government and the media on disability issues—my colleagues include Hannah Sharland, HG and the mighty Nicola Jeffery.

There are also so many freelancers such as Hannah Shewan Stevens, Melissa Parker, Hollie-Anne Brooks and Chaminda Jayanetti. For longer reads, this book is a good start, but there are many others that will give a full picture (see the Bibliography). There's also the case to be made that independent media outlets such as *Byline Times*, *OpenDemocracy* and of course my home, *The Canary*, are much more representative of disabled people.

As well as educating yourself it's important that, if you're able to, you fight for the cause. There are many local disability rights groups and searching in your local area will find you countless; most of these also have online groups and meetings. A national organisation I

CONCLUSION

would definitely recommend supporting is Disabled People Against Cuts. There are lots of ways you can get involved, and it's worth contacting a Deaf and Disabled People's Organisation (DDPO) if you have a particular skill that you think you can offer them.

But the quickest way to get involved is to attend a protest. Direct in-person action undoubtedly gets attention and slowly but surely works. It is however important to note that protest may not always be safe, especially with the unprecedentedly draconian anti-protest laws that are in place at the moment. Thanks to the 2022 Police, Crime, Sentencing and Courts Act, which was passed in response to climate protests, protest can now result in heavier policing and much harsher punishments, including even prison sentences.

It also pays to know your rights on protesting and the adjustments that police must make for disabled people, including providing information in an accessible way and giving you enough time to follow instructions. The Disability Rights UK website is a really good resource on this which all disabled protestors should check out.

If in-person action isn't accessible to you, there are lots of other ways you can get involved online. For disabled people social media has played two important roles in creating change, which work side by side: community and organising. Many disabled people have experienced feeling isolated in their everyday lives. After all, we live in a world which isn't built for us, and that often forces us to stay at home.

Many of us either don't have that many people in our lives who really also understand what we're going through, or don't have ways to meet other disabled people. Much of the internet is an absolute cesspit run by tech supervillains out to destroy anything they see as wrong—namely anyone from a minority feeling loved—but disabled people aren't just lonely. We are undeniably fucking hilarious—after all, there's no humour like gallows humour—and I've been saved from many a meltdown by a witty rage-filled group text.

When I was first coming to terms with my conditions and accepting that I was disabled in my early twenties—despite being ill since the age of eight—I sought out others who were going through the same thing I was. The only disabled people I knew were a good thirty or forty years older than me and in a very different place in their life.

So of course, I sought out an online community. I wrote blogs, became part of Facebook groups and took to Twitter to desperately find connection, a life raft on which to navigate life in those awkward early twenties whilst disabled. For me, disability Twitter was the place where, more than anything, I was believed for the first time. After decades of medical professionals, strangers and unfortunately, even loved ones, treating me like I was exaggerating or making a fuss, this incredible community of—let's face it—strangers told me "we hear you, we believe you".

CONCLUSION

I can honestly say without those online spaces I wouldn't be where I am today. Without Twitter I wouldn't have got most of the work opportunities I have, have been given the voice I have, or have found most of my amazing, brave (but not "inspirational") pals. I wouldn't have connected that my birth control was slowly ruining my life without seeing a near stranger tweet about her boob pain and low moods whilst on the Mirena coil. I wouldn't have realised I had ADHD if I hadn't seen women my age struggling with everyday tasks in the same way I was on, yes, TikTok. I wouldn't have found people like me who never judge me or hold me to non-disabled standards and in turn I would never have discovered the real me who not only accepted my disabilities but allowed my neurodivergent disabled self to thrive without the support of the truly outstanding community I've been able to cultivate over social media.

As well as a way to find and build community, the online world has been an invaluable resource for organising and campaigning, from petitions against benefit cuts to parents organising Instagram campaigns to hold their local authority to account for SEND provision to TikTok videos tagging MPs ahead of the assisted dying debate.

Where in-person meetings can be difficult to coordinate, video calling services such as Zoom have become the go-to for DDPOs and campaign groups. Organisations such as Disabled People Against Cuts are able to host calls for over a hundred activists at a time. Most DDPO actions agreed at these meetings will also have online components, from virtual rallies and solidarity sessions connecting those unable to attend protests, to actual digital campaigning. If an action doesn't have pre-planned social media options it may be worth offering to coordinate something, even a hashtag.

Seeking out what hashtags are already out there and trending, and throwing your weight behind them, is always a great idea. Social media is a perfect place for us to spread awareness and help non-disabled people to learn how their actions can impact us. Sometimes this is about calling out disablist behaviour that's actually taking place online and ensuring that companies and individuals learn from their mistakes; many disabled people have successfully received compensation over unacceptable treatment online.

Sometimes it's bringing public attention to an ongoing frustration of disabled life. Dr Amy Kavanagh started the hashtag #JustAskDontGrab to highlight that non-disabled people can offer support in ways other than manhandling disabled people and trying to lead us places or physically assist us without our consent.

It is also where activists and organisations first report their frustrations with media ableism, often leading to changes in language or articles being pulled together.

For example, in April 2024, Penguin Random House released a polished video announcing a new edition of

CONCLUSION

Roald Dahl's *The Twits* written by BBC Radio 1 presenter Greg James and Chris Smith in which they discussed how they might go about making the characters "revolting" with the illustrator. When the illustrator asked if they should add a glass eye, they both replied, "A glass eye! She needs a glass eye. That's it. What a disgusting pair of twits!"

As was the case for many other disabled people within a second of watching this on social media, I was appalled. Not only at the fact that they would say this so unthinkingly, but that the video made it through a video editor and several departments of the biggest publisher in the world with not a single person blocking it. Having a disabled member of staff who felt able to share their honest opinion could have saved them a lot of trouble.

I and many others immediately flagged the video. Even the Royal National Institute of Blind People released a statement about it, stating, "When there's positive representation of disabilities in children's books, children with disabilities feel seen and heard, and their friends and classmates treat everyone the same. There is nothing at all revolting about prosthetic eyes, we think they're brilliant."

It's unbelievable that we're still living with the trope of the disabled villain—where a bad guy is given a physical disability to somehow hammer home that they're evil, strange or morally inferior. Instead of a celebration day for this new book, or indeed the whole new series which actually involved other disabled people such as Adam Hills and Elle McNicoll, the publisher and the authors had to backtrack and delete the video due to the backlash it received on social media.

The authors said, "We apologise unreservedly. It's [the video] now gone. We understand that words matter and we pride ourselves on championing and welcoming everyone into the magical world of children's books. We would never dream of deliberately setting out to exclude anyone."

If you think that we are all just snowflakes and we should grow up because "they didn't mean harm" and it's not a big deal, then you need to consider what was happening at the same time. In the same week, a school in Aberdeen was discovered to be offering an option for parents to have class photos which digitally edited out the disabled children in the class.

As Frances Ryan said in her column in the *Guardian*, "Behind the erasure of disabled children lies the frightening belief that they don't belong in 'perfect' pictures—or public spaces." It's a slippery slope from calling disability in children's books disgusting to erasing disabled children, and it was thanks to social media that the video, and its offensive message, was taken down so fast before more children could see it.

I've seen many disabled people lament Elon Musk's destruction of Twitter, because for us that little hellsite was the first place where we discovered we weren't alone.

CONCLUSION

But just like we have done many times offline, we rebuild. Who knows what the popular social media will be when this is published but at time of writing it seems Bluesky will hopefully be a better place for us.

* * *

As we've seen from history, disability rights are won and upheld when the power of the disabled community comes together. It's vital that we harness the power in these pages both past and present, continue to dig in, cultivate community and vow to make lasting change for all disabled people.

Key battlegrounds:

- **Living**: Educate yourself on the assisted dying bill and disabled people's concerns with it, and fight like hell to make sure what happens in Parliament doesn't threaten our right to live.
- **Transport**: The Disability Discrimination Act 1995 had the ambition that by 2025, all public transport in the UK would be accessible. Unfortunately, this was dropped when the Equality Act 2010 superseded it. We should all lobby for transport and public and commercial venues to be fully accessible. Follow Motability about the Transport Accessibility Gap.
- **Work**: The Access to Work backlog desperately needs fixing, but we also need to fight for disabled people's right to work safely. All office jobs should have the option of fully working from home.

- **Media and arts**: We need a set of government guidelines and anti-discrimination rules that all media organisations have to follow to ensure that disabled people aren't othered or spoken about with outdated language. Whether you're disabled or not, support disability art with your time and your money, so that we can have a thriving cultural scene that includes disabled stories and disabled storytellers outside of inspiration porn and trauma porn.
- **Law**: The UK has to get back in line with the UN Disability Rights charter, starting by enshrining the principles of the UN Convention on the Rights of Disabled People in law. Ensuring legal and medical representation—to have a consultation role for any law that impacts disabled people.
- **No more benefits cuts** and a shift in the rhetoric used about disabled people by government and politicians. Instead let's see some political energy put into accessible housing and urban planning, SEND funding in the education system, and training for the service sector on their obligations to disabled people.
- **No more apathy** from non-disabled people: get yourself informed and organised in whatever way you can, and always question accessibility and inclusion in every space you enter. The same way we don't stop being disabled at 5 p.m. or at the weekend, our activism doesn't stop either, so buckle up. Have a look around your life and community: is your office inac-

cessible and could you organise a strike until it is? Do the disabled people around you need something to make their life easier? Do you see the disabled people in your life fighting for a cause and feel you could help lend your voice to theirs? There is so much you can do, just don't give up when it gets hard—we don't.

- **Get uncomfortable**: Whether you're disabled or not, be prepared to be challenged on the way you talk or think about disability—"I would rather die than deteriorate that far", "have you tried yoga", etc. These conversations can be hard, and you might not feel comfortable having your compassion or allyship questioned. We're uncomfortable every fucking day of our lives, and we're DONE.

AFTERWORD
THE COMMUNITY SPEAKS

After writing a book that spans more than a century of activism and highlights all the incredible work that disabled people have done to fight for our rights, I knew there was only one way I could possibly end it. The final word has to be left to the community. After all, this book wouldn't be possible if it wasn't for their great work—disabled people in the UK wouldn't have anywhere near the quality of life that they do now, me included.

But of course, there's still work to be done. So much work. As Part Two has highlighted, disabled people are still battling to work, study, go places, be represented and live our goddamn lives.

With this in mind I passed the mic over to the disability community. I asked the many legendary campaigners featured in the book, and my social media followers, one simple question:

What do we want?

"There's an old political slogan, 'Bread and roses' that signifies human beings want the right to live, not just exist. True disability rights does not mean subsistence benefits for baked beans and a care worker for a quick wash. Disabled people want to dance, snog and feel the sun on our faces. Just like everyone else."—Frances Ryan, journalist and author of *Who Wants Normal?* and *Crippled*

"Revolution! (well, a radical restructuring of society) and when do we want it? Eh, now. Soon."—Liz Carr, actor and activist

"For accessibility to be baked into the fabric of how society works, not tacked on as an afterthought if and when we ask for it."—Laura Elliott, author of *Awakened*

"All of our rights under the UN CRPD restored, fully incorporated into UK domestic laws and enforceable by law enforcement and the British judiciary."—John McArdle, Black Triangle

"I want us to move forward in solidarity, breaking down internalized ableism that can lead us to hierarchise disabilities—so we can campaign stronger for a more accommodating world."—Dr Jay Watts, consultant clinical psychologist

"A world where nobody has to give the best (or all) of their health to work—and where I'm remembered. Remember I'm probably isolated at home. Remember my social life is 90% WhatsApp, and I struggle to stay connected to people who only 'do relationships' by spending time IRL. Remember I need notice to hang out; and remember that my being there and enjoying myself doesn't mean I feel well. We live with our conditions 24/7."—Lara Weisweiller-Wu, Senior Editor at Hurst Publishers

"Fundamentally, disabled people need what everyone needs—to be listened to, believed, and whole-heartedly supported. It's really not hard!"—Dr Hannah Barham-Brown, GP, speaker and EDI consultant

"Warm words and being heard is not enough, decision makers need to act on the concerns of people with disabilities. It is only then we will feel truly listened to, and when wider society will start to change their attitudes towards us."—Emma Lewell-Buck, MP for South Shields

"A safety net in the welfare state and to have UNCRDP ratified in UK law and abided by."—Paula Peters, DPAC steering committee

"I want people to take our word on our own reality as authority, instead of the constant arguing, downplaying, demonizing, and gaslighting we have to experience from those in power."—Sam Hatley (via Twitter)

"We want the space to be angry and not do all the heavy lifting to help non-disabled people understand our bitterness."—Ella Maisy Purvis, actor

"An education system where children are happy and not school refusing, one that includes lots of creative elements as well as academic ones. An education system where disabled educators are valued and supported with flexible working patterns, adjustments, sound policies and manageable workloads."—Colleen Johnson, Seat Holder for Disabled Members, National Education Union—National Executive Committee and Chair NEU Disabled Members Organising Forum

"My one hope is to be able to live, without having to fight so hard to be considered worthy of living and of basic humanity. Being disabled is only a small part of who I am, there is so much I want to do and I keep being distracted by an ableist society."—Caro Clarke, Literary Agent at Portobello Literary and Chair of the Association of Scottish Literary Agents

"To be listened to as if we know what we're saying! (Newsflash: we do)."—Jane Stemp, writer

"To have the same working opportunities as anyone else, not to be sidelined by interviews, application and stereotypes."—Caroline Keep, data scientist, University of Central Lancashire

"I would most like dignity, security from the welfare state—without demonisation, and simply being believed/heard."—Lorna

"Acknowledgement from the medical community and leaders of society that they understand, that disabled people are valued and that they will make things better for us."—Liz Meddings

AFTERWORD

"I want non-disabled people to start taking part in disability activism, not just with a pitying post or occasional retweet. I want them to take meaningful action on our behalf. We cannot fight all these battles alone, especially when so many of us are living with energy-limiting disabilities. Yes, we make up 24% of the UK population, but that means there is 76% of people who need to speak up too."—Hannah Shewan Stevens, journalist

"To be treated as an individual. So we could actually live with our partners without being at their financial mercy. Potentially getting trapped in situations we can't escape. Second thing is enough financial support to actually live. Facing homelessness isn't OK."—Katie I, former mental healthcare worker

"The right to let down tyres of whatever c*nt parks on a dropped kerb."—Ted Shiress (via Twitter)

"Peace of mind of knowing our future is as secure as can be whether or not we are able to work."—John Grieve, web designer

"For the law to presume disability discrimination is more likely than not as a starting point, rather than presuming it's a rare and terrible thing."—Becca Jiggens, The Work Inclusion Project

"For our existence to be believed and respected. No intrusive questions or expectation to educate strangers, no justifying everything we do just to make others comfortable, no pity porn or expectation to be inspirational, to be able to live independently and access the support we need without being traumatised in the process. Basically just being able to live with dignity and trusted that we know ourselves best."—Lozza Gilbert, campaigner, speaker and voiceover artist

"access-centred world; person-centred care."—Polly Atkin, author

"Free and fast diagnosis, it doesn't matter how many rights disabled people get if we don't count as disabled."—Eleanor (via Twitter)

"To be seen as adults—I think infantilisation is at the root of the discrimination we face in everything from employment to dating, health and care to benefits, parenting to transportation."—Lucy Webster, journalist, campaigner and author

"Stop thinking that by accepting our reality we are giving up, and let us be unhappy about it sometimes."—Lucinda (via Twitter)

"Social security which allows disabled claimants to retain their level of benefits & independence while living with someone including romantic partners."—Nic (via Twitter)

"Laws that allow us to actually enforce our rights. None of this 'if you ask nicely', 'be grateful' or 'we've said sorry, what more do you want?' bullshit."—Stephen Anderson (via Twitter)

"The ability to join the table, be a part of creating today's world and the future. Enough care, right diagnosis and available treatment, so I can use my energy and time being part of the conversation, not fighting for scraps just to stay alive, invisible to those who decide."—Anja aune (via Twitter)

"To be heard & valued. Not based solely on our ability to work but who we're as people. We laugh, cry & feel pain too. We also want love & all the ups & downs that come with it."—Callum Warren, ParaPhrase Media

"The understanding that accessibility is more than wheelchair access alone. There are so many physical and psychological barriers that stop disabled people participating in society, accessing the businesses and facilities that are essential to daily life."—Germander Speedwell, campaigner and ceramic artist

"A full on societal change is needed, which sounds dramatic and like it'll never happen but it's fundamentally a human right for us to exist peacefully. From government decision makers taking our needs seriously to the media having a strong stance on use of appropriate language to schools teaching acceptance for everyone. We deserve to live an equal, joyful life."—Hollie-Anne Brooks, campaigner and journalist

"We need people to be afraid to fail us. Our rights can only be protected when those in institutions know that if it doesn't happen, there's consequences."—Glen (via Twitter)

* * *

And me? Well, I of course echo everything that's been said above (especially the anger).

I want a world where disabled people don't have to campaign for our rights anymore. I want to live in a world where disabled people are considered human beings and that our disabilities aren't something to overcome, but something that is accommodated so we can live our lives. I want a society where disabled isn't seen as the worst thing a person can be and that, in fact, it's the least interesting thing about us.

I want a government that sees us as people worthy of support whether or not we can contribute to the economy. A welfare system that believes and supports us, without us having to prove we deserve it. I want a press that sees us as worthy of coverage whether or not we're being inspirational. I want my disabled friends and family members to not be afraid or ashamed to be who they truly are.

More than anything I want a world where disabled people don't have to fight just to survive, but one where we can thrive. Disabled people deserve to live happy, sad, messy, sexy, content, full lives. And we deserve a world that encourages us to be able to be our whole selves without scorn, fear or mistreatment.

Until that day comes, we'll be here fighting. Won't you join us? After all, there's nothing about us without ALL of us.

ACKNOWLEDGEMENTS

This book, and my whole book writing career, wouldn't have been possible without my incredible agent, Caro Clarke at Portobello Literary. Caro is a true champion for marginalised writers but even more than that an eternal friend and hype person. Thank you for your incredible research, stern faces, brownies and for (not so) gently nudging me on the right path—but especially the brownies.

Secondly, to everyone at Hurst, but especially my amazing editor Lara Weisweiller-Wu, who saw the potential and need for a book like this when so many weren't prepared to invest in disabled stories that were less palatable.

To my best friend in the whole universe, Gemma Hastings, for always reminding me who the fuck I am when I forget, taking my hand and dragging me headfirst and fearless, and being there to pick me up. I couldn't live this definitely-not-ridiculous life without you and nor would I want to.

ACKNOWLEDGEMENTS

My wonderful family—Mam, Dad, Jodie, Nana, Granda and all the aunties, uncles and cousins, who are endlessly proud of me and put up with me ranting about "this fucking government" every time you see me, I can't promise that will change. Thank you for the meals (especially panack and soup Tuesdays, Auntie Joanne), the distractions and cuppas. My incredible nieces Ella, Paige and Grace: keep fighting for what's right in the world.

The best boy in the world, Rusty, for keeping me sane and giving me a reason to live. You won't be able to read this because you're a dog, but I'll read it to you.

To every single incredible activist who has given me their time so generously over the years whilst I blundered through this and spent more time gassing on Zoom and over email about other things than disability rights. But especially to Ellen Clifford for your constant compassion, fire and wit; John Pring for helping me believe I can write this; Frances Ryan for the email encouragement; and my hero Barbara Lisicki, who is literally the reason I'm writing this book.

To my fellow millennial auntie Cath, famous best friend Ella, my neurospice girl Dawn, and Caitlin for keeping me sane and also letting me very much not be sane.

Mouche, Armadillo, Caravaggio and Geronimo (Sarah O'Brien, Dr Amy Kavanagh, Caro Stickland and Ginny Butcher) for always giving me the space to feel my feelings on disability, no matter how big or small. That will be the last time I ever call you all your real names.

ACKNOWLEDGEMENTS

A big list of other important people (apologies if I miss you, this is feeling like they're going to start playing me off): Toni, Amber and Claire, Ellen Jone, Lozza, Charli, Lou, Mims, Emily, Ella, Jo and the rest of H+H. Melissa, Bond, Hannah, Hollie-Anne, Jasper, Lydia, Faith, Helen and Frankie. Laura Elliot, Elspeth, Lindsay and all the other Porty Literary authors. Steve, Nicola, Hannah Sharland, HG and everyone else at *The Canary*. Anyone involved in the production of gluten-free Jaffa Cakes, Nozeco, or roast potatoes, the cast of *Ghosts*, and Dr Taylor Alison Swift.

Lastly, to my incredible supporters both off- and online (but especially on Twitter/X) for allowing me the space to learn, grow, be angry and celebrate the greatness of disability.

BIBLIOGRAPHY

Foreword by Ellen Clifford

Butler, P. (2016). "UK austerity policies 'amount to violations of Disabled People's Rights.'" *The Guardian*. Available at: https://www.theguardian.com/business/2016/nov/07/uk-austerity-policies-amount-to-violations-of-disabled-peoples-rights

Jayanetti, C. (2025). "DWP's consultation on Disability Benefit Reforms Unlawful, High Court rules." *Big Issue*. Available at: https://www.bigissue.com/news/social-justice/dwp-disability-benefits-reforms-consultation-ruling/

Pring, J. (2017). "UK faces UN Examination: Government cuts caused 'human catastrophe.'" *Disability News Service*. Available at: https://www.disabilitynewsservice.com/uk-faces-un-examination-government-cuts-caused-human-catastrophe/

Trump III, F.C. (2024). "Donald Trump told me disabled Americans 'should just die.'" *Time*. Available at: https://time.com/7002003/donald-trump-disabled-americans-all-in-the-family/ (Accessed: 15 February 2025).

Work capability assessment reform: Update to estimated number of claimants affected. GOV.UK (2024). Available at: https://www.gov.uk/government/publications/work-capability-assessment-reform-estimated-number-of-claimants-affected/work-capability-assessment-reform-update-to-estimated-number-of-claimants-affected

Introduction

"Barbara Lisicki." Wikipedia (2023). Available at: https://en.wikipedia.org/wiki/Barbara_Lisicki

BIBLIOGRAPHY

Charlton-Dailey, R. (2020). "BBC documentary *Silenced: The Hidden Story of Disabled Britain* uncovers how disabled people were shut out of society for decades." *Stylist*. Available at: https://www.stylist.co.uk/entertainment/silenced-the-hidden-story-of-disabled-britain-bbc/472905

—— (2023). "It's vital we teach the next generation about disability history." *The Mirror*. Available at: https://www.mirror.co.uk/news/politics/its-vital-teach-next-generation-30067716

—— (2023). "Shameful: Britain hauled before the UN for violating Disabled People's Rights." *The Lead*. Available at: https://thelead.uk/shameful-britain-hauled-un-violating-disabled-peoples-rights

—— (2024). "What was it like being at the UN Committee on the Rights of Disabled People? F*cking frustrating." *The Canary*. Available at: https://www.thecanary.co/opinion/2024/04/04/uncrpd-uk-government/

Diamond: The Seventh Cut (2024). *The Creative Diversity Network*. Available at: https://creativediversitynetwork.com/wp-content/uploads/2024/09/Standard-main-Report_Diamond-The-Seventh-Cut_CDN_12-Sept-2024pdf.pdf

"Disability facts and figures." Scope (2024). Available at: https://www.scope.org.uk/media/disability-facts-figures

"Disability hate crimes rise to record levels." Leonard Cheshire (2022). Available at: https://www.leonardcheshire.org/about-us/our-news/press-releases/disability-hate-crimes-rise-record-levels

"Disability Price Tag 2023: the extra cost of disability." Scope (2023). Available at: https://www.scope.org.uk/campaigns/extra-costs/disability-price-tag-2023.

Disability Discrimination Act 1995. Legislation.gov.uk. Available at: https://www.legislation.gov.uk/ukpga/1995/50/contents

Disability, England and Wales: Census 2021. Office for National Statistics (2021). Available at: https://www.ons.gov.uk/peoplepopulationandcommunity/healthandsocialcare/healthandwellbeing/bulletins/disabilityenglandandwales/census2021

"Disabled people won't be properly represented in TV until 2041." Televisual (2022). Available at: https://www.televisual.com/news/report-disabled-people-wont-be-properly-represented-in-tv-until-2041/

BIBLIOGRAPHY

Impact of increased cost of living on adults across Great Britain: July to October 2023. Office for National Statistics. Available at: https://www.ons.gov.uk/peoplepopulationandcommunity/personalandhouseholdfinances/expenditure/articles/impactofincreasedcostoflivingonadultsacrossgreatbritain/julytooctober2023

"Justice Gap Widens: Disability hate crime charges continue to drop." Leonard Cheshire (2023). Available at: https://www.leonardcheshire.org/about-us/our-news/press-releases/justice-gap-widens-disability-hate-crime-charges-continue-drop

National LGBT Survey: Summary report. Government Equalities Office (2019). Available at: https://www.gov.uk/government/publications/national-lgbt-survey-summary-report/national-lgbt-survey-summary-report

Pring, J. (2024). "Trio of new disabled MPs join House of Commons." *Disability News Service.* Available at: https://www.disabilitynewsservice.com/trio-of-new-disabled-mps-join-house-of-commons/

Tobitt, C. (2021). "British Journalism Awards winners, Pics and video 2021: ITV's Robert Moore is Journalist of the Year and Guardian Best News Provider." *Press Gazette.* Available at: https://pressgazette.co.uk/news/british-journalism-awards-winners-2021/

Trans lives survey 2021: Enduring the UK's hostile environment. TransActual (2021). Available at: https://transactual.org.uk/trans-lives-21/

UK disability statistics: Prevalence and life experiences. House of Commons Library (2023, August 23). The House of Commons Library. Available at: https://commonslibrary.parliament.uk/research-briefings/cbp-9602/

Chapter 1: My Freedom of Spirit

"A Brief History of Disabled People's Self Organisation, Greater Manchester Coalition of Disabled People." Historic England. Available at: https://historicengland.org.uk/content/docs/research/brief-history-disabled-peoples-self-organisation-pdf

Atkinson, D. (2018). *Rise Up, Women!: The remarkable lives of the suffragettes.* Bloomsbury.

"Bethlem Royal Hospital." Wikipedia. Available at: https://en.wikipedia.org/wiki/Bethlem_Royal_Hospital

BIBLIOGRAPHY

Campbell, J. and Oliver M. (1996). *Disability Politics*. Routledge.

"Cohen, Sir (Benn) Jack Brunel." Oxford Dictionary of National Biography (2011). Available at: https://www.oxforddnb.com/display/10.1093/ref:odnb/9780198614128.001.0001/odnb-9780198614128-e-94524

Fielding, S. (2020). "Overlooked No More: Rosa May Billinghurst, Militant Suffragette." *The New York Times*. Available here: https://www.nytimes.com/2020/10/30/obituaries/rosa-may-billinghurst-overlooked.html#:~:text=2-,Overlooked%20No%20More%3A%20Rosa%20May%20Billinghurst%2C%20Militant%20Suffragette,right%20to%20vote%20in%20England

Hasted, R. (2015). "The Untapped Stories of Disability and the First World War." Heritage Fund. Available at: https://www.heritagefund.org.uk/blogs/untapped-stories-disability-and-first-world-war

Langton, W. *Courage: An account of the lives of Eliza Adelaide Knight and Donald Adolphus Brown* (Geoff Gamble, 2007).

Main, E. (2020). "'Justice not charity'—the blind marchers who made history." BBC Ouch. Available at: https://www.bbc.co.uk/news/disability-52477587

"Our History and Origins." British Deaf Association. Available at: https://bda.org.uk/history/

Reiss, M. (2015). *Blind Workers against Charity: The National League of the Blind of Great Britain and Ireland, 1893–1970*. Springer.

"When Was the First School for Blind Pupils Established in Britain?" Historic England. Available at: https://historicengland.org.uk/listing/what-is-designation/heritage-highlights/when-was-the-first-school-for-blind-pupils-established-in-britain/#:~:text=The%20Liverpool%20School%20for%20the,of%20the%20trade%20in%20enslaved

"William Cuffay, 1788–1870." BBC History. Available at: https://www.bbc.co.uk/history/historic_figures/cuffay_william.shtml

"William Cuffay: 7 things you should know." TUC (2018). Available at: https://tuc150.tuc.org.uk/stories/william-cuffay/

"Workhouses and the Poor Law Amendment Act 1834." Health.org. Available at: https://navigator.health.org.uk/theme/workhouses-and-poor-law-amendment-act-1834

BIBLIOGRAPHY

Chapter 2: Does He Take Sugar?

"Charity History." Disabled Motoring UK. Available at: https://www.disabledmotoring.org/about-us/charity-history

"Creating a National Disability Income." Disablement Income Group (1972).

Du Boisson, M. and Moore B. "Letter to the Guardian: Pensions for Disabled people." Republished on the Disability History Project, Disability Resource Centre (2015). Available at: https://disabilityhistorydrc.blogspot.com/2013/05/letter-to-guardian-from-1965-pensions.html

"Early Ceefax caption." The Teletext Museum (2001). Available at: https://teletext.mb21.co.uk/timeline/early-ceefax-subtitling.shtml

Flintoff, J.P. (2008). "Thalidomide: the battle for compensation goes on." *The Times*. Available at: https://web.archive.org/web/20080513095824/http://www.timesonline.co.uk/tol/life_and_style/health/article3602694.ece

"History of Scope." Scope. Available at: https://www.scope.org.uk/about-us/history

"History of Thalidomide." The Thalidomide Trust. Available at: https://www.thalidomidetrust.org/about-us/history-of-thalidomide/

Mental Health Act 1959. UK Public General Acts. Available at: https://www.legislation.gov.uk/ukpga/Eliz2/7-8/72/enacted

Moore, I. (2012). "Berit Stueland obituary." *The Guardian*. Available at: https://www.theguardian.com/society/2012/mar/19/berit-stueland-obituary

"Obituary: Lord Ashley." *BBC News* (2012). Available at: https://www.bbc.co.uk/news/uk-politics-11167902

"Obituary: Mrs Megan Du Boisson." *The Times* (1969).

Robinson, C. (1967). "D I G in danger." *The Times*.

Ryan, C. (2004). "'They just didn't know what it would do.'" *BBC News*. Available at: http://news.bbc.co.uk/1/hi/health/3589173.stm

Vargesson, N. (2015). "Thalidomide-induced teratogenesis: history and mechanisms." *Birth Defects Research. Part C. Embryo Today*. Available at: https://pmc.ncbi.nlm.nih.gov/articles/PMC4737249/

BIBLIOGRAPHY

Chapter 3: Let Us Live

Baldwinson, T. (2016). "A public history of UPIAS—the Union of the Physically Impaired Against Segregation." Available at: https://tonybaldwinson.com/2016/11/29/a-public-history-of-manchester-upias-the-union-of-the-physically-impaired-against-segregation/

Beesley, L. (ed.) (2022). *Collected Works of Paul Hunt*. TBR Imprint. Available at: https://gmcdp.com/sites/default/files/Collected%20Works%20of%20Paul%20Hunt%20-%20ISBN%20-%20978%201913%20148%20188.pdf

Boyle, A. (1955). "Peace-time Mission of a Bomber 'Ace'". *Radio Times*.

"Founding Statement." Union of the Physically Impaired Against Segregation (1972). Available at: https://disability-studies.leeds.ac.uk/wp-content/uploads/sites/40/library/UPIAS-UPIAS.pdf

Hunt, J. (2019). *No Limits: The disabled people's movement—a radical history*. TBR Consulting.

"Margaret Blackwood, Breaking the Mould." WEA Scotland (2015). Available at: https://wealothianwomensforum.org.uk/BreakingtheMould/mblackwood.html

Roth, A. (2012). "Lord Morris of Manchester obituary." *The Guardian*. Available at: https://www.theguardian.com/politics/2012/aug/14/lord-morris-of-manchester

"The fundamental principles of Disability (audio description)." National Disability Arts Collection & Archive. Available at: https://the-ndaca.org/resources/audio-described-gallery/fundamental-principles-of-disability/

"The Fundamental principles of Disability." Union of the Physically Impaired Against Segregation & The Disability Alliance (1975). Available at: https://disability-studies.leeds.ac.uk/wp-content/uploads/sites/40/library/UPIAS-fundamental-principles.pdf

"Vic Finkelstein." National Disability Arts Collection & Archive. Available at: https://the-ndaca.org/the-people/vic-finkelstein/

Oliver, M. (2011). "Vic Finkelstein obituary." *The Guardian*. Available at: https://www.theguardian.com/society/2011/dec/22/vic-finkelstein

Chapter 4: Coalition

Baar, M. (2017). "Disability Goes Global: The Repercussions of the

BIBLIOGRAPHY

International Year of Disabled Persons (1981)." Global Health, London School of Hygiene and Tropical Medicine. Available at: https://www.lshtm.ac.uk/newsevents/events/disability-goes-global-repercussions-international-year-disabled-persons-1981

Beckett, E. (1988). *Inventing Ourselves*. Routledge.

Blacker, T. (2012). "Spasticus Autisticus revisited." *The Independent*. Available at: https://www.independent.co.uk/hei-fi/views/terence-blacker-spasticus-autisticus-revisited-8099070.html

Chronically Sick and Disabled Person's Act 1970. UK Public General Acts. Available at: https://www.legislation.gov.uk/ukpga/1970/44/

Disabled People's Mini Histories—Episode 1: Too Frightening For Kids TV. Disabled People's Archive (2020). Available at: https://www.youtube.com/watch?v=ZzcfxpKosAg

Disabled Persons (Services, Consultation and Representation) Act 1986. UK Public General Acts. Available at: https://www.legislation.gov.uk/ukpga/1986/33

Evans, J. (1996). *The UK Civil Rights Campaign and the Disability Discrimination Act*. Vienna: European Network on Independent Living (ENIL) Paper.

"Our History." Greater Manchester Coalition of Disabled People. Available at: https://gmcdp.com/our-history

Pring, J. (2012). "Disability movement loses 'visionary leader'." *Disability News Service*. Available at: https://www.disabilitynewsservice.com/disability-movement-loses-visionary-leader/

"The International Year of Disabled Persons 1981, Department of Economic and Social Affairs-Disability." United Nations. Available at: https://www.un.org/development/desa/disabilities/the-international-year-of-disabled-persons-1981.html

Chapter 5: Piss On Pity

"Alan Holdsworth." National Disability Arts Collection and Archive. Available at: https://the-ndaca.org/the-people/alan-holdsworth/

"BCODP Day of Action, London—1988." Disabled People's Archive. Available at: https://disabledpeoplesarchive.com/1988-bcodp-day-of-action-london/

BIBLIOGRAPHY

Brisenden, S. "The Battle for Elephant and Castle." Printed in *Body Shopping— Poems by Simon Brisenden* (2018). SPECTRUM Centre for Independent Living. Available at: https://spectrumcil.co.uk/wp-content/uploads/2018/02/ULO14A-Body-Shopping-Poems-Simon-Brisenden.pdf

Davis K. and Mullender A. (1993). *Ten Turbulent Years: A Review of the Work of the Derbyshire Coalition of Disabled People*. Centre for Social Action, University of Nottingham.

"Johnny Crescendo, Block Telethon Protest." National Disability Arts Collection and Archive. Available at: https://the-ndaca.org/resources/audio-described-gallery/johnny-crescendo-block-telethon-protest/

Lisicki, B. (2018). "Block Telethon 1992—the day we 'pissed on pity.'" National Disability Arts Collection and Archive on Medium. Available at: https://medium.com/@theNDACA/block-telethon-1992-the-day-we-pissed-on-pity-69117b03825a

Parker, M. (2022). "Children in Need shaped me, but I wish it hadn't." *The Unwritten*. Available at: https://www.theunwritten.co.uk/2022/11/18/box-ticking-exercise-children-in-need-shaped-me-but-i-wish-it-hadnt/

Pearson, C. and Watson N. (2007). "Tackling Disability Discrimination in the United Kingdom: The British Disability Discrimination Act." *Journal of Law & Policy*. Available at: https://openscholarship.wustl.edu/cgi/viewcontent.cgi?article=1333&context=law_journal_law_policy

Pring, J. (2023). "Ruth Bashall: Tributes and affection for 'mighty' and 'formidable' activist." *Disability News Service*. Available at: https://www.disabilitynewsservice.com/ruth-bashall-tributes-and-affection-for-mighty-and-formidable-activist/

Rose, D. "The wheelchair warriors." *BBC News*. Available at: https://www.bbc.co.uk/news/extra/8rvpt6bclh/wheelchair-warriors-disability-discrimination-act

Velho, R. (2017). *FIXING THE GAP: an investigation into wheelchair users' shaping of London public transport*. Available at: https://discovery.ucl.ac.uk/id/eprint/1565187/1/Velho%20-%20Fixing%20the%20Gap%20(PhD%20Thesis).pdf

"Who are DAN?" Direct People's Direct Action Network. Available at: https://dan-shop.org/pages/who-are-d-a-n

BIBLIOGRAPHY

Chapter 6: Disabled Anarchist Blues

Arienello K. and Williamson, A. (2007). *The Disabled Avant Garde*. Available at: https://disabledavantgarde.wordpress.com/

"Art and Social Change: The Disability Arts Movement." Midlands Arts Centre (2020). Available at: https://macbirmingham.co.uk/exhibition-archive/art-and-social-change-the-disability-arts-movement

"Baroness Jane Campbell." National Disability Arts Collective and Archive. Available at: https://the-ndaca.org/the-people/baroness-campbell/

Cameron, C. (2009). "Tragic but Brave or Just Crips with Chips? Songs and Their Lyrics in the Disability Arts Movement in Britain." *Popular Music Vol. 28, No. 3, Popular Music and Disability*. Cambridge University Press.

Crescendo, J. "Say it now." *Mouth Mag*. Available at: https://www.mouthmag.com/johnnypoem.htm

"Deborah Williams." DaDaFest. Available at: https://www.dadafest.co.uk/artist/deborah-williams

"Disability music and poetry audio." Disabled People's Archive. Available at: https://disabledpeoplesarchive.com/in-the-archive/audio/

Evans, J. (2003). "The Independent Living Movement in the UK." Independent Living Institute. Available at: https://www.independentliving.org/docs6/evans2003.html

Heaton, T. (1992). "Shaken not Stirred." Shape Arts. Available at: https://www.shapearts.org.uk/news/shape-collection-heaton-shaken

––––– (1994). "Great Britain from a wheelchair." Shape Arts. Available at: https://www.shapearts.org.uk/tony-heaton-gbfaw

"Liz Crow." National Disability Arts Collective and Archive. Available at: https://the-ndaca.org/the-people/liz-crow/

Lupton, D. (2023). "A History of Disability from a Disability Arts perspective." Disability Arts Online. Available at: https://disabilityarts.online/resources/research-and-learning/learning-topics/disability-arts-history/a-history-of-disability-from-a-disability-arts-perspective/

"Mixed reception for disability bill." *BBC News* (2003). Available at: http://news.bbc.co.uk/1/hi/uk/3288685.stm

Rocco, L. "Reflections on the Disability Arts Movement." Shape Arts.

BIBLIOGRAPHY

Available at: https://www.shapearts.org.uk/blog/reflections-on-the-disability-arts-movement
"Sian Vasey." National Disability Arts Collection and Archive. Available at: https://the-ndaca.org/the-people/sian-vasey/
Sutherland, A. (2012). "Paddy Masefield obituary." *The Guardian*. Available at: https://www.theguardian.com/society/2012/jul/24/paddy-masefield-obituary

Chapter 7: Cuts Kill

Black Activists Rising Against Cuts (2010). Available at: https://blackactivistsrisingagainstcuts.blogspot.com/
Briant et al (2011). "Bad News for Disabled People: How the newspapers are reporting disability." Strathclyde Centre for Disability Research and Glasgow Media Unit on behalf of Inclusion London. Available at: https://www.inclusionlondon.org.uk/wp-content/uploads/2015/09/bad-news-for-disabled-people-pdf.pdf
Butler, P. (2012). "How the Spartacus welfare cuts campaign went viral." *The Guardian*. Available at: https://www.theguardian.com/society/2012/jan/17/disability-spartacus-welfare-cuts-campaign-viral
———(2016). "Damian Green dismisses 'offensive' UN report on UK disability rights." *The Guardian*. Available at: https://www.theguardian.com/society/2016/nov/08/damian-green-dismisses-offensive-un-report-on-uk-disability-rights
Cameron, D. (2013). "Crazy situation where you earn more on benefits than you do at work ends NOW." *The Sun*. Available at: https://www.thesun.co.uk/archives/politics/649702/crazy-situation-where-you-earn-more-on-benefits-than-you-do-at-work-ends-now/
"Doctors demand end to work capability assessment." *Benefits and Work* (2012). Available at: https://www.benefitsandwork.co.uk/news/doctors-demand-end-to-work-capability-assessment
"DWP publishes Improving Lives: The Work, Health and Disability Green Paper." Death by Welfare (2016). Available at: https://deathsbywelfare.org/timeline/dwp-publishes-improving-lives-the-work-health-and-disability-green-paper/

BIBLIOGRAPHY

Gentleman, A. (2015). "After hated Atos quits, will Maximus make work assessments less arduous?" *The Guardian*. Available at: https://www.theguardian.com/society/2015/jan/18/after-hated-atos-quits-will-maximus-make-work-assessments-less-arduous

"Grave and systematic violations—our UN Inquiry briefing and responses." Inclusion London (2017). Available at: https://www.inclusionlondon.org.uk/campaigns-and-policy/facts-and-information/equality-and-human-rights/grave-systematic-violations-un-inquiry-briefing-responses/

Gregory, A. (2021). "Austerity in England linked to more than 50,000 extra deaths in five years." *The Guardian*. Available at: https://www.theguardian.com/society/2021/oct/14/austerity-in-england-linked-to-more-than-50000-extra-deaths-in-five-years

"House of Commons Hansard Debates for 15 June 1993." Hansard (1993). Available at: https://publications.parliament.uk/pa/cm199293/cmhansrd/1993-06-15/Orals-2.html

Iain Duncan Smith and Owen Jones, BBC Question Time (2012). Available at: https://www.youtube.com/watch?v=I2dJHLdbrBM

"Incapacity Benefit set for axe." *Daily Mirror* (2007). Available at: https://www.mirror.co.uk/news/uk-news/incapacity-benefit-set-for-axe-518511

Incapacity Benefits: Deaths of recipients. Department for Work and Pensions (2012). Available at: https://assets.publishing.service.gov.uk/government/uploads/system/uploads/attachment_data/file/223050/incap_decd_recips_0712.pdf

"Join the ATOS games!" Disabled People Against Cuts (2012). Available at: https://dpac.uk.net/2012/07/our-atos-games/

Lilley, P. (1992). "*I've got a little list*" speech. Found on the *Deaths by Welfare project*. Available at: https://deathsbywelfare.org/timeline/peter-lilley-secretary-of-state-for-social-security-talks-about-closing-down-the-something-for-nothing-society-and-tightening-up-on-scroungers-and-bogus/

McCardle, J. and Ward, G. (2010). *Black Triangle Campaign*. Available at: https://blacktrianglecampaign.org/about/

Mental Health Resistance Network (2010). Available at: https://mentalhealthresistance.org/

Milland, G. (2009). "75% on sickness benefits are faking." *The Express*.

BIBLIOGRAPHY

Available at: https://www.express.co.uk/news/uk/133880/75-on-sick-benefits-are-faking

Mills C. and Pring, J. (2021). "The Deaths by Welfare project." Healing Justice London. Available at: https://deathsbywelfare.org/

"Notable Black Activists in the Disability Canon." Shades of Noir (2023). Available at: https://shadesofnoir.org.uk/content/notable-black-activists-in-the-disability-canon/

Owen, G. (2016). "Controversial UN task force slams Britain's welfare cuts and says disabled people are 'unfairly bearing the brunt' of austerity." *Mail on Sunday*. Available at: https://www.dailymail.co.uk/news/article-3909276/Controversial-task-force-slams-Britain-s-welfare-cuts-says-disabled-people-unfairly-bearing-brunt.html

Pettinger, T. (2017). "UK Recession of 1991–92." Economics Help. Available at https://www.economicshelp.org/macroeconomics/economic-growth/uk-recession-1991/

Piggot, L. and Grover, C. (2009). "Retrenching Incapacity Benefit: Employment Support Allowance and Paid Work." *Social Policy & Society*. Cambridge University Press. Available at: https://eprints.lancs.ac.uk/id/eprint/28222/1/Retrenching_Incapacity_Benefit.pdf

Pring, J. (2010). "'Terrified' survivors burn Osborne effigy in cuts protest." *Disability News Service*. Available at: https://www.disabilitynewsservice.com/terrified-survivors-burn-osborne-effigy-in-cuts-protest/

——— (2010). "Spending cuts protest sparks birth of new campaign." *Disability News Service*. Available at: https://www.disabilitynewsservice.com/spending-cuts-protest-sparks-birth-of-new-campaign/

——— (2012). "Oxford Circus protest: Campaigners warn government of more direct action." *Disability News Service*. Available at: https://www.disabilitynewsservice.com/oxford-circus-protest-campaigners-warn-government-of-more-direct-action/

——— (2012). "Victory in first stage of 'fitness for work' court case." *Disability News Service*. Available at: https://www.disabilitynewsservice.com/victory-in-first-stage-of-fitness-for-work-court-case/

——— (2013). "Carpet of flowers turns Parliament Square into memorial to WCA victims." *Disability News Service*. Available at: https://www.disabili-

BIBLIOGRAPHY

tynewsservice.com/carpet-of-flowers-turns-parliament-square-into-memorial-to-wca-victims/

——— (2014). "WOW petition debate: Government refusal is due to 'fear of revolt'." *Disability News Service*. Available at: https://www.disabilitynewsservice.com/wow-petition-debate-government-refusal-is-due-to-fear-of-revolt/

——— (2016). "Shadow chancellor backs calls to prosecute Iain Duncan Smith over WCA deaths." *Disability News Service*. Available at: https://www.disabilitynewsservice.com/shadow-chancellor-backs-calls-to-prosecute-iain-duncan-smith-over-wca-deaths/

"Protestors throw 'Blair's blood'." *BBC News* (1997). Available at: http://news.bbc.co.uk/1/hi/uk/41746.stm

Ranson, J. (2019). "Artist Vince Laws brings his devastating attack on the DWP to a top arts venue." *The Canary*. Available at: https://www.thecanary.co/uk/2019/04/25/artist-vince-laws-brings-his-devastating-attack-on-the-dwp-to-a-top-arts-venue/

"Recovery in the Bin Welfare Training." Recovery in the Bin (2016). Available at: https://recoveryinthebin.org/2016/06/12/ritb-welfare-training-june-2016-part-1/

Rose, D. (2011), "Disability: The difficulties of the Hardest Hit." *BBC News*. Available at: https://www.bbc.co.uk/news/uk-15413935

Ryan, F. (2019). *Crippled: Austerity and the Demonization of Disabled People*. Verso.

Sue Marsh v Chris Grayling, *Newsnight* (2012). Available at: https://www.youtube.com/watch?v=S0RZyZKrIJg

Sylvester, R. and Thomson, A. (2008). "Welfare is a mess, says adviser David Freud." *The Daily Telegraph*. Available at: https://www.telegraph.co.uk/news/politics/1577313/Welfare-is-a-mess-says-adviser-David-Freud.html

"Unapologetic Cameron challenged by Andrew Marr over benefits deaths and ILF closure." *Benefits and Work* (2015). Available at: https://www.benefitsandwork.co.uk/news/unapologetic-cameron-challenged-by-andrew-marr-over-benefits-deaths-and-ilf-closure

"We are living in a shirkers paradise in the UK." Originally published in *The Sun*, 2010, referenced on Deaths by Welfare. Available at: https://deaths-

BIBLIOGRAPHY

bywelfare.org/timeline/the-sun-publishes-an-interview-with-iain-duncan-smith-on-benefits-britain/

Welfare Reform Act 2012. UK Public General Acts. Available at: https://www.legislation.gov.uk/ukpga/2012/5/contents

Wikeley, N. (1995). "The Social Security (Incapacity for Work) Act 1994." *The Modern Law Review, 58*. Available at: http://www.jstor.org/stable/1096460

Chapter 8: We Shall Not Be Removed

"A Tribute to Manjeet Kaur." Greater Manchester Coalition of Disabled People (2020). Available at: https://gmcdp.com/tribute-manjeet-kaur

Baker, K. (2022). "Government in court for no sign language at Covid briefings." *BBC News*. Available at: https://www.bbc.co.uk/news/disability-63010384

Bosworth, M. et al. (2021). "Deaths involving COVID-19 by self-reported disability status during the first two waves of the COVID-19 pandemic in England: a retrospective, population-based cohort study." *The Lancet Public Health, Volume 6, Issue 11*. Available at: https://www.thelancet.com/journals/lanpub/article/PIIS2468-26672100206-1/fulltext

Callard, F. and Perego, E. (2021). "How and why patients made Long Covid." *Social Science & Medicine*. Available at: https://pmc.ncbi.nlm.nih.gov/articles/PMC7539940/

Charlton-Dailey, R. (2020). "After disabled people were left to die, I'm terrified of a second wave of coronavirus." *Metro UK*. Available at: https://metro.co.uk/2020/11/02/disabled-people-coronavirus-second-wave-13503388/

—— (2020). "As a disabled person, my healthcare has been forgotten in the pandemic." *Stylist*. Available at: https://www.stylist.co.uk/opinion/disabled-healthcare-nhs-ignored/423005

—— (2020). "New lockdown restrictions are forcing disabled people to make a choice between health and career." *The Independent*. Available at: https://www.independent.co.uk/voices/disabled-lockdown-rules-shielding-unemployment-b1557985.html

—— (2020). "The coronavirus shutdown puts people using birth control

BIBLIOGRAPHY

and contraception at risk." *Metro UK*. Available at: https://metro.co.uk/2020/04/01/coronavirus-shutdown-puts-birth-control-contraception-risk-12484369/

—— (2021). "In The Midst Of The Pandemic, Have Politicians Done Enough For Disabled People?" *Each Other*. Available at: https://eachother.org.uk/in-the-midst-of-the-pandemic-have-politicians-done-enough-for-disabled-people/

—— (2021). "This Is Not Freedom Day for Vulnerable Disabled People Like Me." *The Spill*. Available at: https://www.thespillmag.com/article/this-is-not-freedom-day-for-vulnerable-disabled-people-like-me/

—— (2021). "What Long COVID Awareness Means for People with Chronic Illnesses." *VeryWell Health*. Available at: https://www.verywellhealth.com/long-covid-chronic-illness-research-5201370

—— (2021). "Working From Home Levels the Playing Field for Disabled People. Why are Businesses so Intent on Returning to the Office?" Rooted in Rights. Available at: https://rootedinrights.org/working-from-home-levels-the-playing-field-for-disabled-people-why-are-businesses-so-intent-on-returning-to-the-office/

—— (2022). "Matt Hancock going on I'm a Celeb is a kick in the teeth for disabled people." *Daily Mirror*. Available at: https://www.mirror.co.uk/news/politics/matt-hancock-going-im-celeb-28383052

—— (2023). "Disabled people still feel a collective trauma from start of Covid pandemic." *Daily Mirror*. Available at: https://www.mirror.co.uk/news/politics/disabled-people-still-feel-collective-31338057

—— (2023). "Lockdown files show how the Government let disabled people die. We need to examine that." *Daily Mirror*. Available at: https://www.mirror.co.uk/news/uk-news/lockdown-files-show-how-government-29456746

—— (2023). "NHS covid app closing next month, but pandemic is far from over for disabled people." *Daily Mirror*. Available at: https://www.mirror.co.uk/news/health/nhs-covid-app-closing-next-29574460

—— (2023). "Tories laughed behind our backs during lockdown—we won't let them forget." *Daily Mirror*. Available at: https://www.mirror.co.uk/news/politics/tories-laughed-behind-backs-during-30280187

BIBLIOGRAPHY

—— (2023). "Tories want us to act like Covid is normal now—we must keep protecting each other." *Daily Mirror*. Available at: https://www.mirror.co.uk/news/politics/tories-want-act-like-covid-30788555

"Coronavirus (COVID-19) and the impact on disabled people." Welsh Government (2021). Available at: https://www.gov.wales/coronavirus-covid-19-and-impact-disabled-people-html

"Covid: Deaf woman wins claim over lack of sign language at briefings." *BBC News* (2021). Available at: https://www.bbc.co.uk/news/uk-england-leeds-57998047

"Covid-19 Timeline." British Foreign Policy Group (2021). Available at: https://bfpg.co.uk/2020/04/covid-19-timeline/

"Do Not Attempt Cardiopulmonary Resuscitation DNACPR letter 3 April 2020." NHS England (2020). Available at: https://www.england.nhs.uk/coronavirus/documents/do-not-attempt-cardiopulmonary-resuscitation-dnacpr-letter-3-april-2020/

Elgot, J. and Booth, R. (2021). "Pressure mounts on Johnson over alleged 'let the bodies pile high' remarks." *The Guardian*. Available at: https://www.theguardian.com/politics/2021/apr/26/pressure-mounts-on-boris-johnson-over-alleged-let-the-bodies-pile-high-remarks

Kavanagh, A. (2020). *The Staying Inn*. Available at: https://www.thestayinginn.org.uk/

Lasker, A. (2024). "Covid is doing the rounds again—here's everything you need to know about the new rules." *The Telegraph*. Available at: https://www.telegraph.co.uk/health-fitness/conditions/cold-flu/covid-rules-2024-what-to-do-if-test-positive/

"Long-term effects of COVID-19 (long COVID)." NHS England. Available at: https://www.nhs.uk/conditions/covid-19/long-term-effects-of-covid-19-long-covid/#:~:text=What%20is%20long%20COVID%3F,or%20post%20COVID%2D19%20syndrome

Lott-Lavigna, R. (2023). "Vallance: Sunak likely knew 'Eat Out to Help Out' would drive Covid infections." *Open Democracy*. Available at: https://www.opendemocracy.net/en/covid-19-inquiry-patrick-vallance-rishi-sunak-eat-out-help-out-infections/

"Lynn Stewart-Taylor." Where is The Interpreter campaign, WheelieQueer

BIBLIOGRAPHY

(2020). Available at: https://www.wheeliequeer.net/post/lynn-stewart-taylor-where-is-the-interpreter-campaign.

McGrath, D. (2023). "Boris Johnson denies using 'let the bodies pile high' phrase during pandemic." *The Independent*. Available at: https://www.independent.co.uk/news/uk/boris-johnson-dominic-cummings-protesters-lord-london-b2460644.html

"National Covid Memorial Wall." Covid Bereaved Families for Justice. Available at: https://www.nationalcovidmemorialwall.org/

Pring, J. (2020). "Coronavirus: Lack of engagement with DPOs 'has led to bad policies.'" *Disability News Service*. Available at: https://www.disabilitynewsservice.com/coronavirus-lack-of-engagement-with-dpos-has-led-to-bad-policies/

——— (2020). "Seán McGovern: Tributes paid to 'principled and tenacious fighter for rights.'" *Disability News Service*. Available at: https://www.disabilitynewsservice.com/sean-mcgovern-tributes-paid-to-principled-and-tenacious-fighter-for-rights/

——— (2022). "Roger Lewis: Kindness, decency and dedication to fighting oppression." *Disability News Service*. Available at: https://www.disabilitynewsservice.com/roger-lewis-kindness-decency-and-dedication-to-fighting-oppression/

Ryan, F. (2021). "'We feel forgotten': high-risk groups missed off UK's vaccine priority list." *The Guardian*. Available at: https://www.theguardian.com/society/2021/feb/12/we-feel-forgotten-high-risk-groups-missed-off-uks-vaccine-priority-list

Tapper, J. (2021). "Fury at 'do not resuscitate' notices given to Covid patients with learning disabilities." *The Guardian*. Available at: https://www.theguardian.com/world/2021/feb/13/new-do-not-resuscitate-orders-imposed-on-covid-19-patients-with-learning-difficulties

"The pandemic's true death toll." *The Economist* (2022). Available at: https://www.economist.com/graphic-detail/coronavirus-excess-deaths-estimates

UK health indicators: 2019 to 2020. Office for National Statistics (2022). Available at: https://www.ons.gov.uk/peoplepopulationandcommunity/healthandsocialcare/healthandlifeexpectancies/bulletins/ukhealthindicators/2019to2020

BIBLIOGRAPHY

Updated estimates of coronavirus (COVID-19) related deaths by disability status, England: 24 January to 20 November 2020. Office for National Statistics (2020). Available at: https://www.ons.gov.uk/peoplepopulationandcommunity/birthsdeathsandmarriages/deaths/articles/coronaviruscovid19relateddeathsbydisabilitystatusenglandandwales/24januaryto20november2020

"We Shall Not Be Removed." UK Disability Arts Alliance (2020). Available at: https://www.weshallnotberemoved.com/

Williams, S. (2024). "Long Covid has left me feeling worthless and invisible—and Labour is making it worse." *The Canary*. Available at: https://www.thecanary.co/opinion/2024/11/19/long-covid-uk/

Chapter 9: Heating or Eating

Buckingham, H. (2024). "Most people who use food banks are disabled. We can do better than this—and we must." *Big Issue*. Available at: https://www.bigissue.com/opinion/disabled-people-food-banks-trussell-trust/

Chaplain, C. (2024). "Housing benefits wiped out by soaring rents—as Reeves faces pressure to help." *iNews*. Available at: https://inews.co.uk/news/politics/reeves-pressure-housing-benefit-soaring-rents-3395989

Charlton-Dailey, R. (2023). "Disabled people are missing out on the government's cost of living payments. This needs to change." *Big Issue*. Available at: https://www.bigissue.com/opinion/disabled-people-are-missing-out-on-the-governments-cost-of-living-payments-this-needs-to-change/

—— (2023). "DWP crowing about extra disabled cost of living payment—but it barely scratches surface." *Daily Mirror*. Available at: https://www.mirror.co.uk/news/politics/dwp-crowing-extra-disabled-cost-30291428

—— (2023). "I tried to buy a Christmas dinner with my DWP bonus—it was a disaster." *Daily Mirror*. Available at: https://www.mirror.co.uk/news/uk-news/dwp-christmas-bonus-10-2023-31602686

—— (2023). "It's time the government stepped up to help disabled people in the cost of living crisis." *Big Issue*. Available at: https://www.bigissue.com/opinion/cost-of-living-crisis-its-time-the-government-stepped-up-to-help-disabled-people/

—— (2023). "Labour blames disability benefits fraud and error for lack of

BIBLIOGRAPHY

Cost of Living Support—but they're demonising the wrong people." *Daily Mirror*. Available at: https://www.mirror.co.uk/news/politics/labour-blames-disability-benefits-fraud-29682877

—— (2023). "No one should have to ask whether they can 'do without' medication. But that's where we are as a country." *Big Issue*. Available at: https://www.bigissue.com/opinion/prescription-charges-no-one-should-have-to-ask-whether-they-can-do-without-medication-but-thats-where-we-are-as-a-country/

—— (2024). "Disabled people urge Kendall and Reeves not to go ahead with dangerous WCA changes." *The Canary*. Available at: https://www.thecanary.co/uk/news/2024/10/28/dwp-wca-changes-budget/

—— (2024). "DWP sparks protests by disability activists over benefit sanctions and 'inhumane deaths.'" *Big Issue*. Available at: https://www.bigissue.com/news/social-justice/disabled-dwp-protests-benefit-deaths/

—— (2025). "DWP WCA consultation broke the law—yet Labour planning on making the Tories' changes, anyway." *The Canary*. Available at: https://www.thecanary.co/uk/analysis/2025/01/16/dwp-wca-court-verdict/

"Disability Price Tag 2024." Scope. Available at: https://www.scope.org.uk/campaigns/disability-price-tag

El Dessouky, O. and McCurdy, C. (2023). "Costly differences: Living standards for working-age people with disabilities." Resolution Foundation. Available at: https://www.resolutionfoundation.org/app/uploads/2023/01/Costly-differences.pdf

Elliott, J. and Schmuecker, J. (2023). "On a low income, but not claiming means-tested benefits." Joseph Rowntree Foundation. Available at: https://www.jrf.org.uk/social-security/on-a-low-income-but-not-claiming-means-tested-benefits

Essential Digital Skills Report 2021. Lloyds Bank. Available at: https://www.lloydsbank.com/assets/media/pdfs/banking_with_us/whats-happening/210923-lb-essential-digital-skills-2021-report.pdf

Faith, B. et al (2022). *Digital Poverty in the UK*. Institute of Developmental Studies. Available at: https://opendocs.ids.ac.uk/artlicles/report/Digital_Poverty_in_the_UK/26428945?file=48182248

BIBLIOGRAPHY

Hourston, P. (2022). "Cost of Living Crisis" explainer. Institute for Government. Available at: https://www.instituteforgovernment.org.uk/explainer/cost-living-crisis

Impact of increased cost of living on adults across Great Britain: June to September 2022. Office for National Statistics (2022). Available at: https://www.ons.gov.uk/peoplepopulationandcommunity/personalandhouseholdfinances/expenditure/articles/impactofincreasedcostoflivingonadultsacrossgreatbritain/junetoseptember2022

Jayanetti, C. (2024). "DWP benefit reforms to get people into work are 'smokescreen for cuts', disability activist says." *Big Issue.* Available at: https://www.bigissue.com/news/social-justice/dwp-disability-benefit-reforms-cuts/

Johnson-Hunter, M. et al (2024). "No end in sight for living standards crisis: JRF's cost of living tracker, winter 2024." Joseph Rowntree Foundation. Available at: https://www.jrf.org.uk/cost-of-living/jrfs-cost-of-living-tracker-winter-2024

"Liz Kendall: Don't Continue With WCA Cuts, Disabled People Against Cuts." Disabled People Against Cuts, UK DDPO CRDP et al (2024). Available at: https://dpac.uk.net/2024/10/uk-ddpo-crdp-coalition-and-others-urge-the-government-to-not-continue-cuts-to-the-wca-as-part-of-the-autumn-budget/

"The cost of living impacts access to prescription medicines says RPS." The Royal Pharmaceutical Society (2023). Available at: https://www.rpharms.com/about-us/news/details/the-cost-of-living-impacts-access-to-prescription-medicines-says-rpS

The National Minimum Wage in 2023. Low Pay Commission (2023). Available at: https://www.gov.uk/government/publications/low-pay-commission-report-2022

Chapter 10: Don't Make Me the Problem

Boffey, D. (2024). "Tory Covid contracts worth £15bn had corruption 'red flags', study finds." *The Guardian.* Available at: https://www.theguardian.com/politics/article/2024/sep/09/tory-covid-contracts-worth-15bn-had-corruption-red-flags-study-finds

BIBLIOGRAPHY

Brooks, H-A. (2024). "Why Dragons' Den's latest episode was so damaging." *Digital Spy*. Available at: https://www.digitalspy.com/tv/reality-tv/a46456849/dragons-den-ear-seeds/

Charlton-Dailey, R. (2023), "Email template to complain about ADHD stories." Available at: https://docs.google.com/document/d/1UqjFPzVc5k7LgIvGBQYbBj64kLvj4_t2Y1-XbETN0hk/edit?usp=sharing

—— (2023). "BBC's *A Kind of Spark* is groundbreaking in its portrayal of autistic women." *Digital Spy*. Available at: https://www.digitalspy.com/tv/a43451800/a-kind-of-spark-bbc-review-autism/

—— (2023). "DWP still pushing dangerous 'benefit fraud crackdown.'" *Daily Mirror*. Available at: https://www.mirror.co.uk/news/politics/dwp-still-pushing-dangerous-benefit-30085859

—— (2023). "Press Regulator must create guidelines for reporting disability—or the media will never become less ableist," *Daily Mirror*. Available at: https://www.mirror.co.uk/news/uk-news/press-regulator-create-guidelines-reporting-29286578

—— (2023). "Scope says the media must stop 'destructive disability narrative'—and I agree." *Daily Mirror*. Available at: https://www.mirror.co.uk/news/politics/scope-says-media-must-stop-30113136

—— (2023). "Tories are doing their best to make disabled people the enemy of the taxpayer.'" *Daily Mirror*. Available at: https://www.mirror.co.uk/news/politics/tories-doing-best-make-disabled-31096904

—— (2023). Update on IPSO campaign tweet. Available at: https://x.com/RachelCDailey/status/1629056050774122499

—— (2024). "*A Kind of Spark*'s Ella Maisy Purvis on show's portrayal of complex autistic characters." *Digital Spy*. Available at: https://www.digitalspy.com/tv/a60615161/a-kind-of-spark-season-2-ella-maisy-purvis/

—— (2024). "*Doctor Who*'s Ruth Madeley doubles down on the show's inclusive spirit." *Digital Spy*. Available at: https://www.digitalspy.com/tv/a45983391/doctor-who-shirley-disability/

Code Review: 2023 Editors' Code of Practice Review Report. Editor's Code (2023). Available at: https://editorscode.org.uk/the-code/code-reviews/code-review-2023/

Disability and Crime. Office for National Statistics (2019). Available at:

BIBLIOGRAPHY

https://www.ons.gov.uk/peoplepopulationandcommunity/healthandsocialcare/disability/bulletins/disabilityandcrimeuk/2019#domestic-abuse

Disabled Survivors Too: Disabled people and domestic abuse. SafeLives (2017). Available at: https://safelives.org.uk/research-policy-library/disabled-survivors-too/

"Dragon's Den Series 21 Ratings." Wikipedia (2024). Available at: https://en.wikipedia.org/wiki/Dragons%27_Den_(British_TV_programme)#Series_21

Dupont, C. (2023). "Journalist and editor calls for action to stop ableist reporting in the UK media." Journalism.co.uk. Available at: https://www.journalism.co.uk/news/journalist-and-editor-calls-for-action-to-prevent-ableist-reporting-in-the-uk-media/s2/a1008154/

Glaze, B. (2023). "Rob Burrow's wife joins calls for heroic pal Kevin Sinfield to be knighted." *Daily Mirror*. Available at: https://www.mirror.co.uk/news/uk-news/rob-burrows-wife-joins-calls-30170788

Goldbart, M. (2021). "'Help' Writer Jack Thorne: 'Radical Thinking' Could Make British TV And Film Industry 'World Leader' On Disability." *Deadline*. Available at: https://deadline.com/2021/12/thorne-radical-thinking-disability-1234883405/

Greenslade, R. (2016). "NUJ backs Impress, calling Ipso a 'pointless so-called regulator.'" *The Guardian*. Available at: https://www.theguardian.com/media/greenslade/2016/apr/29/nuj-backs-impress-calling-ipso-a-pointless-so-called-regulator

Hope, R. (2024). "Dragon's Den episode edited after complaints over 'unfounded' claims about treatment of ME." *Sky News*. Available at: https://news.sky.com/story/dragons-den-episode-edited-after-complaints-over-unfounded-claims-about-treatment-of-me-13058392

"Jeremy Vine's C5 show asked if we should stop benefits for people too sick to work—13 favourite responses." *The Poke* (2023). Available at: https://www.thepoke.com/2023/05/26/jeremy-vine-channel-5-benefits/

Lawson, D. (2023). "I'm sorry but all this ADHD doesn't add up." *The Times*. Available at: https://www.thetimes.com/article/all-this-adhd-doesnt-add-up-comment-vqvl9kqvn

Lloyd, T. et al (2021). "The Majority of Women with ADHD are Being Left

BIBLIOGRAPHY

Behind by the Health System." The ADHD Foundation. Available at: https://www.adhdfoundation.org.uk/wp-content/uploads/2021/10/Women-With-ADHD-Call-To-Action.pdf

Mills, K. (2023). "Inside home of teenager found dead in squalor 'after parents let her weight hit 23st.'" *Daily Mirror*. Available at: https://www.mirror.co.uk/news/uk-news/inside-home-teenager-found-dead-29126941

Naish, J. (2023). "Why are so many adults now being diagnosed with ADHD?" *Daily Mail*. Available at: https://www.dailymail.co.uk/health/article-11693601/amp/Why-adults-diagnosed-ADHD-depth-look-condition.html

Parker, M. (2022). "*EastEnders*—Frankie Lewis's attack storyline will help disabled women everywhere." *Digital Spy*. Available at: https://www.digitalspy.com/soaps/eastenders/a41241383/eastenders-frankie-attack-storyline-disability/

—— (2022). "Soap fans reflect on how well storylines reflected their disabilities." *Metro UK*. Available at: https://metro.co.uk/2022/06/19/soap-fans-reflect-on-how-well-storylines-reflected-their-disabilities-16840935/

—— (2023). "Izzy's return to *Coronation Street* after shielding resonates with many disabled people." *Metro UK*. Available at: https://metro.co.uk/2023/01/20/izzys-return-to-coronation-street-resonates-with-disabled-people-18132399/

Partington, R. (2023). "Tax collectors lack ambition, say MPs, as £42bn remains unpaid." *The Guardian*. Available at: https://www.theguardian.com/politics/2023/jan/11/tax-collectors-lack-ambition-say-mps-as-42bn-remains-unpaid

Pring, J. (2023). "Media must be pressured to stop disability discrimination, conference hears." *Disability News Service*. Available at: https://www.disabilitynewsservice.com/media-must-be-pressured-to-stop-disability-discrimination-conference-hears/

Scope on X (Formerly Twitter) (2023). Available at: https://x.com/scope/status/1662025729297481728

Smith, E. (2024). "Hannah Cockroft 'scared' to be disabled in Britain after government decision." *BBC Sport*. Available at: https://www.bbc.co.uk/sport/disability-sport/67984423

BIBLIOGRAPHY

——— (2023). "What should living standards look like for people on benefits, minimum wage, and average earnings?" YouGov. Available at: https://yougov.co.uk/society/articles/45956-what-should-living-standards-look-people-benefits-

Sophie Morgan tweet (2023) posted on Twitter. Available at: https://x.com/sophmorgtv/status/1632011683483774976

Spilsbury, M. (2023). *Diversity in Journalism: An update on the characteristics of journalists*. National Council for the Training of Journalists. Available at: https://www.nctj.com/news/characteristics-of-uk-journalists-examined-in-new-diversity-report

The Editors' Code of Practice. IPSO. Available at: https://www.ipso.co.uk/editors-code-of-practice/

The IMPRESS Standards Code. IMPRESS. Available at: https://www.impress-org.com/standards/impress-standards-code/our-standards-code/

The Unwritten (now offline). Formerly available at: https://theunwritten.co.uk

Young, S. (2014). *I am not your inspiration, thank you very much*. TedX Sydney. Available at: https://www.ted.com/talks/stella_young_i_m_not_your_inspiration_thank_you_very_much/transcript

Zayed, Y. (2024). *TV Licence Fee Statistics*. House of Commons Library. Available at: https://researchbriefings.files.parliament.uk/documents/CBP-8101/CBP-8101.pdf

Chapter 11: A Decent Life

999 phone registration. Deaflink. Available at: https://www.deaflink.org.uk/bsl/services/information/999-phone-registration

"Access for All—improving accessibility at railway stations nationwide." Network Rail. Available at: https://www.networkrail.co.uk/communities/passengers/station-improvements/access-for-all-improving-accessibility-at-railway-stations-nationwide/

"Almost half of Grenfell fire deaths were Disabled people and children." Disability Rights UK (2019). Available at: https://www.disabilityrightsuk.org/news/2021/march/almost-half-grenfell-fire-deaths-were-disabled-people-and-children

Bristol City Council Fair and Affordable Care Policy (draft) (2024). Available

BIBLIOGRAPHY

at: https://files.smartsurvey.io/3/0/B218NC38/Bristol_City_Council_Fair_And_Affordable_Care_Policy_draft_v11.pdf

"Campaign victory: Plans to close rail ticket offices are officially scrapped." Transport For All (2023). Available at: https://www.transportforall.org.uk/news/campaign-victory-plans-to-close-rail-ticket-offices-are-officially-scrapped/

Charlton-Dailey, R. (2022). "I'm Blind but a hotel kicked us out as I 'didn't look disabled'." *Daily Mirror* (print).

—— (2023). "Closing train station ticket offices will stop disabled people from travelling safely'." *Daily Mirror*. Available at: https://www.mirror.co.uk/news/uk-news/closing-train-station-ticket-offices-30339321

—— (2023). "It's vital for disabled people that you oppose train station ticket office closures." *Daily Mirror*. Available at: https://www.mirror.co.uk/news/politics/its-vital-disabled-people-you-30559628

—— (2023). "Woman claims 'Premier Inn would've left me to die in fire because I'm a wheelchair user'." *Daily Mirror*. Available at: https://www.mirror.co.uk/news/uk-news/woman-claims-premier-inn-wouldve-29530574

—— (2024). "Disabled people march on Downing Street to demand accessible housing." *The Canary*. Available at: https://www.thecanary.co/uk/analysis/2024/08/02/accessible-housing-protest/

—— (2024). "Tanni Grey-Thompson's transport nightmare is a waking reality for most disabled people." *The Canary*. Available at: https://www.thecanary.co/opinion/2024/08/29/tanni-grey-thompson/

Clarke, H. and Standley, N. (2023). "Disability campaigners lose legal fight over Grenfell recommendation." *BBC News*. Available at: https://www.bbc.co.uk/news/disability-63839447

"Climate adaptation: appeal considered after High Court rejects legal challenge over government plan." Friends of the Earth (2024). Available at: https://friendsoftheearth.uk/climate/climate-adaptation-appeal-considered-after-high-court-rejects-legal-challenge-over

Disability in Asia and the Pacific: The Facts. UNESCAP. Available at: https://www.unescap.org/sites/default/files/Disability%20The%20Facts.pdf

DPTAC reference frame: working towards a fully accessible railway. Disabled

BIBLIOGRAPHY

Persons Transport Advisory Committee (2022). Department for Transport. Available at: https://www.gov.uk/government/publications/dptac-reference-frame-working-towards-a-fully-accessible-railway/dptac-reference-frame-working-towards-a-fully-accessible-railway

English Housing Survey 2018–19: Accessibility of English homes. UK Government. Available at: https://assets.publishing.service.gov.uk/government/uploads/system/uploads/attachment_data/file/898205/2018–19_EHS_Adaptations_and_Accessability_Fact_Sheet.pdf

Equality Act 2010. UK Public General Acts. Available at: https://www.legislation.gov.uk/ukpga/2010/15/contents

Evennett, H. (2022). *The Equality Act 2010: Impact on disabled people.* House of Lords library. Available at: https://lordslibrary.parliament.uk/the-equality-act-2010-impact-on-disabled-people/

Extra burden of energy among disabled households. Scope (2023). Available at: https://www.scope.org.uk/campaigns/research-policy/extra-burden-of-energy-disabled-households

Geen, E. (2024). "A green future is possible, but only if Disabled people are invited in, Bristol 24/7." *Bristol 24/7.* Available at: https://www.bristol247.com/opinion/your-say/a-green-future-is-possible-but-only-if-disabled-people-are-invited-in/

Habinteg (2023). *Living not existing: The economic value and social value of wheelchair user homes.* Available at: https://www.habinteg.org.uk/download.cfm?doc=docm93jijm4n3930.pdf&ver=4904

Houchen, A. (2023). "Only 22% of London's Tube stations have fully accessible trains." *SW Londoner.* Available at: https://www.swlondoner.co.uk/news/21072023-only-22-of-londons-tube-stations-have-fully-accessible-trains

Lomas, K. (2021). "Disabled councillors face discrimination from City of York Council." York Disability Rights Forum. Available at: https://ydrf.org.uk/2021/07/16/disabled-councillers-face-discrimination-from-city-of-york-council/

Pring, J. (2024). "Disabled campaigners call on government to take seven key steps in response to final Grenfell report." *Disability News Service.* Available at: https://www.disabilitynewsservice.com/disabled-campaigners-call-on-government-to-take-seven-key-steps-in-response-to-final-grenfell-report/

BIBLIOGRAPHY

——— (2024). "Labour's watered-down policy on high-rise evacuation 'is insult to disabled people who died in Grenfell fire.'" *Disability News Service*. Available at: https://www.disabilitynewsservice.com/labours-watered-down-policy-on-high-rise-evacuation-is-insult-to-disabled-people-who-died-in-grenfell-fire/

Ryan, F. (2024). "Think of this: a plan to 'warehouse' disabled people. What kind of nation is Britain becoming?" *The Guardian*. Available at: https://www.theguardian.com/commentisfree/2024/jan/25/warehouse-disabled-people-bristol-city-council

"Save Ticket Offices" campaign. RMT Union (2023). Available at: https://www.rmt.org.uk/campaigns/rail/save-ticket-offices/

The Hidden Housing Market. Habiteng and Papworth Trust (2016). Available at: https://www.habinteg.org.uk/download.cfm?doc=docm93jijm4n1527

"Wheelchair users subjected to decades-long wait for new accessible housing." Habinteg (2022). Available at: https://www.habinteg.org.uk/latest-news/wheelchair-users-subjected-to-decadeslong-wait-for-new-accessible-housing-2004/

Chapter 12: Does the Minister Really Think This Is Supporting People?

Academic year 2023/24—Special educational needs in England. Explore Education Statistics; Department for Education (2024). Available at: https://explore-education-statistics.service.gov.uk/find-statistics/special-educational-needs-in-england

"Access to Work: get support if you have a disability or health condition." Department for Work and Pensions (2019). Available at: https://www.gov.uk/access-to-work

Brewer, M. and Murphy, L. (2024). *Cutbacks ahead: Considering the impact of proposed changes to disability benefits on living standards and the public finances*. Resolution Foundation. Available at: https://www.resolutionfoundation.org/publications/cutbacks-ahead/

Brione, P. et al (2025). "Employment Rights Bill 2024–25: Progress of the bill." House of Commons Library. Available at: https://commonslibrary.parliament.uk/research-briefings/cbp-10174/

BIBLIOGRAPHY

Campbell, G. (2023). "Lowestoft deaf teen pleased British Sign Language to be taught as GCSE." *BBC News*. Available at: https://www.bbc.co.uk/news/uk-england-suffolk-67780306

Charlton-Dailey, R. (2020). "Working and Studying at Home Shouldn't Be Pandemic-Only Accommodations." *Rooted in Rights*. Available at: https://rootedinrights.org/working-and-studying-at-home-shouldnt-be-pandemic-only-accommodations/

——— (2021). "How the Pandemic Helped a Disability Journalist Find Her Groove." *VeryWell Health*. Available at: https://www.verywellhealth.com/pandemic-public-speaking-disabled-5198096

——— (2023). "DWP are telling lies in the Work Capability Assessment consultation." *Daily Mirror*. Available at: https://www.mirror.co.uk/news/politics/dwp-telling-lies-work-capability-31278923

——— (2024). "Disabled people earn £4,300 less a year—but Labour STILL want to force us into work." *The Canary*. Available at: https://www.thecanary.co/uk/analysis/2024/11/07/disability-pay-gap-day/

——— (2024). "Minister reveals the DWP is even sh*tter than we thought." *The Canary*. Available at: https://www.thecanary.co/opinion/2024/05/19/dwp-minister-access-to-work/

Civil Service People Survey: 2023 results, Government efficiency, transparency and accountability. Cabinet Office (2024). Available at: https://www.gov.uk/government/publications/civil-service-people-survey-2023-results

Clare, S. (2017). "Disabled 'losing out on jobs' over Access to Work cap." *BBC News*. Available at: https://www.bbc.co.uk/news/uk-41722225

Clement, C. (2024). "Labour's Mental Health Act reforms will not go far enough towards dignity or real support." *The Canary*. Available at: https://www.thecanary.co/opinion/2024/11/07/mental-health-act-reforms-autism/

Darling, S. (2024). "Access to Work Programme: Question for Department for Work and Pensions, Written questions, answers and statements." Available at: https://questions-statements.parliament.uk/written-questions/detail/2024-10-04/6749

"Disability facts and figures." Department for Work and Pensions (2014). Available at: https://www.gov.uk/government/statistics/disability-facts-and-figures/disability-facts-and-figures

BIBLIOGRAPHY

"Disability pay gap reaches staggering level of £4,300 a year." TUC (2024). Available at: https://www.tuc.org.uk/news/tuc-disability-pay-gap-reaches-staggering-level-ps4300-year

Educational attainment. RNIB (2023). Available at: https://www.rnib.org.uk/professionals/health-social-care-education-professionals/knowledge-and-research-hub/reports-and-insight/educational-attainment-2023/

Employment for blind and partially sighted people in 2019. RNIB (2020). Available at: https://www.rnib.org.uk/professionals/health-social-care-education-professionals/knowledge-and-research-hub/reports-and-insight/employment-for-blind-and-partially-sighted-people-in-2019/

Hall, R. (2022). "'Funding black hole': councils grapple with 'catastrophic' debt for SEN children." *The Guardian*. Available at: https://www.theguardian.com/education/2022/jul/28/funding-black-hole-councils-grapple-with-catastrophic-debt-for-sen-children

Johnson-Hunter, M. (2023). "Our social security system must support households with a disabled person to afford the essentials." Joseph Rowntree Foundation. Available at: https://www.jrf.org.uk/cost-of-living/our-social-security-system-must-support-households-with-a-disabled-person-to-afford/

Jones, E. (2024). Linkedin post about Access to Work. Available at: https://www.linkedin.com/posts/ellen--jones_accesstowork-hr-employeewellbeing-activity-7260257041619808257-46C6/

Keer, M. (2020). "95% of decisions in favour of parents, but nobody wins at the SEND Tribunal." *Special Needs Jungle*. Available at: https://www.specialneedsjungle.com/95-decisions-favour-parents-nobody-wins-send-tribunal

——— (2021). "Councils wasted £253 million fighting parents at the SEND Tribunal since 2014 reforms." *Special Needs Jungle*. Available at: https://www.specialneedsjungle.com/councils-wasted-253-million-fighting-parents-send-tribunal-2014-reforms/

Langford, E. (2020). "DWP lost more disability discrimination cases than any other UK employer, investigation reveals." *Civil Service World*. Available at: https://www.civilserviceworld.com/professions/article/dwp-lost-more-disability-discrimination-cases-than-any-other-uk-employer-investigation-reveals

BIBLIOGRAPHY

"Number of autistic people in mental health hospitals: latest data." National Autistic Society (2024). Available at: https://www.autism.org.uk/what-we-do/news/number-of-autistic-people-in-mental-health-ho-24

"Our Manifesto." British Deaf Association (2024). Available at: https://bda.org.uk/our-manifesto/

Outcomes for disabled people in the UK: 2021. ONS (2021). Available at: https://www.ons.gov.uk/peoplepopulationandcommunity/healthandsocialcare/disability/articles/outcomesfordisabledpeopleintheuk/2021

Prevalence of British Sign Language. RNID (2021). Available at: https://rnid.org.uk/get-involved/research-and-policy/facts-and-figures/prevalence-of-british-sign-language/

Rose, B. (2019). "Disabled Students' Allowances: Over half of eligible students miss out." *BBC News*. Available at: https://www.bbc.co.uk/news/disability-47651296

Schendel-Wilson, C. and Stage, K. (2022). *The State of the Nation in SEND Education: England.* Disability Policy Centre. Available at: https://static1.squarespace.com/static/619e1d7a522f9748f55d6a17/t/636ba10fbeccb906440b3456/1667997969482/SEND+Education+England.pdf

Scott, J. (2023). "Public have 'duty' to work, says minister—as benefits shake-up looms." *Sky News*. Available at: https://news.sky.com/story/autumn-statement-public-have-duty-to-work-says-minister-as-benefits-shake-up-looms-13012681

Signal, N. (2017). "Children with disabilities are being denied equal opportunities for a quality education across the world, including in the UK." University of Cambridge. Available at: https://www.cam.ac.uk/research/news/children-with-disabilities-are-being-denied-equal-opportunities-for-a-quality-education-across-the/

SPANC21 Reporting on Disability. Student Publication Association (2021). Available at: https://www.youtube.com/watch?v=daAdAdxH8_g

Weale, S. and McIntyre, N. (2018). "Thousands of children with special needs excluded from schools." *The Guardian*. Available at: https://www.theguardian.com/education/2018/oct/23/send-special-educational-needs-children-excluded-from-schools

BIBLIOGRAPHY

Chapter 13: Assist Us To Live

Abortion Act 1967. UK Public General Acts. Available at: https://www.legislation.gov.uk/ukpga/1967/87/section/1

Boer, T. (2024). *Written evidence submitted to the committee*. Available at: https://committees.parliament.uk/writtenevidence/117110/pdf/

Carr, L. (2024). *Better off dead? BBC Two*. Available at: https://www.bbc.co.uk/programmes/m001z8wc

Charlton-Dailey, R. (2021). "Spectrum 10k: Why Some Autistic People Are Hesitant About the New Autism Study." *VeryWell Health*. Available at: https://www.verywellhealth.com/why-autistic-people-are-against-spectrum-10k-5199849

——— (2022). "As a pro-choice, disabled woman, I'm torn over why late terminations are legal if the foetus is potentially disabled." *Glamour*. Available at: https://www.glamourmagazine.co.uk/article/heidi-crowter-court-of-appeal-verdict-opinion

——— (2022). "How pro-life campaigners hijacked Heidi Crowter's fight against aborting disabled foetuses." *iNews*. Available at: https://inews.co.uk/opinion/pro-life-campaigners-hijacked-heidi-crowter-aborting-disabled-foetuses-2000505

——— (2022). "Why Channel 4's Disability & Abortion: The Hardest Choice documentary is a hard but important watch." *Stylist*. Available at: https://www.stylist.co.uk/entertainment/disability-and-abortion-the-hardest-choice-channel-4-ruth-madeley-review/699122

Choice at the End of Life bill—briefing from UK DDPO CRDP Monitoring Coalition, DPAC. UK DDPO CRDP Monitoring Coalition (2024). Available at: https://dpac.uk.net/2024/10/choice-at-the-end-of-life-bill-briefing-from-uk-ddpo-crdp-monitoring-coalition/

Elgot, J. (2024). "Mass advertising campaigns on assisted dying spark anger among MPs." *The Guardian*. Available at: https://www.theguardian.com/society/2024/nov/26/mass-advertising-campaigns-on-assisted-dying-spark-anger-among-mps

"Eugenics in Britain." English Heritage. Available at: https://www.english-heritage.org.uk/visit/blue-plaques/blue-plaque-stories/eugenics/

"Euthanasia Program and Aktion T4." Holocaust Encyclopedia. Available at: https://encyclopedia.ushmm.org/content/en/article/euthanasia-program

BIBLIOGRAPHY

Fifth Annual Report on Medical Assistance in Dying in Canada. Health Canada (2023). Available at: https://www.canada.ca/en/health-canada/services/publications/health-system-services/annual-report-medical-assistance-dying-2023.html

Fox, A. (2016). "Why Autism Speaks Dropped The Word 'Cure' From Its Mission Statement." *Huffpost.* Available at: https://www.huffingtonpost.co.uk/entry/cure-for-autism_n_58062f2be4b0dd54ce3522b1

——— (2024). "Starmer 'pleased' to keep promise to Esther Rantzen on assisted dying vote." *The Independent.* Available at: https://www.independent.co.uk/news/uk/esther-rantzen-keir-starmer-bill-prime-minister-ed-miliband-b2623901.html

I am autism commercial. Autism Speaks (2009). Available at: https://www.youtube.com/watch?v=9UgLnWJFGHQ

"Joint Statement." Boycott Spectrum 10K (2021). Available at: https://eu.jotform.com/aucademy/boycott-s10k

Leadbeater, K. (2024). *Terminally Ill Adults (End of Life) Bill.* Parliamentary Bills. Available at: https://bills.parliament.uk/bills/3774

Lord Falconer (2014). *Assisted Dying Bill.* Parliamentary Bills. Available at: https://bills.parliament.uk/bills/1381

Marris, R. (2015). *Assisted Dying Bill (No 2).* Parliamentary Bills. Available at: https://bills.parliament.uk/bills/1631

Parker, M. (2024). "An open letter to my MP Cat Smith over the Assisted Dying Bill." *The Canary.* Available at: https://www.thecanary.co/opinion/2024/11/22/assisted-dying-mp-letter/

Pring, J. (2021). "Autistic campaigners' anger over Spectrum 10K protest lockout and 'scare tactics'." *Disability News Service.* Available at: https://www.disabilitynewsservice.com/autistic-campaigners-anger-over-spectrum-10k-protest-lock-out-and-scare-tactics/

Quinn, B. (2016). "Disability rights campaigners protest at premiere of *Me Before You*." *The Guardian.* Available at: https://www.theguardian.com/society/2016/may/25/disability-rights-campaigners-protest-at-premiere-of-me-before-you

Salhan, S. (2023). "Cambridge-led research into autism a 'field in crisis', BBC report finds." *Varsity.* Available at: https://www.varsity.co.uk/news/25333

BIBLIOGRAPHY

Sharland, H. (2024). "Pro-assisted dying group has its origins in eugenics—and it all revolves around your favourite chocolate company." *The Canary*. Available at: https://www.thecanary.co/long-read/2024/11/19/assisted-dying-debate-uk/

——— (2024). "REVEALED: assisted dying campaign funded by 'charitable' Trust tied to right-wing, dark-money think tanks." *The Canary*. Available at: https://www.thecanary.co/uk/analysis/2024/10/23/assisted-dying-campaign-funding/

Spectrum 10k, University of Cambridge. Autism Research Centre. Available at: https://www.autismresearchcentre.com/projects/spectrum-10k/

"The Assisted Dying Bill is an ableist abomination—not that Kim Leadbeater even realises." *The Canary* (2024). Available at: https://www.thecanary.co/editorial/2024/11/26/assisted-dying-bill-dignity-in-dying/

Topple, S. (2024). "Disabled people need YOUR support fighting against the Assisted Dying Bill." *The Canary*. Available at: https://www.thecanary.co/uk/analysis/2024/11/11/assisted-dying-bill-protest/

——— (2024). "How to get involved with Friday's #AssistUsToLive anti-Assisted Dying action online." *The Canary*. Available at: https://www.thecanary.co/uk/analysis/2024/11/28/assisted-dying-bill-protest-29-november/

Turner, C. (2024). "Extend assisted dying to those without terminal illness, say Labour MPs." *The Telegraph*. Available at: https://www.telegraph.co.uk/politics/2024/10/05/widen-access-to-assisted-dying-say-labour-mps/

Conclusion: Just Ask

"Access to elected office fund." UK Government (2015). Available at: https://www.gov.uk/access-to-elected-office-fund/eligibility

Charlton-Dailey, R. (2024). Post on Twitter. Available at: https://x.com/RachelCDailey/status/1776267342772625751

"Disabled people's protest rights: what you need to know." Disability Rights UK. Available at: https://www.disabilityrightsuk.org/resources/disabled-people%E2%80%99s-protest-rights-what-you-need-know

Kavanagh, A. (2018). "Blind activist wants to change how people interact with those with disabilities." *Sky News*. Available at: https://news.sky.com/

BIBLIOGRAPHY

story/blind-activist-wants-to-change-how-people-interact-with-those-with-disabilities-11481119

Police, Crime, Sentencing and Courts Act 2022. UK Public General Acts. Available at: https://www.legislation.gov.uk/ukpga/2022/32/contents

Quantock, G. (2022). "It's appalling that less than 1% of MPs are disabled—things need to change." *Daily Mirror*. Available at: https://www.mirror.co.uk/news/uk-news/its-appalling-less-1-mps-27391412

RNIB (2024). Post on Twitter. Available at: https://x.com/RNIB/status/1776209679279882354

Ryan, F. (2024). "Cropped out, banned, airbrushed: the school photos that show the ugly face of Britain today." *The Guardian*. Available at: https://www.theguardian.com/commentisfree/2024/apr/04/school-photos-disabled-children

INDEX

Aberdeen Press and Journal, 51
ableism, 10, 31, 41, 70, 124
  eugenics, xviii, 226–45
  in media, 3, 65–9, 78–9, 82, 83, 155–82
abortion, 231–4
Abortion Act (1967), 231
Access for All, 195–6
Access to Elected Office Fund, 249
Access to Work Fund, 149, 218–23, 259
accessibility, 84, 185–204, 264
  arts and culture sector, 80, 82, 174
  criminal justice system, 72, 151
  education sector, 185
  emergency services, 186
  healthcare sector, 185–6
  housing, 186–92
  public transport, 3, 12, 70–74, 142, 181, 195–9, 247, 259
  services, 58, 72, 76, 151, 185–6, 192–5
  workplaces, 157, 183, 219
Acuseeds, 158–9, 175
ADAPT, 66
ADHD, 158, 170, 177, 179–80, 219, 255
Adult Suffrage Society, 25
Advisory Committee for Welfare of the Blind, 28
AIDS, 131
Airlie, Angie, 187
All Work Test, 90
Anti-Discrimination Bill (1983), 58

INDEX

apathy, 260–61
Araniello, Katherine, 84
Arts Council England, 82, 84
Arts Council Wales, 84
arts movement, 78–85, 169, 260
Ashcroft, Jonathan, 147
Ashley, Jack, 37
Aspel, Michael, 65
Asquith, Herbert Henry, 23
'Assist Us To Live', 51, 243
Assisted Dying Bill (2024), 51, 235–45, 247, 255, 259
Association of British Commuters, 197
Astor, Nancy, Viscountess, 27
asylum seekers, 131
asylums, 17–19, 38
Atkin, Polly, 268
Atos, 103, 110–11
Auberger, Mike, 66
austerity (2010–19), 10, 87, 94–114, 163, 165, 188–9
autism, 122, 158, 169–70, 210, 227, 228–31
Autism Genetic Resource Exchange, 229

Autism Research Centre, Cambridge, 228, 230–31
Autism Speaks, 229
Ayling-Ellis, Rose, 173

'Bad News for Disabled People' (2011 report), 100
Bangladeshi people, 9
Barham-Brown, Hannah, 192–4, 265
Barnes, Colin, 20
Baron-Cohen, Simon, 228–9
Barr, Genevieve, 174
Bashall, Ruth, 70
Battle of Ypres (1917), 29
Beckett, Elsa, 56
bedroom tax, 102
Bellingcat, 176
benefits, *see* welfare state
Benefits Defence workshops, 112
Benefits Street (2014 TV series), 5, 10
Bermuda, 97
Bethlem Asylum, London, 17–18
Better Off Dead? (2024 documentary), 235
Big Issue, The, 144, 151, 252

INDEX

Billinghurst, Rosa May, 6, 22–4
Birmingham, West Midlands, 97
Black Activists Rising Against Cuts, 96
Black communities, 97, 182, 223
Black Disabled People's Association, 97
Black Friday (1910), 23
Black Triangle, 96, 240, 244, 264
Blackwood, Margaret, 32–3, 50–51
Blair, Tony, 91
Blind March (1920), 26–7
Blind people, 26–8, 194–5, 212–13
Blind Persons Act (1920), 27, 28
Blind Veterans UK, 29
Block Telethon (1990–92), 65–9, 78, 82, 83, 231
Blue Badges, 39, 40, 199–201, 203
Bluesky, 243, 259
Boxer, Giselle, 158–9, 175
Boycott Spectrum 10K, 230
Brackenby, Sam, 98
'bread and roses', 263

Brexit (2016–20), 142, 165
Brisenden, Simon, 61
Bristol Climate and Nature Partnership, 103
Bristol Reclaiming Independent Living, 188–9
British Broadcasting Corporation (BBC), 35, 78–9, 81, 84, 157, 166
  Children in Need, 64, 66–7
  Doctor Who, 170–71
  Does He Take Sugar?, 35
  Don't Take My Baby, 170
  Dragons' Den, 158–9, 175
  EastEnders, 159–60, 173
  Kind of Spark, A, 169–70
  Panorama, 217
  Poor Dear, 81
  Question Time, 107, 172
  Strictly Come Dancing, 177–8
  We Might Regret This, 173
British Council, 55–6, 57, 61, 66, 76–7
British Deaf and Dumb Association (BDDA), 26, 211

INDEX

British Deaf Association, 26, 211–12
British Legion, 29
British Sign Language (BSL), 119, 186, 210–12, 219, 221
Brooker, Alex, 172
Brooks, Hollie-Anne, 158, 252, 269
Broomfield, Abigail, 146
Brown, Donald Adolphus, 24
Brown, Kate, 70
Bruno, Frank, 68
Burnell, Cerrie, 4
Burnham, Andy, 198
Burnip, Linda, 98, 99
Burrow, Rob, 168
Byline Times, 252

Cambridge Autism Research Centre, 228, 230
Cameron, David, 95, 98, 103, 109, 111, 112–13, 221
Campaign for Accessible Transport, 70–71
Campbell, Jane, Baroness, 76–7, 82, 239
Canada, 237–8

Canary, The, xiv, 135, 176, 210, 220, 238, 243, 252
'Cap in Hand?' (1990 conference), 64
capitalism, xix, 87, 91, 94
Cardiff, Wales, 72
care, *see* social care
care homes, 43–4, 119, 121, 123, 135, 188
Carr, Liz, 47, 83, 84–5, 235–7, 240, 244, 264
cerebral palsy, 31, 173–4
Changing Perspectives, 244
charity, 3, 63–9
Chartist movement (1838–57), 21–2
Chemie–Grünenthal, 36
Chesterfield, Derbyshire, 61, 200
Child and Adolescent Mental Health Service (CAMHS), 210
Children in Need, 64, 66–7
Children Poverty Action Group, 35
'Chip on Your Shoulder' (Stanton), 78
Christchurch by-election (1993), 73–4
Christian far right, 233–4
Christmas, 147

INDEX

Chronically Sick and Disabled Act (1970), 48–50, 199
Churchill, Winston, 74
Circle Pictures, 81
Civil Rights movement (1954–68), 5, 46
Civil Service People Survey, 217
Claddag, 190
Clapson, David, 110, 113
Clean Air Zones, 203–4
Clarke, Caro, 266
Clement, Charli, 210
Clifford, Ellen, 103, 124–5, 131, 149, 150–51, 240, 241, 242
Climate and Disability Programme, 203
Climate Change Act (2008), 203
climate crisis, 202–4, 253
Coalition, 81
coalition government (2010–15), 10, 87, 94–111
Cockroft, Hannah, 157
Cohen, Benn Jack Brunel, 29
Cold War (1947–91), 90–91

Coleman, Lisa, 111
comedy, 78, 82, 254
Communist Party of Great Britain, 25
Conservative Party, xviii, 7, 73, 88–90, 94–114
  austerity programme (2010–19), 10, 87, 94–114, 163, 165, 188–9
  Brexit (2016–20), 142, 165
  cost of living crisis (2021–), 143, 148, 165
  Covid-19 pandemic (2020–22), 115–39
  welfare state and, 88–9, 94–114, 163–7, 188–9, 215, 217, 221
de Cordova, Marsha, 146
Coronation Street, 174
cost of living crisis (2021–), 6, 141–52, 165, 172
Costly Differences, 142–3
Covid-19 Bereaved Families for Justice, 138–9
Covid-19 pandemic (2020–22), 1, 6, 8, 10, 12, 115–39, 161–2, 165

INDEX

clinically vulnerable people, 120–23, 127
death toll, 127, 131–2, 138–9, 161, 166
disablement and, 117, 132–5
Do Not Resuscitate orders, 121–3, 135, 162, 226
Eat Out to Help Out, 126, 128, 137, 161
'freedom day' (2021), 130
herd immunity strategy, 116, 118
home working, 213–15
Inquiry (2022–), 126–7, 136–7
lockdowns, 116, 117–21, 123, 124, 127–8
Long Covid, 133–5, 137, 138
parking restrictions, 199–201
Partygate (2021–2), 136
PPE, 123, 125
public funds and, 165
shielding, 117–18, 123, 127, 128, 136, 137, 215
social distancing, 136, 215

testing, 130, 137, 138
vaccine programme, 129, 137
Creative Diversity Network, 155
Crippled (Ryan), 100
Criptic Productions, 81
Crow, Liz, 78
Crowter, Heidi, 231–4
Cuffay, William, 21–2
Cummings, Dominic, 135
Cure Autism Now, 229
Curtis, Rachel, 146
'Cuts Kill', 97–8

Dahl, Roald, 256–7
Daily Express, 93, 166
Daily Mail, 175
Daily Mirror, 165, 166, 175, 192, 197, 215, 248–9
Disabled Britain, xiv, 2, 176, 248–9
Daily Star, 166
Daily Telegraph, 93, 175, 180
Davies, Mims, 219
Davies, Rhian, 166
Davis, Ken, 62
Deaf and Disabled People's Organisations (DDPOs), 240, 250, 253, 255–6

INDEX

Deaf people, xv, xvi, 26, 37–8, 119, 173, 186, 210–12
  British Sign Language (BSL), 119, 186, 210–12, 219, 221
Deaths by Welfare Timeline, 94–5, 113
Debois, Jane, 176
Declaration of Human Rights, 55
Degener, Theresia, xiv
Denmark, 109
Department for Education, 208, 211
Department for Environment, Food and Rural Affairs, 203
Department for Health and Social Security, 61, 111, 231–2
Department for Work and Pensions (DWP), 92, 93, 217–18
  Access to Work fund, 149, 218–23, 259
  austerity programme (2010–19), 94–114
  cost of living crisis (2021–), 145–52
  'Employment of Disabled People' (2024 report), 207
  home working and, 215–16
Department, The (Pring), 113
Derbyshire Coalition (DCDP), 62, 63
Derbyshire Direct Action Now Network (DDANN), 63, 65, 69
Diamond report, 155
Dickens, Charles, 19–20, 66
Difference North East, 215
digital literacy, 149, 216
Digital Spy, 158, 169, 171
Dignity in Dying, 243
Dimbleby, David, 107
Direct Action Network, *see* Disabled People's Direct Action Network
Disability & Abortion (2022 documentary), 232
Disability Action Plan, 249
Disability Alliance, 51
Disability Arts in London, 81
Disability Arts Online, 123
Disability Benefits Consortium, 99

INDEX

Disability Discrimination Act (1995), 3, 4, 13, 58, 74, 82, 170, 183–4, 205, 247, 259

Disability Living Allowance, 39, 101, 105

Disability News Service, 98, 103, 120, 146, 159, 191

Disability Pay Gap Day, 206

Disability Policy Centre, 208

Disability Politics (Campbell and Oliver), 20, 77

Disability Rights Commission, 75

Disability Rights UK, 120, 240, 244, 253

Disability Wales, 152, 156–7, 166, 240

Disabled Avant-Garde, 84

Disabled Britain, xiv, 2, 176

Disabled Drivers' Association (DDA), 40

Disabled Drivers' Motor Club (DDMC), 39–40

Disabled Motoring UK, 40

Disabled People Against Cuts (DPAC), 98, 124, 132, 253, 255–6
  Atos protests (2012), 103
  Terminally Ill Adults Bill (2024), 240, 242, 244
  UN investigation (2013–16), 108
  Welfare Reform Act (2012), 102
  Work Capability Assessment protests (2024), 150, 152

Disabled People's Archive, 57

Disabled People's Direct Action Network (DAN), 2–3, 69, 70–74, 76, 79, 151
  Blair's blood protest (1997), 92
  Christchurch by-election (1993), 73–4
  Oxford Circus protest (2012) 102
  public transport protests (1993–5), 70–73

Disabled People's Steering Group, 58

Disabled Peoples' International (DPI), 55

Disabled Person's Transport Committee, 196

Disabled Persons Act (1944), 30

INDEX

Disablement Income Group (DIG), 32–5, 43, 50, 56
Distillers, 37
Do Not Resuscitate orders, 121–3, 135, 162, 226
Docklands Light Railway, 70
Doctor Who, 170–71
Does He Take Sugar? (radio programme), 35
domestic abuse, 160
Don't Take My Baby (TV series), 170
Douglas Haig Memorial Homes Trust, 29
Dove, Joy, 110
Down's syndrome, 122, 159, 227, 231–4
Dragons' Den (TV series), 158–9, 175
driving, 39–41, 199–201, 203
Du Boisson, Megan, 32, 33–4, 35, 50
Duncan Smith, Iain, 95, 99, 105, 107, 111
Dury, Ian, 54–5, 80
dyslexia, 136
dyspraxia, 249

EastEnders, 159–60, 173
Eat Out to Help Out, 126, 128, 137, 161
Economist, The, 138
Edinburgh, Scotland, 51
Editors' Code of Practice, 175
education, 185, 206, 207–13, 248, 255, 260, 265–6
Education, Health and Care Plan (EHCP), 209
Elephant and Castle, London, 61
Elliott, Laura, 264
Elsegood, Sue, 69, 70, 92
Emergency Evacuation Information Sharing, 191
emergency services, 186
Emmerdale, 173–4
Empathy Quotient, 228
employment, 7, 74, 205–7, 267
  home working, 213–16
  see also welfare state
'Employment of Disabled People' (2024 report), 207
Employment Rights Bill (2024), 224
Employment Support

Allowance, 92, 106, 107, 112, 127, 145
endometriosis, 128
English Housing Survey, 186
Equality Act (2010), 82, 105, 184, 193, 205, 259
Erasmus Microman (TV series), 59
ethnicity, 9, 97, 223
eugenics, xviii, 34, 226–45, 247, 255, 259
Eugenics Society, 243
euthanasia, 34, 235–45, 247, 255, 259
Eyles, Priscilla, 230

Facebook, 254
Fair and Affordable Care Policy, 188
Fibromyalgia, 133
financial crisis (2008–9), 94
Financial Times, 176
Finkelstein, Vic, 46, 56, 80, 135
First World War (1914–18), xvii, 28–9, 39, 49
Fitton, Jack, 62
food banks, 144
Foxcroft, Vicky, 219

Freaks (1932 film), xiii
Freud, David, 93
Friends of the Earth, 203
Fundamental Principles of Disability, 51

Gabsi, Adam, 191
GCSEs, 211, 213
Geen, Emma, 203–4
General Election (1992), 73
General Election (2024), 219
Geneva, Switzerland, xiv
Gentleman, Amelia, 110
Geschwind, Daniel, 229
Get Britain Working, 217
Gilbert, Lozza, 268
Gill, Andy, 76
Glastonbury Festival (1993), 78
Global South, 54
Godalming, Surrey, 35
Good Omens (TV series), 85
Govind, Thorrun, 144
Graeae theatre company, 55
Graham, Errol, 108, 110
Granada, 59
Grayling, Chris, 106
'Great Britain from a

INDEX

Wheelchair' (Heaton), 83
Great Depression (1929–39), xvii
Greater Manchester Coalition of Disabled People (GMCDP), 56–9, 81
Greater Manchester Council, 58
Greaves, Mary, 50
Greece, 35
Grenfell Tower fire (2017), 189–92
Grey-Thompson, Tanni, 196, 198
Grey's Monument, Newcastle, 151
Grieve, John, 267
Grover, Chris, 91
Guardian, The, 33, 35, 45, 49, 176, 189, 209, 252
guide dogs, 194–5

Habinteg Housing, 186
Hadi, Fazilet, 120
Haig Housing Trust, 29
Hain, Peter, 92–3
Hancock, Matt, 135–6
Hardest Hit coalition, 99
Harpe, Wendy, 82
Harris, Kyla, 173
Harrison, Mark, 120
hate crimes, 10
Hatley, Sam, 265
Hayward, Robert, 73–4
healthcare, 21, 108, 144, 185–6
  see also Covid-19 pandemic
Heath, Edward 'Ted', 41
Heaton, Tony, 83–4
Hennessy, Joe, 40
herd immunity, 116, 118
Het Dorp, Netherlands, 45
Hill, Milliedrette, 97
Hills, Adam, 172, 258
Hirst, Natasha, 156–7
Hogg, Tina, 98
Holdsworth, Alan, 65–9, 71–2, 78–9, 170
Holocaust (1941–5), 227
home working, 213–16
House of Commons, *see* Parliament
House of Lords, *see* Parliament
housing, 102, 186
Houston, Cherylee, 174
Hulme, Georgia, 190
Human Rights Act (1998), 203

INDEX

Hunt, Jeremy, 165
Hunt, Judy, 46
Hunt, Paul, 43–6, 49, 80, 135

i Paper, The, 233, *see also Independent*
'Improving Lives' (2016 green paper), 111–12
Incapacity Benefit, 90–92, 94
Inclusion London, 187–8, 191, 244
Independent, 176, 252, *see also i Paper, The*
Independent Living Fund, 41, 111
Independent Monitor for the Press (IMPRESS), 176
Independent Press Standards Organisation (IPSO), 175–80
Industrial Revolution (c. 1760–1840), 19, 25
iNews, 152
influencers, 250
inspiration porn, 167–8, 260, 268
Instagram, 158, 177, 255

Institute for Government, 142
International Year of Disabled Persons, 53–5
Internet
 access to, 149, 216
 social media, 149, 158, 179, 253–9, 264–5
intersectionality, 56, 182, 250
Invalid Tricycle Association, 40
Invalidity Benefit, 87–90
Irish Sign Language, 211
Islam, 9
ITV, 64, 65, 166
 Coronation Street, 174
 Emmerdale, 173–4
 Telethon, 64–9, 78, 82

James, Greg, 257
Jarrow March (1936), 26
Jayanetti, Chaminda, xiv, 151, 252
Jeffery, Nicola, 252
Jeremy Vine Show, 164
Jiggens, Becca, 267
Jillings, Daniel, 211
Johnson, Babs, 66
Johnson, Boris, 94, 115–16, 118, 126, 130, 136, 172

INDEX

Johnson, Colleen, 266
Jolly, Debbie, 98, 99
Jones, Ellen, 220
Jones, Owen, 107
Jones, Rosie, 171
Jordan, Kevin, 203
Joseph Rowntree Foundation, 145, 152, 207
journalism, 156–8, 160, 162–7, 175–82, 248

Kaur, Manjeet, 131
Kavanagh, Amy, 126, 256
Keep, Caroline, 266
Kendall, Liz, 152
Kennington, London, 61
Kind of Spark, A (McNicoll), 169–70
Knight, Eliza Adelaide, 24–5

Labour Party, xviii, 1, 8, 25, 27, 48–9, 110, 131, 147, 165
   accessibility and, 187–8, 190–91
   climate crisis and, 203
   Employment Rights Bill (2024), 224
   New Labour, 91–4, 96, 101–2
   Terminally Ill Adults Bill (2024), 241–2
   Work Capability Assessment and, 151–2, 215, 217
Last Leg, The (TV series), 172
Laws, Vince, 112
Leadbeater, Kim, 235, 238
learning disabled people, 122
Led By Donkeys, 138–9
Leeds Marathon, 168
legal vs moral obligation, 37
Leonard Cheshire, 10
Leveson Inquiry (2011–12), 176
Levete, Gina, 80
Lewell-Buck, Emma, 248–9, 265
Lewis, Roger, 132
LGBTQ+ community, xvi, 8–9, 56, 131, 233, 250
Liberal Democrats, 74, 109
Lilley, Peter, 88–90
Lisicki, Barbara, 1, 2, 10, 61–2, 65–9, 71–3, 78–9, 114, 170
Lisney, Eleanor, 98
literacy, 19

INDEX

Little Red Schoolbook (Andersen et al.), 35
live captioning, 37–8
Liverpool School for the Indigent Blind, 25
Lloyd George, David, 27
Lloyd's Bank, 149
Local Housing Allowance, 152
Lomas, Katie, 200–201
London, England
　accessibility in, 181, 198–9
　media sector in, 181, 214
　Paralympic Games (2012), 55, 103–4
London Disability Arts Forum, 78, 81
London Underground, 198–9, 243
Long Covid, 133–5, 137, 138
Low Capability for Work Related Activity (LC-WRA), 148
Low Emission Zones, 203
Lubran, Holly, 174
Lupton, Dave, 98
Lynch, Mick, 198

Mad Pride, 98

Madeley, Ruth, 10, 170–71, 232–4
Mail on Sunday, 109
Major, John, 89, 91
Maloney, Mary, 74
Manchester Town Hall, 58
March on Wheels (1974), 51
Marsh, Sue, 106
Martinez, Francesca, 171–2
Marxism, xvii
Masefield, Paddy, 82
Master and Servant Act (1823), 22
May, Theresa, 95
McArdle, Brian, 107
McArdle, John, 95–6, 264
McDonnell, John, 110, 152
McGovern, Alison, 220
McGovern, Seán, 131–2
McKenna, Denise, 98
McNicoll, Elle, 169, 258
McRae, Isabella, 252
Me Before Euthanasia, 240
Me Before You (Moyes), 240
Meddings, Liz, 266
media, 155–82, 251–2, 260
　journalism, 156–8, 160, 162–7, 175–82, 248
　television, 9–10, 59, 155–60, 167–75

INDEX

welfare state and, 162–7
Medical Assistance in Dying (MAiD), 237–8
Medicines Act (1968), 36–7
Medium, 68
Members of Parliament, 9, 27, 34, 37–8, 48, 146, 248–9
meningitis, 117
mental health, xviii, 38, 96, 112, 210, 212, 218, 227
Mental Health Act (1959), 38
Mental Health Resistance Network, 96, 105
Metro, 175, 252
Metropolitan Tailors' Charter Association, 21
Mikado, The (Gilbert and Sullivan), 88
Milland, Gabriel, 94
Millington, Pete, 98
Mills, China, 95
Minister for the Disabled, 49, 164
Ministry of Labour, 30
Mirena coil, 255
Mobilise, 40
Moore, Berit, 32, 33, 35
Moore, James, 173, 252
moral vs legal obligation, 37
Morgan, Sophie, 177–8
Morris, Alf, 48–50
Morrison, Ellen, 128–9
Morrison, Elspeth, 68, 81
Motability, 39, 41, 192
Moyes, Jojo, 240
multiple sclerosis, 32
Musk, Elon, 258–9
Muslims, 9
myalgic encephalomyelitis (ME), 133, 158

narcolepsy, 117
National Adaptation Programme, 203
National Autistic Society, 210
National Centre for Independent Living, 76
National Charter Association, 21
National Council for Training of Journalists, 156
National Disability Arts Collection (NDACA), 80, 82
National Disability Arts Forum, 81

National Disability Council, 74
National Education Union, 2, 266
National Fire Chiefs Council (NFCC), 191
National Health Service (NHS), 32, 95, 121, 123, 137, 144, 161–2
National League of the Blind, 26–8
National Union of Industrial and Professional Blind, 28
National Union of Journalists, 156, 176
Nazism, 227
neoliberal economics, 87, 91, 94
neonatal conjunctivitis, 28
Netherlands, 45, 238
neurodivergence, 9, 136, 169–70, 208–10, 255
  eugenics and, 227–31
New Labour, 91–4, 96, 101–2
Newcastle, Tyne & Wear, 151
Newsnight, 106, 236
No Limits (Hunt), 46
non-disabled people
  activism and, 236, 260, 267
  awareness and, 256, 260, 265
  carers, addressing of, 35, 195
  experts, 26, 48, 236
Norwich, Norfolk, 71
Not Dead Yet UK, 81, 239–40, 242, 244
'Nothing About Us Without Us', 48, 80
Novara Media, 176
Noyce, Eleanor, 252

O'Connor, Emma, 190
O'Sullivan, Michael, 110
Ofcom, 158–9
Office for Budget Responsibility (OBR), 150
Office for National Statistics (ONS), 7, 143, 160, 161, 207, 223
Oliver, Mike, 77
Olympic Games (2012), 103
OpenDemocracy, 252
Orange Badges, 199
Orbital, 55
Osborne, George, 98, 111

INDEX

Oxford Circus protest (2012) 102
Oxford Street shut-down (1990), 70, 72

Paget-Jones, Angharad, 194–5
pan-impairment movement, 32, 41
Pankhurst family, 6, 25
Panorama (TV series), 217
Papworth Trust, 186
Paralympic Games, 55, 103–4, 196
Parker, Melissa, 66, 243, 252
Parliament, 9, 27, 34, 37, 38, 48, 248–9
  Abortion Act (1967), 231
  Anti-Discrimination Bill (1983), 58
  Blind Persons Act (1920), 27, 28
  Chronically Sick and Disabled Act (1970), 48–50, 199
  Climate Change Act (2008), 203
  Disability Civil Rights Bills (1982–95), 73
  Disability Discrimination Act (1995), 3, 4, 13, 58, 74, 75, 82, 170, 183–4, 205, 247, 259
  Disabled Persons Act (1944), 30
  Equality Act (2010), 82, 105, 184, 193, 205, 259
  Hardest Hit protests (2011), 99
  Human Rights Act (1998), 203
  Mad Pride protest (2010), 98
  Master and Servant Act (1823), 22
  Medicines Act (1968), 36–7
  Mental Health Act (1959), 38
  Motability event (2023), 192
  Poor Law Amendment Act (1834), 20
  Race Relations Act (1965), 4, 75
  Sex Discrimination Act (1975), 4, 75
  10,000 Cuts protest (2013), 104
  Terminally Ill Adults Bill

INDEX

(2024), 51, 235–45, 247, 255, 259
Welfare Reform Act (2007), 92
Welfare Reform Act (2012), 101–3
Partygate (2021–2), 136
Paulley, Doug, 203
Penguin Random House, 256–7
Pennick, Katie, 198
Pepper, Penny, 252
Perego, Elisa, 134
Personal Emergency Evacuation Plans (PEEPs), 190–91
Personal Independence Payment (PIP), 101, 102, 105, 145
Personal to the Planetary fellowships, 204
Peters, Paula, 239, 265
petitions, 21, 55, 62, 110, 145–6, 251
Piggott, Linda, 91
'Piss On Pity', 3, 65, 67–8
Player, Katie, 174
Police, Crime, Sentencing and Courts Act (2022), 253
policing, 72, 151

Poor Dear (TV series), 81
Poor Law Amendment Act (1834), 20
post-traumatic stress disorder (PTSD), 29
poverty, xviii, 7, 26, 90, 94, 164, 223
Premier Inn, 192–5
prescriptions, 144
Press Complaints Commission, 175
Press Recognition Panel, 176
Pring, John, xiv, 95, 113, 159, 191
protests, 6, 12, 31–2, 251
  Birmingham austerity protest (2010), 97
  Blair's blood protest (1997), 92
  Blind March (1920), 26–7
  Block Telethon (1990–92), 65–9, 78, 82, 83, 231
  Boycott Spectrum 10K (2021), 230
  British Council Day of Action (1988), 61
  Chartists, 21–2

INDEX

DWP cuts protests (2024), 150–51
Hardest Hit protests (2011), 99
Inclusion London protest (2024), 187–8
Jarrow March (1936), 26
Mad Pride protest (2010), 98
March on Wheels (1974), 51
Oxford Circus protest (2012) 102
Oxford Street shut-down (1990), 70, 72
pan-impairment movement, 31–2, 34, 41, 51
public transport protests (1993–5), 70–73
suffragettes, 6, 22–5
10,000 Cuts protest (2013), 104
Terminally Ill Adults Bill (2024), 243–4
Westminster Bridge shut-down (1995), 71
Proudlock, Tracey, 70
Public Assistance Institutions, 21
public transport, 3, 12, 70–74, 142, 181, 195–9, 247, 259
Pupil Referral Units, 208
Purdy, Debbie, 236
Purnell, James, 93
Purple Tuesday, 194
Purse, Ben, 27–8
Pursglove, Tom, 164
Purvis, Ella Maisy, 169, 265

Quantock, Grace, 248–9
Question Time, 107, 172

Race Relations Act (1965), 4, 75
Radio Times, 44
Rae, Anne, 81
railways, 195–9, 247
Rantzen, Esther, 242
Rayner, Angela, 188
recession (1990–92), 90
Reclaiming Our Futures Alliance, 120
Recovery in the Bin, 112
Reekie, Paul, 96
Reeves, Rachel, 152
Refugee Participatory Action Research, 131
remote work, 213–15
Remploy, 30, 132
Renke, Sam, 252

INDEX

Rennie, Sarah, 190
Resolution Foundation, 142
Retrenching Incapacity Benefit (Grover and Piggott), 91
'right to die', 51, 235–45, 247, 255
'right to exist', 52
'Rights Not Charity', 63
Rights Now!, 56, 74
RMT, 197–8
Robinson, Charles, 33
Rowley, Katie, 119
Royal British Legion, 29
Royal College of Psychiatrists, 19
Royal Commission, 26
Royal National Institute for Blind People (RNIB), 212–13, 257
Royal Pharmaceutical Society, 144
Rushton, Edward, 25
Russian Revolution (1917), xvii
Ryan, Frances, xiv, 100, 188–9, 252, 258, 264

SafeLives, 160
Save Our Ticket Offices, 197–8

Scope, 7, 31, 141, 164, 204
Scotland, 50–51
Scottish Veterans Garden City Association, 29
segregation, 43–52
self-harm, xviii
Sensing Climate, 204
sex, 167, 169, 173, 270
sex difference theory, 228
Sex Discrimination Act (1975), 4, 75
Shaban, Nabil, 59
'Shaken Not Stirred' (Heaton), 83
Sharland, Hannah, 243, 252
shell shock, 29
Sherlock, Karen, 107
Shiress, Ted, 267
Shonibare, Yinka, 84
Silenced (2021 documentary), 4
Silent Witness (TV series), 85
Simpson, Joe, 65
Sinfield, Kevin, 168
single-use plastic straws, 202–3
Smith, Chris, 257
Smith, John, 103
social care, 12, 38, 50, 57, 76–7, 95, 108, 188–9

at-home, 38, 76–7, 125, 128, 146, 188
care homes, 43–4, 119, 121, 123, 135, 188
Social Democratic Federation, 25
'Social Justice Not Charity', 27
social model, 46–7, 77, 80, 135
South Africa, 48
South Bank Centre, 84
South Bank, London, 65
Southampton University, 90
Sp*sticus Autisticus' (Dury), 54–5, 80
Spartacus Report (2013), 105–6, 162
Special Educational Needs and Disabilities (SEND), 208–13, 255, 260
Special Needs Jungle, 209
Spectrum 10K, 228–31
Speedwell, Germander, 269
Speight, Ed, 54
spina bifida, 160
Spinal Injuries Association (SIA), 56

Spitting Image (TV show), 89
St Dunstan's, 29
stair lifts, 44
stand-up comedy, 78
Stanton, Ian, 59, 78, 81
Starmer, Keir, 178, 188, 215, 241–2
Statutory Sick Pay (SSP), 127
Stay Safe East, 70, 187
Staying Inn, The, 126
Stemp, Jane, 266
stenograph machines, 38
Stevens, Hannah Shewan, 167, 168, 252
Stewart-Taylor, Lynn, 119
Stickland, Caroline, 197, 199
Strictly Come Dancing (TV series), 177
Stride, Mel, 215
Student Publication Association National Conference, 214
Stueland, Berit, *see* Moore, Berit
Stylist, 128–9, 232
suffragettes, 6, 22–5
suicide, xviii, 96, 98

INDEX

assisted dying, 51, 235–45, 247, 255, 259
Sun, The, 99, 175
Sunak, Rishi, 126, 136, 137, 148, 163, 215, 217
Sutherland, Allan, 70
swine flu, 117

'Talkin' Disabled Anarchist Blues' (Stanton), 78
Tarrant, Chris, 3, 68, 69
Tate Modern, 84
Telethon, 64–9, 78, 82
television, 9–10, 59, 155–60, 167–75
   inspo porn/trauma porn binary, 167–8, 260, 268
10,000 Cuts and Counting (2013), 104
Terminally Ill Adults Bill (2024), 51, 235–45, 247, 255, 259
thalidomide, 35–8
Thalidomide Society, 37
Thatcher, Margaret, 87, 89, 91
Then Barbara Met Alan (2022 film), 10, 170
Thom, Jess, 220–22
Thompson, Gill, 110
Thorne, Jack, 170, 174
TikTok, 158, 179, 255
Times, The, 33–4, 175, 180
Timms, Stephen, 146
Titford, Kaylea, 160
Tomlinson, Justin, 120
Topple, Steve, xiv
Touretteshero, 220
Trade Union Congress (TUC), 27, 131, 206–7, 223
trade unions, xv, 27, 197–8
Trafalgar Square, London, 27, 34, 41
Tragic but Brave, 78
trains, 195–9, 247
trans people, 8–9
Transport Accessibility Gap, 259
transport
   driving, 39–41, 199–201, 203
   public transport, 3, 12, 70–74, 142, 181, 195–9, 247, 259
Transport for All, 198
Transport for London, 199
trauma porn, 167, 168, 260, 268
Trotsky, Leon, xvii
Trott, Laura, 215

INDEX

true crime reporting, 19
Trump, Donald, xviii
Truss, Liz, 142–3
Trussell Trust, 144, 147
Tubman, Harriet, xvii
Turner, Alison, 108, 110
Twits, The (Dahl), 256–7
Twitter, 105–6, 119, 125, 158, 177, 196, 243, 254–5, 258–9

Ukraine War (2022–), 142
Uncut UK, 102
Underlying Health Condition, 174
unemployment, 7, 90
Union of the Physically Impaired (UPIAS), 46–52, 57, 77, 80
Unite, 152
United Nations
 Committee on Rights, xiv–xv, 1
 Convention on Rights (2007), 1, 108–9, 239, 260, 264, 265
 Economic and Social Commission, 202
 International Decade of Disabled Persons (1982–93), 53
 International Year of Disabled Persons, 53–5
 Universal Declaration of Human Rights (1948), 55
 World Health Organization, 54
 World Programme of Action, 53
 Year of Human Rights, 34
United States, xvii, xviii, 5, 46, 134
Universal Credit, 101, 112, 145, 148, 217
University College London, 134
University of California, 229
University of Cambridge, 228–31
University of Glasgow, 100
University of Leeds, 20
Unwritten, The, 2, 166–7

Vasey, Sian, 81
Very Nazi Queer Faust, A (Laws), 112
Verywell Health, 134, 229
Vicinanza, Laura, 187

INDEX

Victorian period (1837–1901), 19
Vine, Jeremy, 164

Waddington, Victoria, 70
Wales Online, 166
War on Welfare petition (2014), 110
Ward, Gail, 96
Warren, Callum, 269
Watts, Jay, 264
'We Exist. Help Us Live', 51
We Might Regret This (TV series), 173
We Shall Not Be Removed, 123
Webster, Lucy, 268
Weisweiller-Wu, Lara, 265
Welfare Reform Act (2007), 92
Welfare Reform Act (2012), 101–3, 105
Welfare Reform and Work Act (2016), 111
welfare state, xviii, 5, 10, 19, 32, 33, 76–7, 87–114, 158, 162–5, 260
   All Work Test, 90
   austerity programme (2010–19), 10, 87, 94–114, 163, 165, 188–9
   cost of living crisis (2021–), 145–52
   deaths and, xv, 94–6, 98, 104, 107–14, 172
   Disability Living Allowance, 101
   Employment Support Allowance, 92, 106, 107, 112, 127, 145
   Incapacity Benefit, 90–92, 93, 94
   Invalidity Benefit, 87–90
   Local Housing Allowance, 152
   media and, 162–7
   Personal Independence Payment (PIP), 101, 102, 105, 145
   Statutory Sick Pay (SSP), 127
   Universal Credit, 101, 112, 145, 148, 217
   Welfare Reform Act (2007), 92
   Welfare Reform Act (2012), 101–3, 105
   Welfare Reform and Work Act (2016), 111
   Work Capability Assess-

ment, 92–4, 96, 101–2, 104–5, 106, 148, 215–16
Westminster Bridge shut-down (1995), 71
Whiting, Jodey, 110
Wikeley, Nick, 90
Williams, Deborah, 82
Williams, Sam, 135
Williams-Finlay, Bob, 98
Williamson, Aaron, 84
WinVisible, 244
witch trials, 169
women; women's rights
neurodivergence and, 169, 179, 229
suffrage movement, xvii, 6, 22–5
Women's Social and Political Union (WSPU), 22–5
Work Capability Assessment, 92–4, 96, 101–2, 104–5, 106, 148, 215–16
Work Inclusion Project, 267
workhouses, 17, 19–20
working class, 21
World Health Organization, 54

Yellow Badges, 39
York, North Yorkshire, 200–201
YouGov, 142, 163

zero-hour contracts, 223–4